# PORTFOLIOS

# PORTFOLIOS
## PROCESS AND PRODUCT

Edited by
Pat Belanoff
and
Marcia Dickson

*With a Foreword by Peter Elbow*

BOYNTON/COOK PUBLISHERS
HEINEMANN
*Portsmouth, NH*

**Boynton/Cook Publishers, Inc.**
A Subsidiary of
**Heinemann Educational Books, Inc.**
361 Hanover Street, Portsmouth, NH 03801–3959
Offices and agents throughout the world

The following chapters have been published previously:
*Chapter 1*: "State University of New York at Stony Brook
Portfolio-Based Evaluation Program," by Peter Elbow and Pat Belanoff, first appeared
in *New Methods in College Writing Programs*. Ed. Paul Connolly and Teresa Vilardi.
New York: MLA, 1986.
*Chapter 2*: "Using Portfolios to Increase Collaboration and Community in a Writing
Program," by Pat Belanoff and Peter Elbow, is reprinted with permission of the
authors and publisher from *WPA: Writing Program Administration*, 9.3 (1986): 27–40.

Every effort has been made to contact the copyright holders for
permission to reprint borrowed material. We regret any oversights
that may have occurred and would be happy to rectify them in future
printings of this work.

**Library of Congress Cataloging-in-Publication Data**
Portfolios: process and product/edited by Pat Belanoff and Marcia
    Dickson; with a foreword by Peter Elbow.
        p.     cm.
    Includes bibliographical references.
    ISBN 0–86709–275–0
    1. Educational tests and measurements—United States.  2. English
language—Writing—Evaluation.   I. Belanoff, Pat.   II. Dickson.
Marcia.
LB3051.P6146   1991
371.2′6′0973—dc20                                          91–3804
                                                             CIP

Designed by Hunter Graphics.
Printed in the United States of America.
92  93  94  95     9  8  7  6  5  4  3

# Contents

# Foreword

Peter Elbow

I would like to call attention to the historical context for the interest in portfolios that the present volume represents. In the last three or four decades, there has been a huge growth in assessment in education. This development—what I cannot help calling a preoccupation with testing—may in fact be the biggest development in education in the last fifty years, crescendoing to the accountability movement of the seventies. Greg Anrig, head of the Educational Testing Service, recently tried to persuade the state of Georgia not to use a mass statewide test for graduation from kindergarten—and failed. He is arguing against mass testing for higher education and not having much success ("Testing and Student Performance"). The Department of Education spends more on the National Assessment of Educational Progress than on any other item. More money for testing clearly means less money for teaching in most education budgets—some of which are actually shrinking. It is often easier these days to get money out of administrations, school boards, towns, states, and the federal government for testing than for teaching.[1]

In an interesting newer development, assessment has expanded massively in the last decade from elementary and secondary education into higher education. Almost 70 percent of colleges and universities currently use assessments other than teacher grades, (more often community colleges than others); the majority of the testing is for basic skills, but many institutions are looking to assessment of long-term outcomes among graduates—one in four already doing so, half planning it (these figures are from a survey conducted by the American Council on Education, see El-Khawas).

At least one state, Missouri, requires public universities to give tests of general knowledge to entering freshmen and to give similar follow-up tests to determine how much the students have learned (*New York Times*, 5 Mar. 1990 B6). As the Chronicle of Higher Education reports, "the National Governors' Association . . . says 24 states now require assessment and another 12 are debating whether to follow. It cites Florida and Tennessee as two states that have seen student test scores rise as a result of assessment programs" (10 Aug. 1988: 1).

In response to this growing preoccupation with testing in higher education, there has grown up an interesting movement of skeptical inquiry into testing. Many people in higher education find themselves saying what boils down to this (my summary may be unfair to some of them/us, but it is true): "It's okay to barge into the classrooms of our colleagues in elementary and secondary schools and force their students to take standardized, multiple-choice tests, which they have no say over choosing or scoring — with no outcome but a computer printout of two- and three-digit scores in the mail four to eight weeks later. It's okay to try to compute the educational output of one school teacher compared to another, and to let those tests dictate what they must teach and how they should teach it. But now that you're trying to make *my* students take tests that I have no say over and trying to measure how much *my* students have learned from me compared to how much my colleagues' students have learned from them — perhaps I had better look into this assessment business and think hard about it." We in higher education used to feel we were exempt: that we could close our doors and do what we wanted, choose what to teach and how to teach and how to test. Most of all, if we said students passed or failed, they passed or failed. Meddling with our professional evaluations was grounds for litigation. But now structures like that mandated by the Florida legislature are not uncommon: the decision as to whether a sophomore graduates to junior status in English is determined not by the grades of English faculty but by a statewide writing test.

One of the most effective forums for this inquiry into assessment has been an ambitious series of annual conferences sponsored by the American Association of Higher Education. More than a thousand people from around the country came to their first "Assessment Forum" in June 1986 — far more than the planners expected. Most of the participants are involved in assessment programs on their campuses — sometimes committed to them, sometimes feeling stuck with them. Though these conferences are large heterogeneous gatherings, which it is risky to sum up, I would characterize the spirit of them not so much as "Wait a minute, we've got to stop this assessment mania" (thought there has been some of that), but rather, "Assessment is unavoidable and often desirable, but we've got to find better ways to do it than have been used in the past."[2]

Portfolio assessment, then, is one notable mode of alternative assessment. The growth in portfolio assessment in the last few years is remarkable. Portfolios are starting to be used in all sorts of ways to assess writing — and also used for assessment in most other subjects. Portfolio assessment probably counts as a fad — though I hope not *only* a fad. I am bemused that because Pat Belanoff and I started experimenting with portfolios as a substitute for proficiency exams in a freshman writing course at Stony Brook in the early 1980s and because we wrote it up and speculated about the implications of it, we are sometimes treated as "assessment people." We experience ourselves to be ambivalent about assessment.

But portfolio assessment is the kind of assessment that seems to suit people who are ambivalent or even hostile to assessment. And yet, because the practice is defensible on hard-nosed methodological grounds, it has also come to interest "real" assessment people.

This book centers on the use of portfolios as a mechanism for teachers to work together on evaluating student writing in order to hammer out some communal agreements or community standards: portfolio grading in this book means *collaborative grading*. The goal is not always to reach genuine consensus. Sometimes it is more of a structure to help teachers create temporary compromises and thereby communicate their standards and criteria better to each other — in order to invite a subtler growth of community discourse, to invite a socially constructed knowledge. (From the adversarial ways that some people write about the social construction of knowledge, I sometimes wonder if they are really interested in the sweaty work of actually compromising with other live bodies who disagree, or if they would rather work alone and declare, as a point of theory or ideology, that what they produce unilaterally is "really" socially constructed.)

But, in this foreword I will not talk in particular about portfolios for collaborative grading. I will speak about the use of portfolios *in general* for assessment — apart from whether portfolios are graded collaboratively or unilaterally. I want to explore some reasons why the portfolio assessment of writing seems so promising compared to assessment by writing exam.

Above all, to grasp the nettle of jargon at the start, it's a matter of improved *validity*. That is, portfolios give a *better picture of students' writing abilities*. Most writing assessments — even those that use actual writing samples produced in response to carefully tested prompts and that are graded by sophisticated holistic scoring—look at only one piece of writing in one genre done on one particular day. We all sense (and research backs it up; see, for example, Cooper, *The Nature and Measurement of Competency in English*) that we cannot trust the picture of someone's writing that emerges unless we see what he or she can do on various occasions on various pieces. And if we want to know about a student's *general* or *overall* writing ability, rather than just her skill in narrative or argument, we need to see her writing in various genres. Thus, most exams give us only the most blurred or distorted picture of the student's actual writing capability. Think about what happens when a student has a bad day or the test question touches a nerve or seems completely boring. Think how much more we can trust the picture we get from three to a dozen pieces done in different genres on different occasions.

Indeed, the use of portfolios throws light on the very process of measurement or evaluation. For portfolio assessment occupies an interesting in-between area between the clean, artificial world of carefully controlled assessment ("Take out your pencils. Don't turn over your books till I say 'go.'") and the swampy real world of offices and livingrooms where people actually write things for a purpose and where we as actual readers look at texts and cannot agree for the life of us (sometimes for the tenure of us) about what they mean and how good they are. Or, to put it differently, the use of portfolios highlights the tension between *validity* and *reliability*. Let me explain.

When a portfolio increases validity by giving us a better picture of what we are trying to measure (the student's actual ability), it tends by that very act to muddy reliability—to diminish the likelihood of agreement among readers or graders. That is, if we are only looking at single pieces of writing by students—all written under the same conditions, all in exactly the same genre, all answering the same question—we are much more likely to agree with each other in our rankings than if we are looking at portfolios containing three or a dozen pieces by each student, all of them different kinds of writing written under different conditions. When all the writing is alike, it is easier to agree about it. What a mess portfolios make, then, for psychometricians looking for reliable scoring. What a problem for holistic testers who've been bragging to professional psychometricians about good reliability scores on holistic readings.

But in this very *difficulty* about reliability, we see another benefit of portfolios—another reason why portfolio assessment appeals to many thoughtful people in our profession. For the truth is that many of us cannot help feeling that if reliability is high — if readers all agree about the worth of a piece of writing — something must be fishy. One of the main findings in literary theory and composition theory in recent years is that people consistently disagree in their interpretations or evaluations of texts, and we have no agreed-upon basis for settling such disputes. Neither literary theory nor philosophy gives us grounds for deciding on right or even better readings of texts. The very fact that carefully run holistic scoring sessions achieve high inter-reader reliability scores is simply an indication that all these people are not reading the way they normally read. "Good" holistic scoring usually means that readers must park their own standards at the door. This situation makes me want to suggest a new piece of testing jargon: "mirror validity." Whereas good normal validity means that the assessment gives a good picture of what we are trying to look at, good "mirror validity" would mean that the assessment gives a good picture of how we actually look at pictures — the assessment does justice to the way readers actually read.

So if assessment is to bear any believable relationship to the actual world of readers and responders, then reliability *should* be under strain. Given the tension between validity and reliability — the trade-off between getting good pictures of what we are trying to test and good agreement among interpreters of those pictures — it makes most sense to put our chips on validity and allow reliability to suffer. Notice how conventional writing assessments take exactly the opposite tack: they give us lots of agreement among readers but it is agreement about a faint, smudged, and distorted picture of the student's writing ability.

Perhaps I shouldn't criticize these writing exams too much. After all (depressing though this fact may be), the biggest force that has helped to inject much more actual *writing* into the English curriculum — rather than exercises on grammar and drills and discussions of good and bad writing — has probably been the growth of state and national assessments, which ask for *writing* rather than just answers on multiple-choice questions. Still, I can't resist going one step further in my criticism of these writing exams and pointing out that the "actual writing" that they call for is almost invariably done in response to a question that the student has never seen before; that there is no time for mulling the topic over beforehand, reading about it, discussing it with others, or writing exploratory drafts; that there is no time for feedback on drafts; and worst of all, that there is no time for substantive rethinking and revising. In short, not only do most writing assessments give us an unsatisfactory picture of the student's skill, the picture they give us is of the student using a skill that most of us would not really call *writing*.

It is nice to see unexpected reinforcement for this view from the field of mathematics:

> You will be interested to know that the Education Department of California recently established the ruling that mathematics teachers should not rely simply on tests to measure students' knowledge. Portfolios or files of students must contain at least two other types of evidence than that given by standardized or criterion-referenced tests, since these cannot adequately indicate students' understanding of concepts, ability to identify problems, and capability for handling alternative manipulations of mathematical notions. How ironic that the field the public thinks of as the most fixed would be the first to say that students' abilities to reflect on information, connect concepts, and put them into action make the difference. (Shirley Brice Heath, personal communication, 24 Jan. 1989)

Another benefit of using portfolios for assessment: they tend to promote a richer and more sophisticated understanding of writing. That is, if we are judging a portfolio containing various pieces of various sorts, we are less likely to fall into thinking that "writing" is one thing, less likely to think that we can rank John and Mary along one continuum with regard to something called "writing" — and more likely to realize that we have to talk about John's being strong in certain writing abilities or kinds of writing (e.g., using lively language or telling-stories language) and Mary strong in other writing abilities (e.g., using complex, interesting syntax or giving arguments). When we look at only a single sample from John and Mary, we are more tempted to think simplistically and assume that we can rank humans along a single continuum. In short, the use of portfolios exerts a subtle pressure against holistic grading and in favor of analytic grading, against single measures of intelligence or skill and in favor of the idea that humans have multiple intelligences and skills. Of course, nothing *stops* people from taking portfolios and ranking them holistically on scales of one through six, but in my view the experience of the richness of the portfolio helps us notice the perversity of that procedure.

Perhaps the most important benefit of portfolio assessment, and the one most richly illustrated in this book, is that it appeals to *teachers*: people who are not professional psychometricians but who (like Pat Belanoff and myself) nevertheless find themselves having to assess in a more systematic way than simply giving course grades. (The new movement in assessment tends to be made up of such amateurs rather than professionals in testing.) The fact is that teaching and testing often seem to be at odds. Why? For one thing, assessment tends to drive the curriculum, to wrest it out of the hands of teachers, and this makes teachers naturally resent it. "Is this going to be on the test?" ask the pesky students—and, of course, after we get over our annoyance, how can we blame them? But if the answer is no, then they feel little incentive to learn it; and we, correspondingly, feel a pressure not to teach it. For example, if (as is the case) the neatly structured five-paragraph essay works best on most writing exams, and if it is counterproductive to engage in exploratory writing (in which you allow yourself to get genuinely confused and genuinely question some of your own feelings and assumptions), then those exams put an obvious pressure on us as teachers in a direction that most of us do not want to go. When these tests have high stakes, as they often do (for example serving as the only gateway for all Florida college students to enter upper-division status), they put a heavy weight on teachers (especially untenured, adjunct, or graduate instructors—and most especially those at two-year colleges where there is enormous pressure to graduate students into four-year institutions) to focus their writing courses on the narrow and limited kinds of writing tasks demanded by the test.

Most of all, then, portfolio assessment is attractive to teachers because it *rewards* rather than punishes the essential things we try to place at the heart of our writing courses: exploratory writing, in which the writer questions deeply and gets lost; discussion with peers and with teacher; feedback on drafts from peers and teacher; and extensive, substantive revision. Students know that their portfolios of finished pieces will have a better chance of passing or getting a high evaluation if they have made use of all elements of a rich writing process. Thus, portfolio grading helps the learning climate because it reinforces continuing effort and improvement: it encourages students to try to revise and improve poor work rather than feel punished by it or give up. In a writing course, portfolios invite students to invest themselves and try for what is exciting, rather than playing it safe by writing "acceptably" or defensively.

Another important benefit of portfolio grading stems from the fact that testing often embodies a kind of adversarial stance. Testing is a process of "checking up on" students to see who is smart and who is dumb, who has been working hard and who has been goofing off. Assessment is also often informed by an adversarial stance toward *teachers*: not just because people don't trust teachers' grades (as indeed we often cannot), but because legislators, school boards, and colleges often feel that they need evidence about which teachers, schools, or programs are effective and which are not. This was clearly how things worked at Stony Brook, forcing the instituting of a proficiency exam. In short, assessment often seems to treat students and teachers as "the enemy" and heightens the adversarial dimension of schooling ("How well have you studied?" "How well have you taught?").

But assessment does not have to be this way. Portfolio assessment in particular is ideal for inviting students and teachers to be allies in the assessment process. Portfolio assessment takes the stance of an *invitation*: "Can you show us your best work, so we can see what you know and what you can do—not just what you do not know and cannot do?" And also an invitation to teachers: "Can you show us your students' best work—what they can do, not just what they cannot?"

For these reasons, then, I am excited that portfolio assessment has captured the interest of so many people. It seems to me inherent in the genre that it is infinitely malleable and variable. Standard kinds of assessment that try for more precision cannot be much fiddled with or bent, but this is just what portfolio assessment cries out for. So this collection of explorations of different ways portfolios have been used should be of great help to others who want to work out versions of their own.

## Notes

1. This situation leads many of us to the expedient of trying to figure out innovative forms of testing to help address the teaching deficit. People devise writing exams that help students explore and think about the writing process—for example, a placement test that builds in not just exploratory writing but also sharing drafts with peers and revising; or a proficiency exam that helps students think about genre and audience by having them write, say, a letter, a story, and an essay all about the same material. It is helpful to realize finally that a test can still function as a good test—and also as teaching—even if we don't evaluate every activity and piece of writing in it (see Grant and Kohli).

2. The AAHE publishes many interesting talks from these conferences (American Association of Higher Education Forum, One Dupont Circle, Suite 600, Washington, D.C. 20036.) AAHE has also recently published a list of short summaries of uses of portfolio assessment in various colleges and a longer list of people interested in portfolio assessment. It is also worth mentioning Archbald and Newman's small helpful book, which explores alternative methods of assessment—though aimed at secondary education. (Much of this paragraph and the paragraph it footnotes are taken from my "Goals and Testing" in *What Is English*.)

# Acknowledgments

We didn't have husbands who typed the manuscript nor children who played quietly while we worked, but we still have a few people whose help and support we'd like to acknowledge:

- Peter Elbow, who started it all for us;
- The graduate students and teachers in the Stony Brook writing program;
- Ohio State University at Marion for the special grants that made interstate collaboration possible;
- Lynda Barry and Suellynn Duffey, who read and commented on early drafts of papers;
- Richard Larson, who gathered the preliminary references for our bibliography on portfolio assessment.

# Introduction

In this book we've collected articles that Stephen North would call "practitioner lore." You'll find mention of Bakhtin occasionally and Stanley Fish at least once, but for the most part, the theory our contributors call upon reflects the work of Emig, Britten, Elbow, Murray, and others who are directly interested in what goes on in the composition classroom, in the writing-across-the-curriculum program, or in the teaching practicum. In this collection even the lore becomes specialized, for portfolios change depending upon who's being tested, what's being tested, and how those test results are being used. These differences exist even when the tests claim to be for the same kinds of students and the same kinds of purposes; the portfolio proficiency test at Michigan must differ from the one at Stony Brook. The very creation of a portfolio system, embedded as it inevitably is within the academic context of a unique institution, ensures its individual character. Lifting prompts, rubrics, and instruction sheets from other colleges won't work.

Most of us who are responsible for our schools' assessment programs have recognized what students have known for a long time: statistically accurate opscan tests don't tell us much about a student's writing ability. The literature on large-scale testing and prompt creation will not help a teacher determine whether a basic writer's skills merit a try at the school's freshman composition course. Psychometric testing, statistical theory, and numerical analysis can tell an administrator much about an institution's student population, but they can tell a teacher little about whether or not her or his twenty-five students understand the process of drafting, revising, and proofreading.

Teachers and institutions, for whatever reasons, need to assess students in the setting in which they function; awareness of this necessity lay behind our original call for the papers that have come together in this collection. The growing interest on the part of the state and federal authorities in standardization of assessment has a dangerous potential to locate decisions outside individual campuses. It is our hope that this book will help faculties find ways to institute assessment programs that satisfy outside interests without undermining the uniqueness of each institution. We do not need to acquiesce in what others dictate. We can assess and still remain true to what we have learned over the past thirty years about how students learn to write.

Admittedly, portfolio assessment breaks most of the conventional rules for good testing practice: it's messy, bulky, nonprogrammable, not easily scored, and time consuming (though, as you'll see, it's not as bad in these areas as its detractors paint it). Yet portfolio assessment appeals to the scientist in the academy as well as to the humanities professor. It certainly appeals to the business college dean. Why? The reason portfolio exams continue to crop up all over the country comes to this: portfolio assessment alone builds a textured, multi-layered, focused measure of the writing ability students can demonstrate when given time to revise papers, and portfolio assessment alone can map the process students go through as they write.

These are big claims. But those of us who have worked with portfolios can claim even more.

Portfolio assessment may not represent the only way, but it is certainly one of the best ways, to bring about faculty consensus (perhaps it's best to stop short of using the word *uniformity*) in grading. In truth, as William Condon and Liz Hamp-Lyons point out in Chapter 20, portfolio assessment affects internal controls on teachers and classrooms in terms of the standards and consensus that external controls seek to impose but fail to achieve.

However, no one who has participated in a series of portfolio-grading sessions will pretend that this consensus is easily developed. The chapters in this book may be lore, but they don't reveal incantations that will magically transform cranky old-timers or flighty TAs (or flighty old-timers and cranky TAs) into model examiners. Reading these chapters will provide no overnight understanding of the complexities of assessment or instant appreciation of student texts, just as instituting a portfolio in the classroom will not immediately produce startling improvement of student writing. We promise no miracles—just a lot of hard work, with a few side benefits. But primary among those benefits is a negotiated understanding of what proficiency represents in the context for which the portfolio was devised. Consensus. And, as in a negotiated peace, consensus doesn't represent everyone getting what he or she wants, but it does represent the best minds of the community hammering out an agreeable compromise.

Even when the student texts we examine differ vastly, the collaborative decision making that arises from routinely grading portfolios together makes us more attuned to one another. We all seem to accept that when students write collaboratively, they become part of a larger community of writers, in which they learn from each other and create products that they could not have produced alone. In much the same way, the more we grade with others, the more attuned we become to community standards and the more likely we are to award grades fairly to all. Even though we know, for example, that we are passing a paper because of the quality of its language, we can become aware that the rest of the group would fail it for faulty thinking, and we can then recognize that all of us need to rethink and perhaps adjust our standards. And the greatest benefit of all comes when we return to our classrooms enriched by new ways of commenting on student texts which have come to us during discussions with our colleagues.

The essays in *Portfolios* depict the ways in which various academic communities have come to grips with collaborative assessment. We've divided the book into four sections: portfolio proficiency testing, portfolio program evaluation, portfolios in the classroom, and the politics of portfolio assessment. In the first section we reprint two articles that describe the first large-scale writing-portfolio proficiency project in this country—the work done by Peter Elbow and Pat Belanoff at the State University of New York, at Stony Brook. These essays set forth the thought that informed the creation of this first portfolio exam and the basic structure of its functioning. An addendum by Pat traces its later evolution.

The chapters that follow describe various portfolio proficiency tests used to judge student writing. Dennis Holt and Nancy Westrich Baker explain Southeast Missouri State University's portfolio option to graduation proficiency testing; David Smit, Patricia Kolonosky, and Kathryn Seltzer take us through the complex process of implementing the portfolio system at Kansas State University; Roberta Rosenberg outlines how Christopher Newport College meets the state of Virginia's mandated criteria for writing competence; and Patrick Scott reveals how reformed examination procedures in the British schools affect the students' willingness to write and write well. We also include in this section Bonnie Hain's suggestions for replacing M.A. comprehensive exams and theses with departmentally controlled portfolio examinations and Joan Wauters's proposal for an equitable assessment for Alaska's diverse college population.

The second section discusses portfolios designed to assess programs: Karen Mills-Court and Minda Rae Amiran, of the State University of New York College at Fredonia, show how portfolios can be used to track students' growth as they work toward a degree. Anne M. Sheehan and Francine Dempsey explain their use of portfolios as a means of validating requests for college credit on the basis of specific life experiences. Judith Remy Leder traces her business students' writing in order to determine whether or not the business program has successfully imparted the skills they want their graduates to acquire. Finally, Richard Larson sets forth an analysis of how portfolios helped his school assess students' learning in its general education program.

The third section of our collection discusses portfolios in the context of the individual classroom. Jeffrey Sommers's article summarizes and discusses two types of classroom portfolios: one modeled upon the artist's portfolio and the other a "holistic" portfolio, which traces a student's development as well as the best of the student's writing. The rest of the essays in this section demonstrate the practical uses and creative applications of these two distinctive portfolios. Kathy McClelland joyfully reports her release from the tyranny of grading; Pamela Gay describes the freedom that a biology portfolio brought to basic writers; and Sharon Hileman and Beverly Case prove that a portfolio can make developmental English a student-centered activity. Roberta Camp and Denise Levine explain how the Educational Testing Service and the New York City Writing Project have used portfolios to develop middle-school students' awareness of the writing process. Not only have they provided a forum for student writing, they have promoted the type of self-reflection that many college teachers want to see in their more mature postsecondary students. Kerry Weinbaum's description of the portfolio she created with her eighth-grade students demonstrates that it's not only college instructors who struggle with issues of authority, creativity, and ownership of text. And Wendy Bishop's careful recreation of her experiences with graduate students and portfolios establishes that students of any age engage with the subject they're studying if they must confront not only the teacher's attitudes toward grading, but also their peers' attitudes toward the subject.

The final section focuses on the political aspects of portfolio assessment, for we know — as do all the contributors here — that politics is always an issue. Here, in brief, William Condon and Liz

Hamp-Lyons describe the problems they encountered as they developed Michigan's portfolio system and the positive outcome of that process. Chris Anson and Robert L. Brown, Jr., report what can go wrong and offer some suggestions for staying out of the traps that they have already discovered. For those whose recalcitrant faculty fear that portfolios violate the tenets of academic freedom, Marcia Dickson extends a cautionary tale, and Cherryl Armstrong Smith contributes a caveat about the whole idea of testing — portfolios included.

We know our readers will select out of these chapters their own set of ideas. We have been struck by the following.

1. Portfolios are particularly appropriate vehicles for metacognitive awareness. Both students and teachers can see a term's work and can hardly resist reflecting on what has happened over a period of weeks. Such metacognitive awareness is basic to further learning.

2. Portfolios are used for remarkably similar reasons, even though the portfolios and the systems in which they are embedded may differ greatly.

3. The standards for portfolio evaluation grow out of teachers' own interactive experiences with one another and with their students; standards are not imposed from the outside.

4. The specifics of individual portfolio systems are important to their authors; one assumes that this is because these specifics encode intentions, goals, and ideas unique to individual schools.

5. And, finally, portfolio assessment inevitably involves its users in larger issues of teaching, learning, institutional goals, and student individuality. Portfolios enable assessment, but they also reach out beyond assessment and engender changes that could not have been foreseen.

We would like to acknowledge the remarkable patience of our contributors, not just as they waited to hear from us, but, more importantly, for the manner in which they documented the countless hours they devoted to make their programs work. It's not easy to insist upon a complex form of assessment when all about you are insisting that there has to be a cheap, quantifiable, instant, valid, reliable, and universal measure of student writing ability. They have proven that none of us can appropriate another's system nor uncover an ideal one; all of us, in collaboration with colleagues, must develop our own. In the process, as many of these articles demonstrate, all involved inevitably become more committed and enthusiastic as they work out their own particular form of portfolio assessment. We hope that the enthusiasm will be catching and that reading about the variety of tasks for which our authors have used portfolio assessment will act as a springboard for other people, generating ideas, commitment, and enthusiasm—just as Peter and Pat's original paper was a springboard for the projects of our contributors.

# I

# Portfolios for Proficiency Testing

# State University of New York at Stony Brook Portfolio-based Evaluation Program

Peter Elbow and Pat Belanoff

We seek here to give an accurate and practical description of a portfolio-based evaluation system we have just instituted. But we can be more accurate and practical if we avoid giving a static picture and instead suggest the inevitable historical flux: the experiments that preceded this system and the inevitable opportunities for modification in the future.

## An Instructive History of Writing Evaluation

In the early years of the university (less than thirty years ago) the writing requirement at Stony Brook was a two-semester freshman course taught almost entirely by faculty members in the English department. Then, in the late 1960s, the requirement was reduced to a one-semester course. With the rapid expansion of the university, and one thing and another, that course began to be taught largely by graduate students. Before long, the limit of twenty students per section in writing courses was raised to twenty-five. All the while, writing skills of entering freshmen were probably declining.

Throughout the period, the crucial evaluative decision about proficiency in writing was in the hands of individual teachers — first faculty members, then TAs. It was assumed that teachers would not pass students who were not proficient—who could not write well enough for college or well enough for other university writing assignments.

In the mid-70s, faculty members from around the university began to complain that students came to them who had passed the required writing course but who nevertheless were unable to write acceptably. In response to this problem a proficiency exam was put in place in 1977. Passing the course no longer satisfied the writing requirement; the requirement was to pass the exam. With this change, the crucial decision about proficiency in writing was taken out of the hands of the individual teacher and given to examiners who did not know the student.

The goal of the proficiency exam was not just to reduce inconsistency in grading but in particular to keep up standards—or even push them up. Proficiency exams are inevitably attempts at quality control aimed not just at students but also at teachers. The Stony Brook exam, still a requirement for juniors and seniors who entered the university under that legislation, gives students two hours to write a persuasive or argumentative exam from a choice of three questions.

Though the exam was instituted as a move toward increased rigor, the legislation allowed students who passed it on entrance (it was given as a placement instrument) to be exempted from taking a writing course. Thus ironically, over the years (because of various factors, some of them economic), the exam ended up serving to exempt more and more students from any instruction at all in writing.

Standing back and looking at this story, we are struck with the idea that perhaps there would never have been a need for this added procedure for evaluating writing (a procedure in addition to individual teachers giving grades) if the university had still provided two semesters of instruction—particularly if they were taught by faculty members. Might this be true generally? That we get more evaluation of writing as we get less instruction?

## Problems with Proficiency Exams

As so many schools are discovering, proficiency exams have problems. First of all, there is serious doubt as to whether they do the very thing they are supposed to do, that is, accurately measure proficiency in writing. The research movement that gives high marks to holistic scoring for validity (but see Charmey) also shows that no matter how accurately we may evaluate any sample of a student's writing, we lose all that accuracy if we go on to infer the student's actual proficiency in writing from just that single sample. We cannot get a trustworthy picture of a student's writing proficiency unless we look at several samples produced on several days in several modes or genres. That is, not only may students not perform up to capacity on any one occasion, there is no one generic thing we can call "writing" (see Cooper). Besides, faculty members continue to complain about the lack of skill in students who pass the exam.

And even if proficiency exams gave a perfectly accurate measure of writing proficiency, they seriously undermine, by their nature, our teaching of writing and send a damaging message about the writing process. A proficiency test tells students that they can do their best writing (demonstrate their proficiency) with fifteen minutes of thought on some issue just sprung on them, followed by writing, followed (sometimes) by some cosmetic revising and copyediting. No drafts, no discussion of the issue with others, no trying out drafts on readers, no getting responses. Surely few of us ever write anything that matters to us in this fashion. But students who pass are encouraged to believe that they can write anything this way, and students who fail are encouraged to believe this is the process they need to learn.

In addition, when a proficiency exam embodies a university requirement, the whole university can be seen as saying to students, "Here's a serious matter (single-parent families, care of the elderly, the relation of books in the real world). Tell us what you think about it in approximately five hundred words; we know you can give it the attention it deserves; and then you can go home." The writing is unconnected to the study of any material and cut off from connection with any ongoing conversation. Is that how we want students to approach serious intellectual issues?

In short, our experience as teachers and our knowledge of recent research in the field made us uncomfortable with the proficiency exam we found in place here. We also began to notice at conferences that others, too, often introduced accounts of their proficiency exams with a disclaimer and some slight gesture of embarrassment.

Thus we began to experiment with portfolios to evaluate writing — portfolios prepared in a writing class but read by outside readers. We were looking for a kind of quality control — not only to avoid inconsistency but to hold up standards (for we do not disagree with this goal behind proficiency exams) — yet also for a way to avoid the problems of proficiency exams. For four semesters we experimented with a relatively small number of sections. In the fall of 1984, along with a new university writing requirement we'd been working for, we made portfolios an official procedure in all sections of EGC 101. The new requirement says that every student must get a C or higher in 101 or else take it again. The portfolio system says that no students can get a C unless their portfolios have been judged worth a C not only by their teacher but also by at least one other teacher who does not know them.

## Brief Overview of the Portfolio System

Our handout for all students in 101 is useful here for an overview:

> The portfolio system gives you a chance to satisfy the University writing requirement on the basis of your best writing, writing you have had a chance to think about and revise, and it helps us increase consistency in grading.
>
> At the end of the semester you will submit a portfolio of writing from the course: three revised pieces and one in-class piece. These will be judged by examiners who don't know you: 101 teachers other than your own. In order to get a C or higher in the course, your portfolio must pass. You must repeat the course if you do not get a C or higher. (Note that you are not *guaranteed* a C if your portfolio passes; your grade may be pulled down by other factors such as missing classes, or missing deadlines, or consistently unsatisfactory work on assignments.)
>
> At mid-semester you get a chance for a trial dry run on one paper. If it passes, that counts: include it in your final portfolio as it stands (though you may revise if you wish). If it fails, you can revise it and resubmit it in the final portfolio.
>
> Each paper must have an informal but typed introductory cover sheet that explains what you were trying to accomplish and describes some of your writing process, e.g., what feedback you got and what changes you made in revising.
>
> Portfolios will fail if they contain more than a very few mistakes in grammar, punctuation, spelling, or typing. You will also fail if you have more than a few sentences that are so tangled that the meaning is unclear to a general reader on first reading. This level of correctness and clarity may be harder for some of you to achieve than for others—especially those of you who come to English as a second language. But we insist on it because you all *can* achieve it: you all have a chance for feedback and careful revising.
>
> The examiners must be confident that the work you submit is

really yours. This is why we ask for an in-class piece of writing on which you've had no help. Instructors will not forward portfolios to the examiners unless they are confident it is *your* work—and thus will insist on seeing lots of your in-class writing and also insist on seeing the successive drafts of all your writing. They won't accept new pieces on new topics at the last moment that you haven't worked on earlier as part of the course.

The Three Revised Pieces

1. A narrative, descriptive, expressive piece, or an informal essay. The emphasis is on writing from your own experience. (Fiction is fine, not poetry.)

2. An academic essay of *any* sort—except for one restriction: the essay must be organized around a main point, not just organized as a narrative or description or a rendering of experience. Thus, for piece #1, you could write an informal essay that just tells a story with a "moral" added at the end—or just describes a scene with a brief conclusion at the end. Such essays can be excellent writing, but for category #2 we are insisting on a different kind of essay—one that most university professors require when they assign writing in a subject matter course: an essay organized in terms of an idea (such as a claim you are arguing for) or an intellectual task (such as comparing, contrasting, defining, or analyzing).

3. An academic essay which analyzes another essay: that tells *what it is saying* and *how it functions* or *how effectively it says it*. You might analyze a newspaper editorial, a published essay, an essay written by someone in your small group, or you might even analyze one of your own essays. This is practice in close reading and in being able to explain how prose works on readers.

# Modes of Writing

We've continually adjusted and tinkered with the kinds of writing we ask for, trying to embody the commitments we stand for as a program, yet trying not to hem in teachers too much.

Modes 2 and 3 above obviously represent our commitment to academic discourse, to the kinds of writing that other faculty members will assign. Indeed we suggest that teachers might want a paper that students could use in another course for mode 2.

Mode 1 represents our strong commitment to imaginative or expressive writing—writing that tries to render or communicate one's own experience rather than explain or analyze it. We feel this mode of writing is currently under attack as inappropriate at the university level. But as Britton shows, expressive writing is the matrix from which skill in other modes derives; English departments are committed to the *study* of imaginative writing as perhaps the best expression of the human spirit; and personal or creative writing is the only mode through which most students can become sufficiently excited with writing to keep it up when not obliged to write — which is the only way they'll ever become genuinely skilled. If we don't give students practice in this kind of writing, no one else in the university will.

We've had some misunderstandings about the distinction between the kind of informal essay acceptable for mode 1 and the more formal one required for modes 2 and 3: teachers occasionally tell students that an essay fits the latter categories when readers feel it does not. We've been reluctant to emphasize words like *formal* and *academic* because of what they often do to student prose. Probably we should talk more about audience and the discourse of various communities.

Some teachers like to use category 1 for the mid-semester dry run: they want to start with what is easier and more fun and build up to what is harder. Other teachers use category 2 or 3 for the dry run in order to get an early start on what usually needs more work and to prevent overconfidence about mid-semester results. Out of this dilemma rise some current experiments in using more than one dry run piece.

We decided not to evaluate the cover sheets: they must be there but students are not penalized if they are done poorly. We made this decision because we are committed to the usefulness of the process writing or "metawriting" called for by cover sheets, yet we don't want to emphasize it too much for students or teachers who hate it. Also we want to reduce as much as possible what readers have to evaluate. Cover sheets are more for students and teachers than for outside readers — though when the writing is borderline it can help the reader to look at them. And readers are invited to allow them to count favorably in borderline cases.

Similarly, poor in-class writing does not count against a student (though we don't much talk about that to students). It represents a symbolic guard against plagiarism. Our main guard is that the individual teachers should not forward writing they are not confident of. Again we let it count favorably in borderline cases. This decision represents our desire not to penalize students for writing they've not had a chance to revise (though some would say that our view does not pay enough heed to "exam writing" as an important mode that students need practice in).

## The Evaluation Process

At mid-semester teachers meet to discuss sample papers and agree on some verdicts — a "calibration" section. Then teachers distribute their students' actual mid-semester dry run papers to each other for a reading. The judgment is a simple binary Yes or No, Pass or Fail, worth a C or not. No comments or marks are made on the papers (except to circle unambiguous mistakes in mechanics — especially if a paper fails for that reason). A brief comment is paperclipped to failing papers — usually only a few sentences. (It is not the job of readers to diagnose or teach — only to judge. It is the teacher's job to interpret these comments to the student when necessary.)

If the teacher agrees with the verdict, the process is finished — and this is the case with most papers. But a teacher who disagrees can ask for a second reading from another reader. If that second reading is the same, the teacher can either go along with the two readers or else seek a third reading to validate his or her perception. However, the stakes are not high at mid-semester. A failure doesn't count against anyone, as this is a time for teachers and students to get used to the process; in fact, teachers tend to prefer stern verdicts at mid-semester to make sure students are not lulled into false security.

At the end of the semester the evaluation process is repeated but with full portfolios: the calibration meeting with sample portfolios; first, second, and occasionally third readings; comments only on failed portfolios. Again judgments are binary, and we treat portfolios more or less as a whole instead of making separate verdicts on each paper. (We say that a portfolio shouldn't pass if one paper is definitively weak even if the others are very strong, but we purposely leave this matter somewhat inexplicit, believing that there needs to be room for judgment here.) But this time the gun is loaded: a student whose portfolio fails must repeat the course. Nevertheless, if the two concurring readers agree that the failure is due to one paper, the student may revise that paper and resubmit the portfolio. We treat the inevitable appeals to our office from students the way we treat appeals about grades. That is, we consent to hear stories or read papers when it seems important, for we feel we must be as loyal to students as to teachers. On those occasions when we see something genuinely out of line (rather than just a reasonable verdict that we might have called differently), we go back to the teacher or reader or group and ask them to look again — perhaps saying nothing more, perhaps telling our sense of the difficulty.

Note that though there is a lot of machinery, we try hard to keep it as quick and simple as possible. Because judgments are only Yes or No (instead of 1 through 4 or 5 as with most holistic scoring), because we read portfolios as a whole giving only one verdict, and because there are no comments except brief ones on failing portfolios, readings are surprisingly fast. Many strong portfolios can be read very quickly — some of the papers even skimmed.

## An Emphasis on Small Collaborative Groups of Teachers

Small groups of teachers are presently the main vehicle for the functioning of the portfolio system. We invite teachers to form into their own groups of four or five according to friendship or interest (and we group those who prefer random groupings). These groups meet to read papers from each others' classes at mid-semester and portfolios at the end of the semester. They decide on their own specific deadlines and on which of the three kinds of papers should come in at mid-semester (or decide to disagree — allowing a mixed bag of genres). Some groups decide to require a second dry run paper three-quarters through the semester — or to ask for two papers at a slightly late mid-semester date (in an effort to give students more sense of how they are doing).

A few teachers have complained that we give too much autonomy to the small groups — in particular that the crucial evaluative decision is too exclusively rooted in the small face-to-face group. They would prefer more work in larger groups (as, for example, when Elbow treats the Teaching Practicum as one large portfolio group for the fifteen or so new TAs each fall who are teaching in the program for the first time). This complaint stems from a justifiable nervousness that different groups will evolve different standards (and a couple of groups have gotten the reputation among teachers of being "harder" or "easier"). More pointedly, there is the fear that standards will be compromised because readers in a small group often will know who the teacher is for a particular paper and therefore may feel pressured to pass it if they know the teacher wants it passed — because the teacher is their friend or is particularly defensive or edgy. (We both know from experience with the system that it hurts when your own student's portfolio is failed and you think it deserves to pass: you are deeply involved with this student and gratified by his or her enormous progress.)

These are serious worries raised by conscientious teachers, and we feel them ourselves—though the majority prefers the emphasis on small groups. (In fact we suggested having a larger group this last time and only five volunteered.) Did we start off giving too much autonomy to small groups because of our strong predilection for giving teachers their head and because of Stony Brook's strong tradition of total teacher autonomy? Perhaps. Anyway, we've made three policy changes this year that provide somewhat greater commonality or corporate functioning to the portfolio system:

1. We now have large meetings in the middle and at the end of the semester to read sample papers or portfolios. All teachers must attend. We agree on, or negotiate verdicts for, sample papers or portfolios. The change helps keep standards more consistent since formerly we left this calibrating function to individual groups.

2. We are now instituting a programwide response sheet to attach to all failing dry run papers and all failing portfolios. These forms will present, as it were, a common voice of the program to augment the more local voice of the reader or small group and will have checkable boxes that represent programwide categories as to weaknesses in portfolio papers—though of course individual readers will also write a short comment in a space provided. (We have seen occasional comments that were *too* cryptic or idiosyncratic.)

3. Portfolios may now be revised if they fail with only one weak paper. The old policy increased pressure on readers not to fail an unsatisfactory portfolio if it somehow seemed clear from internal evidence or from special pleading from the teacher that the student was really quite skilled and diligent and should not have to repeat the course. Our new policy makes it easier to stick by tough standards—to say, "This isn't good enough"— but still give students a chance to redeem themselves. (This rewrite policy represents a compromise between those who wanted to allow *all* failing portfolios to be revised and those who wanted to stick with our original no-rewrite policy.)

In effect, these additions of programwide consistency are designed to save our emphasis on small collaborative groups for evaluating writing proficiency. Perhaps in the end we will conclude we should jettison that emphasis altogether and use an evaluative mechanism that is more "pure" or ETS-like—less messy. But we would find that sad.

For one thing, we want these small groups to have a prominent place in our program so they can function in other ways too—not just for portfolio business. We encourage groups to form around an interest in a particular technique or approach to teaching, even to do a bit of research. We think teachers need small groups to discuss other teaching matters and for just plain gossip and support. Most teachers like them.

As for impurity in evaluation, we could take a kind of amateur "aw shucks" line and say that we don't need perfect evaluation; we care more about teaching than about evaluation; we're satisfied that this evaluation is much more consistent than the grading of individual teachers and so we don't worry that it is less consistent than some God- or machinelike objectivity. But our reading and talking with others in the field of evaluation and our experiments over more than three years tempt us to take a more uppity line. We suspect that this "impure" process may in the end represent better evaluation.

That is, on the one hand we obviously seek a kind of objectivity and quality control—we seek an evaluation process that involves outside readers with negotiated common standards. But on the other hand, because of our lively sense of the imperfections in the science of evaluating writing proficiency, we seek frankly *not* to seal off entirely the possibility of "leaks" or "pollution" into the evaluative procedure from the teacher who knows the student.

Yes, the whole portfolio system makes for messes—since it puts "objective" examiners in the same room with the student's own teacher and gets them tangled up in discussions of specific papers where the teacher may be personally involved. The system thus makes trouble. (Though in fact we've had little rancor.) But this is nothing but the trouble that results from putting out on the table what has always been in the closet in programs that evaluate with proficiency exams or leave evaluation wholly in the hands of the individual teacher. It helps to have some of these messy discussions in large meetings led by the directors of the program, but there is something to be said for letting some of them also go on in more private small groups where of course there is some impure negotiating. We think this allows for more growth in teaching in the long run.

## A Different Model of Evaluation

About half the mid-semester papers fail. At the end of the semester about ten percent of the portfolios fail, but that goes down to about five percent after some are rewritten. (The number of students who must retake the course is slightly higher because a certain number of them fade away toward the end of the semester and don't complete the course — or fail for other reasons.)

We see the portfolio as a way to ask for better writing and to get more students to give it to us. By giving students a chance to be examined on their best writing — by giving them an opportunity for more help — we are also able to demand their best writing. For example in our first semester of small-scale experimenting, we discovered that when we only explained the system to students and waited till the end of the semester to evaluate (no dry run), many of them failed who obviously didn't need to fail. They hadn't put in enough time or care because they clearly hadn't understood or believed that we were requiring good writing to pass — better writing than writing exams tend to ask for, perhaps better writing than their teachers had required for a C. (We noticed an interesting difference between the experience of reading a failing proficiency exam and a failing portfolio: the failing proficiency tends to make us sad that perhaps the student "couldn't do it"; the failing portfolio tends to make us mad that the student didn't put in enough time and care.)

This sounds like raising standards and raising the passing rate at the same time. Something fishy here. But evaluation by portfolio sets aside the traditional model of evaluation or measurement (norm-referenced) that leads us to assume that grades should ideally end up distributed along a bell curve. This model of measurement aims to rank or differentiate students into as many different grades as possible, for it is a tradition of "measuring" minds; the ideal end product is a population distributed along a bell-shaped curve (as in IQ scores or SAT scores). Our portfolio process, on the other hand, builds on a different model of evaluation or measurement (criterion-referenced or mastery-based or competence-based evaluation). This more recent tradition assumes that the ideal end product is a population of students who have all finally passed because they have all been given enough time and help to do what we ask of them. (See McClelland on competence testing; also Grant et al.; also Elbow on the effects of a competence approach on teachers.)

## Problems

We keep hoping that all problems can be tinkered away through further adjustments but no doubt many are inherent in the approach.

- The system makes more work for teachers. We have done all we can to keep readings from being too onerous or time consuming:

judgments are only yes/no, portfolios are judged as a single unit, cover sheets and in-class writing need not be read (usually), and comments are given only to failing portfolios—and then only brief ones. But the work remains.

- It puts more pressure on teachers and makes some feel anxious— especially those using it for the first time. If your student fails a proficiency exam, it's easy to say, "Well, I'm not teaching exam writing," but if your student fails the portfolio you are liable to feel—at first anyway—as though *you* have failed.

- Some teachers feel it dominates the course too much: as though they are having to "teach to the portfolio," as though it is too much in their minds and their students' minds, as though they are reduced to spending the whole semester on three main pieces and therefore narrowing their focus. We try to avoid this, we want an evaluation system that one can "teach to" without having to change or "pollute" one's teaching at all, a system that lets you teach almost any course. This feeling of constraint is felt most by teachers the first time they use the system, but it is also felt by a few very experienced and competent teachers.

- Some teachers feel that our reliance on groups puts strains on their relations with other teachers in the group when they disagree over verdicts.

- Some teachers feel that the emphasis on revising—and especially the opportunity to revise some failed portfolios—babies or coddles students too much and lets lazy students get by with help and nagging from teachers and help from peers.

## Strengths

But the program continues to present more advantages than problems:

- The portfolio process judges student writing in ways that better reflect the complexities of the writing process: with time for freewriting, planning, discussion with instructors and peers, revising, and copyediting. It lets students put these activities together in a way most productive for them. And it doesn't insist that students be judged on all their efforts.

- The message to students is that thinking and writing are enhanced by conversation with peers and teachers—and that first responses, although valid, need not be final ones. It also tells them that their reactions and opinions about serious matters deserve time and attention.

- It makes teachers allies of their students — allies who work with them to help them pass. Teachers become more like the coach of the team than the umpire who enforces and punishes infractions. One teacher commented, "They don't blame me for the standard they've been asked to reach. I think because of this I have a very good relationship with my students and I'm more comfortable in the role of helper than that of judge." (See Elbow, "Embracing Contraries.")

- It draws teachers together, encourages discussion about ways to help students and about standards. Inevitably, this makes standards more consistent and teachers more conscious of their teaching methods.

- It emphasizes some important complexities of audience — showing students, for example, that we usually write for more than one reader and often for readers who do not know us. Many students come to college convinced that English teachers are hopelessly idiosyncratic and rarely agree — that one teacher's rules and expectations rarely match another's. We want students to realize that teachers can agree on evaluations even if their criteria may be somewhat different. We all write for audiences of individuals who agree on some things and disagree on others — "interpretive communities." Both students and teachers need more experience and talk about this crucial issue.

- Thus the portfolio addresses a critical, professionwide problem in evaluation that most teaching sweeps under the rug. That is, to grade a paper is to interpret and evaluate a text, yet our profession now lacks (if it ever possessed) a firm theoretical disciplinewide basis for adjudicating between different interpretations or evaluations of a text. No wonder we are uneasy in our grading. In this situation, the only source of at least some trustworthiness in grading comes from the kind of negotiation in a community that the portfolio procedure sets up. Such negotiation of a text helps teachers make connections between the teaching of writing and the study of literature.

## Experiments with the Placement Exam

It was interesting for us, without special training in evaluation and testing, to find a proficiency exam in place, to go to meetings of the National Network on Testing and read its newsletter (and other material on testing), and gradually to conclude that no one really had the answer about the evaluation of writing. This realization was empowering and gave us courage to experiment.

Having done so with the portfolio and lived to tell the tale (so far, anyway), we are now experimenting with the placement exam that all students take on entrance to the university. Instead of giving students two hours for one essay as we have done in the past, we are now asking for four writing tasks: (1) twenty minutes of exploratory writing or freewriting about an extended quotation; (2) a one-sentence summary of the quotation; (3) a one-hour essay on the topic of the quotation; (4) twenty minutes of informal, retrospective process writing about the writing the student has already done on the exam.

We find this approach serves the two goals of testing that we're also trying to serve with the portfolio process. First, it improves trustworthiness of evaluation, since the readers can base their judgment on more than one piece in more than one mode. Second, it sends the message we want to send to students about the richness and multiplicity of writing as a process.

In the end we see the portfolio system as a way to try to serve two contrary but desirable goals. On the one hand, we want some programwide commonality, not only in the evaluation of proficiency but also in getting teachers to work together under some common guidelines. On the other hand, we want to provide as much autonomy as possible to individual teachers and small groups of teachers.

# 2

# Using Portfolios to Increase Collaboration and Community in a Writing Program

Pat Belanoff and Peter Elbow

We began by asking how our system of evaluation by portfolio reflects our philosophy as writing program administrators. But we quickly realized that we had never really articulated our philosophy, so the question became more subtle and empirical: Looking back at the gradual development of our portfolio system, what can we learn about our philosophy? Trying to answer this second question, we came to realize how deeply *collaboration* and *community* lie at the heart of our system — and that we are even more indebted to the work of Ken Bruffee than we had realized (though we had always acknowledged indebtedness).

## Collaboration and Community Among Students

Testing tends to emphasize solitary work. One of the main features of most testing situations is a set of safeguards to prevent students from helping each other. The physical setting for proficiency exams here highlighted the solitary nature of assessment: students being herded in large numbers into large lecture halls for a two-hour exam. The paradox was vivid: hundreds of students in the same room — breathing, grunting, and in the warmer months sweating and smelling — all working together yet none really working together at all.

Yet more and more research has shown that much if not most writing in the world has a significant collaborative dimension. In the sciences, business, industry, and the professions, joint authorship is common — often even the norm. Drafts are always going around for collaborative kibitzing. Often the "wrong person" even gets the byline. (For example, no one seems to feel anything strange about judges publishing opinions as "theirs" which are really written by their clerks. Indeed, the judge tends to feel the "decision" or "opinion" is indeed his. Cultural conventions determine much. The aristocratic dinner-party hostess feels that the dinner prepared by her cooks is "her" dinner.)

It is the traditional and romantic link between writing and literature that has given us the cultural model of writing as something produced by the lone toiler in the garret, suffering to get it perfect — and finally bringing it forth as wholly and jealously "his." But even in the humanities and literature, we see, if we look closely, a strong collaborative dimension to most writing. It's not just that most scholars share drafts for help from colleagues and editors. Even the lone artist in his garret — we see more and more — is writing out of a community. Bruffee points us to the theoretical work of people like Vygotsky and Bakhtin, inviting us to look at "solitary work" through a different lens and see an essentially communal and dialogic dimension in it. And the collaborative dimension of literature is palpable in certain flowerings such as in Elizabethan England or Paris in the '30s: writers often felt themselves consciously mining a single creative vein — overtly borrowing and responding to each others' texts.

Thus we look for ways to foster student collaboration in courses in our program: not just sharing drafts and getting feedback from peers, teachers, and tutors in the Writing Center but also a sense of a community of support. We believe that a sense of community helps students learn better and with more pleasure. (Unless students continue to write by choice after the course is over, they'll never improve very much.) And yet our students come to us deeply habituated to think of all school work as solitary and all evaluation as competitive. "My grade," most students reason, "can only be better to the extent that my neighbor's grade is worse." Therefore, students are often reluctant to help their peers on important graded work because it feels as though they will be hurting themselves.

We were instinctively troubled, then, by a testing procedure that worked at cross purposes to our teaching — a proficiency exam that said to students, "Your real writing, your writing that counts, is writing that you do alone, with no time for real revision, without discussing the topic with others, without sharing drafts, without getting feedback, and without in any sense communicating with real readers." Because it's a slow, tough battle to change such individualistic attitudes, we sought a testing process that reinforces collaboration — that rewards students for learning to get help from others on their writing.[1]

Many students do in fact have trouble producing papers that pass the portfolio without help. This is especially striking at the level of copy-editing: it's not just the weak or non-native students who need help to remove all surface mistakes (indeed few of us can successfully copy-edit our own texts; we seldom publish without the help of an editor). But students need help at all stages of writing: generating ideas, clarifying them, focusing, presenting them coherently, and so forth. We want them to walk out of our course and on to other courses — and out into the rest of their lives — with the experience of having had to get feedback from teachers, Writing Center tutors, friends, and relatives in order to get their papers good enough. To some this sounds like cheating, but we insist that it is what people need to learn if they're going to write effectively in a world in which collaborative writing is becoming the norm.

*Cheating.* The word needs to come up. Indeed "collaboration" itself is a word that can connote illicit connections (and not just in wartime France). Since we don't see a simple rule or abstract principle to distinguish between cheating and legitimate collaboration, we make the issue one of human judgment at the one-to-one level — rather than a matter of "test security." That is, the student's own teacher does not forward a piece to the portfolio process unless she is confident it is the student's "own work" — as she sees the matter in a context where collaboration is emphasized. Thus teachers insist on lots of draft writing and in-class writing from students; it is a program principle that students turn in drafts with final revisions; and students may not change topics at the last minute for revised papers. (We also stress cover sheets that ask students to acknowledge help.) This system will not catch a student who gets a roommate or a mother to do all his revising. Traditional proficiency tests prevent this kind of cheating, but at a price of undermining a good writing process.

We could guard against cheating more if we gave more weight to the in-class portfolio writing piece. We've tended not to penalize students for poor in-class writing in their portfolio. We could make the in-class piece serve as explicit practice for exam writing. Or we could allow students to revise their in-class writing over a number of classes—but with no collaboration. We could even allow students to get feedback before revising, but have all this activity take place in class. This is an intriguing possibility we hadn't articulated to ourselves till writing this essay: It wouldn't undercut collaboration or community—just make it function in a slightly different way.

## Collaboration and Community Among Teachers

Too much teaching occurs in isolation (at all levels of education). Teachers go into their classrooms and close their doors. Among the many sad effects of this isolation is the "grading fallacy." Teachers working in isolation slip too easily into believing that they *know* what an A paper is and what an F paper is—that they are calling on grading standards made in heaven. A teacher who is uncertain or perplexed about her grades often feels flawed or inadequate in some way.

And yet of course there are enormous disparities among teachers' grades—especially on something as slippery as writing. And so, whereas isolated teachers often drift into having too much faith in their own grades, the students of isolated teachers often drift into skepticism or even cynicism: a sense that evaluation is nothing but an accident of teachers' personalities. Such students think that getting good grades is nothing but psyching out idiosyncrasies—figuring out what particular teachers "like" or "want."

As an antidote to teacher isolation, our portfolio system brings teachers together to work as colleagues. All meet at the middle and end of the semester to discuss sample papers and try for agreement. And they come together at least twice more in the semester in smaller portfolio reading groups to evaluate dry-run papers and portfolios.

Some teachers who have always been troubled by grades experience great relief at discovering others who are also uncertain. They are even pleased to discover the striking disparity of standards that sometimes emerges. Other teachers, however, feel disturbed and adrift when we are at loggerheads in a large meeting over a particularly vexing borderline paper. They are disturbed to feel moving sand under the foundation—as though everything is arbitrary and anarchic. One powerful faction gives powerful arguments for failing the sample paper; someone even blurts out, "How can anyone who considers himself literate and professional possibly give this paper a C?" But another group gives strong arguments for passing it, and the blurter discovers that the defenders of the paper are not just the flakey wimps he suspected but also include a colleague he respects as more perceptive and learned than himself.

There can be painful moments in these meetings, hurtful words. ("It's not the paper that flunks; it's the assignment!") Yet as the semesters of experimenting and official use have passed, we as writing program administrators have gradually come to treasure these difficult moments. The other day when the heat was rising in the room, one of us couldn't resist saying: "We're sorry you are having a hard time, but we're having a ball!" It's such a relief to see all this disparity of judgment as interaction between people — as heads butting against other heads. When the disparity of standards is locked inside solitary heads, it's only visible to students who compare notes and to administrators looking at different teachers' grade sheets. When a newcomer complains, "Why do you encourage all this chaos and disagreement?" it's fun to be able to reply, "We're not making it, we're just getting it out in the open instead of leaving it swept under the rug."

We're getting better at chairing these meetings: trying to induce people to use the "believing game" with each others' perceptions; trying to keep people from prematurely digging in their heels and calling each other idiots. For we sense that the hurtful behavior often stems from anxiety: understandable anxiety at the threat to their confidence in their own standards or their own teaching. ("Might I have let some of my students down?")

On some samples we actually reach consensus, but on others teachers remain divided. Here's where it's important for us to intervene, get a quick vote to show where the numbers lie (sometimes the discussion can fool you), and say, "Fine. We're split. Here's a picture of where our community disagrees; this is a paper that will pass in some groups and fail in others; nevertheless, this picture can give you some guidance when you go off to make your individual verdicts. We're gradually giving each other a sense of this community's standards." For even though it is the disagreement that is most obvious at such moments, we, from where we sit, see vividly that the discussion itself has produced much more agreement in grading and community standards than we used to have when all teachers graded alone.[2]

In short, the portfolio process is helping us move toward community, toward some commonality of standards — but only over a period of semesters and years. Theorists who talk about "communities of discourse" (who tend to work alone) like to assume that communities of discourse "always already" exist. Though in one sense they do, in another and important sense, they only exist to the extent that they are earned through time and turmoil.

This gradual movement toward some commonality is earned by

teachers learning to understand and even give some credence to the perceptions and estimations of others. They learn that some teachers are not as disturbed by messed-up sentence structures as others are. They learn that some attend more to details than to the overall picture. Some are especially beguiled by particular topics or put off by particular approaches to topics. As teachers talk about all this among themselves, they learn from each other. They become a bit less disturbed about differences of judgment and even realize that there is some valuable balancing off of one person's standard against that of someone else who has a slightly different set of priorities. And then too, they alter their own standards a bit. Someone may discover, for example, that she's been paying too much (or too little) attention to slips in usage. Individuals know that their opinions and their standards will help form those of the group. They usually discover that each of them offers something special. If one person in the group is known to be the toughest, and she passes a paper, the others can feel comfortable about the rating. If a group member who has a particularly good sense of logic criticizes the logic of a paper, other group members accept the decision—and may even deliberately seek out that person if logic seems crucial. One of the nicest things is that when a perplexing portfolio fails, the student's teacher ends up with more to tell the student because the group has usually discussed the work.

These large and small group collaborative meetings, then, tend to chip away at the grading fallacy. Where grading-in-isolation invites teachers to be complacent about their own individual grading standards—and punishes them for being uncertain (since uncertainty is so paralyzing when you are trying to grade in isolation)—these collaborative meetings invite teachers to be uncertain and open in making judgments and punishes dogmatism about grades.

Teachers tell us that they carry some of the power of this collaboration and community back into the classroom. As they teach (whether the door's open or closed), they don't feel so isolated. Sometimes the effect of collaboration is direct: as a teacher reads a paper or ponders a distinction, she relies on an insight from a small or large portfolio meeting; she has more experience than her own to fall back on. But even without such direct help, teachers know they are part of a larger group which in some way comes into the classroom with them; they speak in their own voices but the voices of their colleagues play a role in how they speak.

In portfolio groups we are not trying to agree on standards for all grade levels from A to F. We are just trying to agree on whether papers are good enough for a C or not: just trying to give ourselves a bit of a foundation for our subsequent solitary grading by trying to agree about that crucial line which divides papers we can affirm as "satisfactory college work" and those we call wanting. We don't even have to agree on reasons or diagnoses for turning thumbs up or down. Nevertheless, when a teacher on her own is trying to decide whether to give a B or a B+, she really isn't alone; somewhere in her mind the values of her portfolio group are at work. And if she has doubts, she knows these are appropriate, not a sign of some deficiency.

Of course, we also recognize the problems in all this. Some teachers have told us that when they work in small groups they sometimes know the teacher for the paper they are reading and therefore find themselves reluctant to fail it. The teacher is dogmatic and will badger; or the teacher is insecure and will complain and feel undermined by the failure of her student. Another problem is a possible difference of standards from group to group. A group has occasionally gotten a reputation for toughness or easiness.

To some extent, we can't overcome these problems no matter what our system is. Teachers will always be insecure, teachers will always differ in their standards. Our portfolio system doesn't create these difficulties — it merely brings them out in the open where we all must recognize them and cope with them in some way. We try to deal with the potential inequality of standards among groups by means of discussing samples in our large meetings before each evaluation period. And the portfolio system cannot easily become inbred because groups only stay intact for a year or so because of changes in schedules and teaching assignments. The nicest thing is that the problem of standards is no longer just ours as program administrators — the teachers themselves become concerned about it and feel a need to work toward progress.

We've debated with teachers the pros and cons of small vs. large portfolio reading groups. Large groups create an anonymity which reduces the chance that a particular reader will judge a particular paper on the basis of who the teacher is. But large groups tend to diminish the sense of community. Last year, we gave teachers the option of joining a large anonymous group or forming their own smaller groups. Most opted for the latter, valuing the feel of the small group. Here are comments from a couple of teachers when we asked them to write to us about this question:

> I feel that if we only meet in larger semi-formal groups, the give and take which is needed to see that there are other ways to handle a topic will be lost.

> When two of my students' papers failed and I felt they should have passed, I asked for second and third readings, and then got into a heated discussion with the other group members who read the papers. At the end of the discussion, both of the papers still failed, but I was satisfied with the failures. I learned some things in the discussion about my own standards (in certain ways they were too low) by explaining why I thought the papers should pass. In addition, we as a group got more clear on what our standards were.

Our colleague, Professor Sheryl Fontaine (whose field is research in composition), wrote, "I've worked in many anonymous readings and don't feel they were any more reliable than the [small] portfolio groups."

## Collaboration Between Students and Teachers

In addition to collaboration among peers (that is, among students and among teachers), the portfolio system also promotes a more complex non-peer collaboration between teachers and students. It complicates the authority relationship and we think it promotes what might be called "collaborative leadership": the kind of collaboration one finds between player and coach or between writer and editor. Though some players hate their coach, both parties share the common goal of winning games. Writer and editor share a common goal: publication and success with readers. In these non-peer relationships, reality rewards both parties for working together — and punishes them for working at cross purposes.

The portfolio throws the teacher somewhat into the role of coach or editor because the crucial decision as to whether the student is eligible to get a C or obliged to repeat the course depends on someone other than the teacher. The teacher becomes someone who can help the student overcome an obstacle posed by a third party and is thus less likely to be seen by students as merely "the enemy."

This interesting dynamic ends up giving the teacher a kind of added power — psychologically speaking, anyway. That is, if a student doesn't cooperate — if he doesn't come in for a conference or if he tries to con the teacher or hide his weaknesses — he won't get as much help. The teacher on the other hand, can remove herself from the role of enemy and decrease the chances of a student's getting mad at her for all the work he has to do to bring his writing up to snuff. The portfolio system permits the teacher to say things like this:

> You have made enormous progress here, I'm excited at how much better your writing is than at the beginning of the semester. I know

how hard you've worked. But I have to tell you that I fear your piece will not get a C from the portfolio readers.

This piece of yours works for me. When I read it I hear you, I feel the force of your concerns, I am won over. But I suspect some of your success depends on my having gotten to know you and your concerns and my having read some of your drafts and exploratory writing. I suspect your piece won't work so well for a reader who is a stranger to you.

The leverage here is sometimes ascribed to the "good cop/bad cop" game ("I'd like to give you a break but my buddy is a mean son of a bitch"), but it isn't just a game with the portfolio system. The "bad cop" is really there in the person of the anonymous portfolio reader. The teacher is communicating the real situation.

But because the portfolio system complicates the authority relationship, it also turns out to give the teacher less power. That is, in addition to playing the "good cop/bad cop" game, the teacher must also play the "cop-handcuffed-to-the-prisoner" game. Virtually every teacher who has worked with the portfolio has gotten burned once. It hurts to have to come back to a student and say, "I'm sorry, but I seem to have misled you. Your portfolio didn't pass." (Even after going back for third and fourth readings!) Thus teachers learn to say, "I think this is good work, I like it, I would give it a C. But we'll have to see what portfolio readers think."

We like what this does to the use of grades in a writing course. Teachers retain almost complete power over grades. (They can give any grade they wish on papers; they can give any course grade they wish to students who pass the portfolio; they can give any grade below a C to students who do not pass.) But the portfolio makes teachers a bit less likely to give grades on weekly papers—and instead concentrates their energies on useful comments. We like this because students often ignore comments when there is a grade; and teachers often write better comments when they're not having to justify a grade. Comments under the portfolio system are more likely to be experienced as real communication: something the teacher wants the student to act on and something the student has a need to understand.

We recognize that many students don't like not getting those weekly grades—at first, anyway: "I have the right to know exactly where I stand!" But the portfolio system finally provides the answer we've all been waiting for: "I'm sorry but I don't know exactly where you stand. Where you stand depends partly on unknown and not fully predictable readers. The best I can do is give you honest feedback and advice." This is finally a writerly answer: the answer that all writers must face. Students have always known that their

English teachers' standards varied from teacher to teacher—but they thought that meant we weren't any good at our job. We can make them understand that we don't have to agree exactly on standards or on taste in order to make communal decisions. We think this is an important lesson for students to learn. It helps free them to develop their own personal standards — without which they'll never care about writing or write really well.

Notice how this complex authority relationship ("Who's in charge here, anyway!") helps students understand more about the complex reality of *audience* in writing. People seldom write just for one reader whom they know and who has been teaching and helping them all along; people must usually write for multiple readers — some of whom they don't know and who don't know them and who will differ from each other in their tastes and standards. The portfolio forces this situation on students in a serious way: Those unknown and not fully predictable readers count.

But there is also a problem with this invisible handcuff between teachers' and students' wrists. Teachers sometimes begin to feel so identified with their students that they feel they've failed when their student fails. Indeed, the portfolio system can suck teachers into feeling too responsible — especially in the first semester they teach in the system — and giving too much help. In such cases, that failing paper hurts all the more because in some sense it really is the teacher's paper. Failing papers can make teachers angry at their group members — or so hurt that they begin to distrust themselves as teachers. Such reactions test critically the sense of community among the teachers. Still, we think the price is payable. Too often, in today's schools and colleges, students look on the teacher as the enemy (and vice versa). It would be a big gain if students could begin to see teachers as helpful — as people who lead, prod, stimulate, and otherwise ease them into their adult lives — not just as people who constantly mark them down for their mistakes. (Because the portfolio system can trick teachers into feeling that they are responsible for their students' texts, it is a powerful force for teaching teachers not to appropriate student texts.)

## Collaboration Between Writing Program Administrators and Teachers

We think the portfolio helps us deal with an essential conflict in program administration: Is it our program or the teachers'? On the one hand it's ours and we want it that way. We want to maintain control and impose coherence and uniformity. We can't give the reins entirely to teachers because we have a commitment to students and to the teaching of writing—and a hankering for our own agenda too. On the other hand, we need to give the reins to teachers too. If teachers don't experience their courses as wholly theirs—and even to some degree the program as theirs—they will not invest themselves or do their best teaching. (And they'll be more likely to fight us about everything.) The portfolio permits genuine collaboration between us and our teachers.

On the one hand, the portfolio permits us to invade teachers' classrooms. The portfolio more or less forces them to emphasize drafts and revisions—and almost forces them to use peer feedback. It also obliges them to work on three kinds of writing. (Our categories are enormously broad, but nevertheless a few teachers would otherwise skip expressive/imaginative writing or analyses of a prose text.) And the portfolio takes away the teacher's control over the crucial "gateway" C/C− decision. But on the other hand, everything else is up for grabs: assignments, method of teaching, books, order of treatment, and more. The portfolio leaves so much free—or at least we are gradually learning to make it function so—that most teachers feel little constraint. Indeed, we've gradually realized that the best measure for whether the portfolio is working is whether teachers stop feeling they are "teaching a portfolio course" and instead just feel they are teaching "their" course—within its framework.

Besides, although the impetus to have a portfolio came from us, the evolution of it has depended largely on suggestions and complaints from teachers:

- We started out with no dry-run papers, but teachers in the first small experimental semester realized students didn't understand—or really believe—the standards required of them.

- Till this year, we insisted that one paper be submitted at mid-semester. But teachers said that sometimes they and their students became too preoccupied with the portfolio too early in the semester and they'd rather ask for two papers two-thirds of the way through the semester. We allow groups to make their own decisions on timing.

- We started out insisting on four revised papers but reactions from teachers led us to reduce the number to three.

- When we first turned to an analysis paper, some teachers used a literary text. This turned out to create problems for teachers (weaker student papers; greater disagreement about verdict).

We reacted by going to the other extreme (from poetics to rhetoric) and insisting on an analysis of an argument. That (frankly, to our surprise) was quite a problem for most teachers, so now we've agreed to broaden the category: analysis of any prose text. Some teachers use argument and some literary texts.

- We started out with portfolio decisions as final. But teachers pointed to unjust outcomes because of a student getting bad advice from them, and this led to a policy more in keeping with a mastery approach: If a portfolio fails because of only one weak paper, the student can revise it once more and resubmit.

At least once a semester we have a meeting for all teachers specifically to talk about how the system is working and how it could be improved.

We are "imposing our will" by pushing teachers toward some commonality of standards, but we are inviting standards to emerge from them. We probably couldn't impose standards on the community if we tried. We sometimes refer to our large meetings as "calibration sessions," but that is really a misnomer. For in a true holistic scoring session, the leaders impose their standards: they choose the "anchor papers" and readers must leave their own standards and criteria at the door. The impressive speed and validity in careful holistic scoring depend on this imposed authority. But we're not trying for impressive validity. (We're not trying for speed in our large discussion meetings: We just treat a couple of papers in a session; we do want speed in the actual judging of portfolios, however—which is why readers judge portfolios as a whole and just make a crude binary Yes/No decision). But we think that these more collaboratively achieved standards—however slow and limited—permeate people's teaching more than the standards in holistic scoring with authorized "anchor papers" or "range finders" laid on. Besides, we're not tempted to set standards ourselves since we doubt they exist apart from actual papers in an actual community of readers. Once the community has judged papers, we can say to those who press us: "Here's a record of the community's judgment: here are passing papers and here are failing ones." Our standards are embedded in those decisions—but it's not just us speaking when we say that; it's the whole group.

## Concluding Thoughts:
## The Importance of Experimenting

We are committed to experimenting because we insist on treating perplexity as a virtue. And we feel indebted to WPA and the National Testing Network for, in a sense, sanctioning our perplexity—by telling us, in effect, that there may be a lot of wisdom and scholarship about evaluation and writing program administration, but no one has really figured out how to do it right. There's no single right way to do it. There's room for plenty of experimentation and new knowledge. Therefore we better give ourselves permission to experiment—and in the naughty sense of the word too, that is, to fool around. There are so few "perks" or advantages to our job, there's so much we can't do because of human recalcitrance or financial lack; why not give ourselves permission to try things different ways because it seems interesting—well before we can know whether they will work. The very fact that so much of our program is collaborative, that so much of what we do aims toward creating community, makes us feel somewhat safer in indulging our impulses to experiment.

We suspect this process of experimenting will continue. Now that the portfolio has finally become an official part of the University's writing requirement, and now that we are writing to a national audience about how important it seems to us—and some people are interested in trying it out elsewhere—we'll probably wake up one of these mornings and find that it doesn't work for us or that the teachers we work with have to make a major change. What is most likely is that some other writing program, in adapting it to their setting, will work out some deft but powerful transformation so that it comes out completely different and much better. We know it can be better, and we know too that any system which remains in place very long begins to be perceived as something to outwit—an obstacle rather than a doorway.

We hope, therefore, that our experiments can encourage writing program administrators to feel that they are in one of the best positions for conducting research and developing new knowledge—rather than one of the worst, as we'd feared. WPAs can be braver about experimenting if we provide courage to one another by collaborating as members of an even larger community than the ones each of us can build on our own campus.

## Notes

1. One of the important reasons why students see school as an arena for individual, solitary, and competitive endeavor is the deep "norm referencing" assumption in assessment and measurement: the assumption that trustworthy assessment should always distribute the population along a bell-shaped curve. It's worth consciously shaking ourselves loose from this assumption. The work in competence-based education, mastery learning,

and criterion-referenced testing showed the value of tests built on a completely different model: The goal is not to rank students into finely discriminated degrees of success, but to make a simple binary judgment as to whether something has been mastered or not; and the goal is not just to measure, but in fact to intervene and increase the chance that the student will learn. Our portfolio could be described as a mechanism for trying to goose as many of our 101 students as possible into writing well enough to get a C (not only for their own good but so we don't have to teach them again).

2. We wonder whether this whole complex process of negotiation about interpretation and judgment might not be an argument for keeping writing programs in English Departments: places where people are concerned with interpreting and evaluating texts, where disagreement about interpretation is viewed as healthy and productive, and most of all where priority is given as much to imagination as to reason in accounts of the reading and the writing process.

## Addendum

Pat Belanoff

Stony Brook's portfolio system has now been in place for six years. We've made some changes in the system, but through these years the system has changed us and our classroom more than we have changed it.

First: how we've tinkered a bit with the system itself. Fairly early on, we made some minor adjustments in the categories or genres required for the portfolio. Originally, we limited category 1 papers (narratives, descriptions, expressive pieces, informal essays) to prose. Three years ago an eloquent graduate student—himself a poet—convinced a majority of us that the ability to shape language into poetry can have beneficial effects on even the most academic of writing. Thus, we began to allow poetry into the portfolio.

Opponents of this change argued then (and continue to argue) that we don't know how to judge poetry. This indeed sounds like an indictment, rather than a reason, since almost all our teachers are English majors with—one would think—considerable experience in reading poetry. Why is it we distrust our judgment of poetry most? One of the things we've discovered from our years of doing portfolio readings is that we agree most on text analyses and least on narratives—that is, we agree most on that very genre in which we ourselves write. Because we and our teachers have narrowed its form—perhaps unnecessarily—the genre of text analysis has become more definable. This very narrowing allows us to agree on just how successful a particular text analysis is. Few of us write narratives, and even fewer have written poetry. Is that the reason we fear it? Perhaps. Whatever the case, very few students have opted to include poetry in their portfolios and few teachers have encouraged it.

Nonetheless, the presence of the poetry option gives teachers and students permission to write poetry in the class; and, given current interest in the value of metaphoric thinking, perhaps writing poetry (or, at the least, poetic writing) should be encouraged in all writing classes. Additionally, the function of form in poetry may very well draw attention to aspects of language which students often seem quite unaware of.

In a related decision, we broadened the text analysis category to include analyses of poetry as well as of prose. I have no empirical knowledge of how many students have submitted papers based on poetry, but my sense is quite a few. Stretching the term *text* even farther, but in ways compatible with modern critical theories, some of our teachers permit (and even encourage) students to analyze films and music for this category.

Two more serious and interwined issues have engendered much debate among our teachers with no solid resolution. The basic debate has centered on the help students get while revising and polishing pieces for the portfolio. Our policy has been to encourage them to get as much help as possible. Some students get quite a bit—from the teacher, from a tutor in our writing center, or from classmates, a roommate, family member, or friend. "How much is too much?" is the question we're asking ourselves now. At what point does a piece of writing cease to be a student's own? How much should a student be able to do on her or his own?

These questions tie into a number of current theoretical concerns. Knowledge, says Kenneth Bruffee, is a social construct (647). Is not the language in which knowledge inheres also a social construct? How much of all our language *is* our own? If a student engages in conversation about a piece of writing and is able to incorporate parts of that conversation into a revision that thereby becomes a more effective piece of writing, to whom shall we give the credit? Bakhtin notes that all our language shows traces of where it has been (293). It may not be possible to draw a clear line separating our ideas from the ideas of others whose words we've heard or read: all writing is collaborative. How much actual language can one person supply to another without undercutting that other's claim to authorship? But this argument is not inclusive enough, for students get help with actual language as well as with ideas. Should we be passing papers in which someone other than the acknowledged author has changed all *alots* to *a lots*, all *could of*s to *could have*s, and so forth? Again, what constitutes authorship?

The secondary debate intertwined with this debate on authorship focuses on the importance of the in-class writing piece in the portfolio. Thus far, we have given it very little weight. But we do recognize it as a piece of evidence testifying to how much a student can do alone. We also recognize that if we begin to weigh it too much in our overall judgment of a portfolio, we'll be back to square one where proficiency hinges on one piece of writing done within a limited period of time with little or no time for revision—exactly what we devised the portfolio to replace!

Still, a few of our teachers are experimenting this semester with putting more emphasis on the in-class piece. They're asking students to practice it, their rationale being that this is the sort of writing students often have to do for short-answer examinations. Against that, others note that those examinations are devised to test specific knowledge—not writing ability. Nonetheless, we'll be looking at what occurs in these revised-in-class pieces to see if we want to give them added weight of some kind in the overall portfolio. Frankly, I'm uncomfortable about this development, but perhaps some new way will emerge.

At the same time some teachers are testing these waters, we're trying to make a case to non—composition faculty that either students' in-class writing should be judged differently from writing they have a chance to revise and reconsider or they should be given a specific period of time in which to revise the in-class piece. I suspect we're not being very successful with this campaign. Most faculty expect students to produce fairly error-free prose without revision.

Another important issue we struggle with continually is the stress surrounding submission of portfolios. One of the problems with standardized testing is the irrational anxiety it creates for quite a few students—an anxiety that subverts abilities and intelligence. Unfortunately, we have discovered that for some students (and for some teachers), the portfolio system extends this anxiety over a longer period of time. In some classes, students become obsessed with the revision process. I hear this when I read the student evaluations at the end of the term and I despair a bit. And teachers can become just as anxious as their students.

Our original vision had been to see the portfolio as a collection of the students' papers, from which a selection would be presented to an outside reader. We had envisioned that some papers the students started would not be revised into final form, but we certainly expected that more than three papers per semester would be brought through several drafts to a final version. Thus, each student should have choices for submission to the outside reader. Unfortunately, what seems to happen too often is that more attention is spent on the papers for the portfolio than on other papers written during the semester. Such an emphasis is not apparent in all classes, but it is apparent in too many. It is especially true of the classes of beginning teachers who feel most vulnerable. Our more experienced teachers have developed strategies for lessening the impact of portfolio stress on themselves and on their students. Next year with the help of some of these more experienced teachers, we're going to put major effort into finding ways to lessen this anxiety.

But we know too that some degree of anxiety isn't all bad. Listen to how anxiety works through this student's experience:

> At first I felt the portfolio was a pain in the butt, because I couldn't think of a topic for my essays. I was so happy when I finished the first essay. When I got to the second essay I almost had a heart attack. The persuasive essay took me two weeks just to find a topic. The last essay wasn't that bad. After I finished typing I was happy that I had finally finished my portfolio. I think that the portfolio is a very good idea, because each person in class has two chances to pass the proficiency exam. I didn't enjoy doing the portfolio because of its length, but after I finished and I looked at what I had completed I was impressed.

Another vexing undercurrent is that the passage of time has lessened teachers' sense of ownership of the system. Initially, almost every phase of the program was discussed and voted on by our teachers. The small cadre of part-time teachers who have been with us a number of years work out of their awareness of their own part in creating the system. But since our teaching is done almost solely by graduate students, we have a large staff turnover. Teachers currently entering the program (new graduate students) come into an already established system and many of them tend to feel it as "company policy." We have to keep working against the resulting tendency to "go through the motions" and give only lip service to the system. We're often not as successful as we'd like to be. And being graduate students in English, many of them are "antisystem" by nature and thus resist systems almost instinctively. The challenge for us is to find ways to direct whatever resistance there is into ways of improving the system itself.

This resistance has its own history. It tends to manifest itself negatively at first in noncommitment. But the resistance grows most strongly in students' second year of teaching, as though they were gaining some perspective that allowed them to criticize. (This perspective tends to affect all their work as graduate students, not just their teaching.) Graduate students at Stony Brook often move into teaching other classes by the end of their second year — introductory literature courses or advanced composition courses. Additionally, some of them serve as tutors in our Writing Center or as assistants to faculty in large literature classes. They then often return to the teaching of EGC 101 at the end of their third year or during their fourth year. Many of them return to the course with far more appreciation of our portfolio system. Judging by conversations I've had with some of these students, I would surmise that their experiences on the receiving end of grading in their own graduate courses make them more appreciative of our portfolio system. They come to understand how very difficult it is to give grades fairly; they see firsthand how regular faculty decide on grades and they're not always impressed.

But even as I write this, a group of four graduate students, on their own initiative, is exploring a modified approach to our midsemester dry-run evaluation. After dividing up all their papers and making their decisions, they plan to read all failing papers in a group and come to a collaborative decision on each one. They will then divide up the failing papers and conference with each others' students. During these conferences, they will be able to communicate their personal reactions to the paper as well as the reactions of the other members of the group. This experiment grows out of these teachers' unhappiness with the effects of midsemester failure on their students — effects that dampen enthusiasm carefully nourished during the first half of the semester. These teachers hope that the more personal approach will lessen the impact of failure. Those of us who have been here for a while believe that this personal contact will also enrich the wider sense of audience that the portfolio groups are designed to create. But most significantly, teachers are making this piece of our system their own by remaking it slightly. This promises well for the continued health of our program.

Nonetheless, the issue of ownership of the system is ongoing and we need to learn to cope with it. If loss of a sense of ownership is inevitable, how do we counter it? Devise another whole new system? And, if it's not inevitable, what have we been doing that has led some students to feel uncommitted?

This brings me to my final point — a point of envy. As I've already said, almost all teaching of writing at Stony Brook is done by graduate students. Even though some of them may not be enamored of the system at first, they haven't the status to protest the invasion of their classrooms that the portfolio mandates. Thus, they accept the portfolio system because they have no choice. But, as I've already said, a certain percentage of them become quite enthusiastic; in fact, when hired at other schools, our graduates begin to involve faculty there in discussions that they hope will lead to some kind of similar system. Meanwhile, our system has only minor influence on our faculty, thus demonstrating its kinship with much else that develops within writing programs at many colleges and universities and does not affect other teaching.

I've had quite a few conversations with faculty at a number of schools as they attempt to establish portfolio systems in programs in which writing is taught by a combination of part-timers and faculty. Part-timers cannot be asked or expected (exploited as they too often are) to give even an extra hour of time. And it is far more difficult to get a system such as ours (or some variation of it) accepted when faculty are involved; they are accustomed to being unchallenged in their own estimations of students' work. In fact, a number of schools have almost gotten systems in place, only to have them blackballed at the last moment. Nonetheless, once a system gains a foothold in such circumstances, it has a far healthier growth than ours, because it begins to work its magic on full-time faculty. This is why I'm envious. Our system is confined to the composition faculty at Stony Brook; it's a kind of "other" in the English Department. Some of our faculty, in truth, know very little about it and, I suspect, would not approve if they did understand it. All is not negative, though, for a number of departments *are* using a portfolio to certify competence in writing within their disciplines — the third level of our writing requirement. We have been able to give them some help and advice on doing this.

As I read back over this, I fear I may be sounding negative about the recent history of our portfolio system. But these problems can never outweigh the benefits. Our teachers seem to talk a great deal about evaluation, but when I listen closely I realize that what they're really talking about is feedback. Their evaluations are almost always geared to finding language to guide revision. Since their own students are being judged by these others with whom they're sitting around and evaluating papers, they listen intently so that they can apply the reactions in their own comments on their own students' papers. Evaluation and feedback merge; the community strengthens. As one of our teachers says, "When I'm responding to students' papers, I'm often surprised to hear someone else's words mixed up with my own — words I'd heard during a portfolio grading session. I don't feel alone like I used to."

Another positive development that continues to flourish is that teachers spend far less time on grading papers than they used to. In fact, most teachers don't grade papers at all. If they feel constrained to give some kind of judgment, they'll usually use a system of checks, check-minuses, and check-pluses. Becasue they've learned to be content with this, their students learn to accept it also. Freed from justifying grades, they have more energy for commenting. This result is one I've also heard expressed by teachers teaching at other schools using portfolio evaluation.

And, finally, even when the anxiety is a bit higher than I would like, students have the sense that they're working the way "real" writers work—creating drafts, talking to others, revising, getting nervous about final products, meeting deadlines, and so forth. And that's what was most important for us back when we started. That writerly tone to our classes constantly motivates us to cope with whatever problems arise. After all, we created our system for our undergraduates, not for ourselves. If it works to make them better writers, we've accomplished our purpose. We knew at the outset that we had not created a perfect system; the passage of time has shown us the wisdom of that knowledge. But it has also shown us that our most important aims are being realized and that our system is inherently flexible enough to keep itself vital and to inspire variations of itself at schools throughout the country.

# 3

# Portfolios as a Follow-up Option in a Proficiency-Testing Program

Dennis Holt and Nancy Westrich Baker
*Southeast Missouri State University*

All students at Southeast Missouri State University must pass a test of writing proficiency in order to graduate. Responsibility for administering the test belongs to the Writing Outcomes Program, an academic support unit that is also responsible for writing-across-the-curriculum and a writing center. The centerpiece of proficiency assessment is a holistically scored essay exam consisting of two impromptu expository essays written in a controlled setting. The exam is administered, scored, and reviewed in accordance with the recommendations of Ed White in *Teaching and Assessing Writing* (23–26). Prompts are pretested; only trained readers score; and results are constantly reviewed for reliability and validity. Despite this, and even though students may take the exam as many times as necessary, we don't believe that graduation should be denied solely on the basis of one's inability to negotiate the special demands of the exam. We have therefore begun to pilot a portfolio option — an alternative test of proficiency for students who believe that their performance on the impromptu exam is not an accurate indication of their writing ability.

Before discussing the portfolio option in detail, it will be helpful to review some essential facts about the impromptu proficiency exam. All students must sit for this exam after completing seventy-five hours of coursework. Most students have taken the exam once before, in their first or second year at the University, as the final in a required composition course. The first part of the exam asks for a personal essay on a specified topic. The second part includes approximately two pages of readings that students have not previously seen. The readings focus on an issue related to the topic introduced in the first part, and students are asked to write a persuasive essay on the issue raised by these readings. The second essay, unlike the first, requires students to incorporate textual references into a developed argument. A recent exam, for example, employed the following prompts:

> *Part One*: Think of a material possession you own, something that was bought or given to you that you would hate to be without. Write a brief essay of approximately two pages in which you explain why you value this item so much, showing the reader exactly in what ways the item proves its worth. Be sure to *show* how the item is valuable to you, giving examples to illustrate your ideas.
>
> *Part Two*: Madonna sings, "This is a material world, and I am a material girl." Write an essay in which you answer the following question: Do people in our country place too much emphasis on material things? Support your opinion with information and examples from your personal knowledge and experience. Refer to the readings at least twice, but remember that you are to express your own opinion and back it up with your own ideas, using the information from the readings only as it relates to your point of view.

The use of two prompts on a single topic not only provides us with two kinds of writing, a personal and a persuasive essay, but also engages students in a prewriting task, the writing of Part One, which should help them to prepare for the more demanding analysis required by Part Two. Students are given fifty minutes to complete the first essay and seventy minutes to complete the second. The two writing sessions are separated by a short break. The essays are scored holistically on a six-point scale by faculty from across the disciplines. Between the two essays twelve points are possible, and a combined score of seven is required to pass.

As we have mentioned, students who fail the exam may retake it as many times as necessary until they pass. Or, if they like, they may submit a writing portfolio. There are three ways to prepare the portfolio: first, by gathering together representative samples of writing completed for classes in the semester subsequent to failure; second, by signing up for a series of three three-hour exams permitting ample time for revision; and third, by enrolling in a course (e.g., EN-230) specifically designed to produce portfolios. (This last option is similar in philosophy and procedure to Elbow and Belanoff's EGC 101 course at Stony Brook.)

Though promising, the portfolio option is a minefield of problems, not the least of which is image. Whereas we see the portfolio project as a humanizing effort, some faculty and administrators see it as an attempt to lower standards. If the proficiency test is sound, why trouble with portfolios? Either the test works or it doesn't, they suggest. Isn't it that simple?

We don't think so. We believe that one should not ignore the problems of reliability and validity inherent in this type of writing assessment. We can always improve the test, but no one can make it perfect. If the test were used only for program assessment or to make formative evaluations, this would not concern us. But the fact that the test is a barrier to graduation makes the margin of error a matter of special significance. To inform students on the basis of two impromptu writing samples that they must take Composition I before taking Composition II is one thing; to inform them that they cannot graduate is quite another.

Three specific concerns, each in its own way related to the validity of the test, have been voiced: one concerns the exam's impromptu nature, another its stress on product rather than process, and a third its apparent conflict with basic assumptions of writing-across-the-curriculum. Fundamentally, the proficiency exam tests the ability of students to write an impromptu expository essay at a predetermined time on a topic not of their choosing with little opportunity for substantial revision. It is a test of students' ability to think and write quickly in a stressful situation. Granted, failing students may take the test again. And tutors are available at the Writing Center to review their essays and help them prepare to sit for the exam again. But what of students (for example, many ESL students) for whom impromptu writing on a generic topic is a special, perhaps unfair, burden? And how confident can we be about borderline scores? A student who receives an average score of 2 on the two essays is unlikely to write proficiently outside of the exam situation. But we should not be so confident about our judgment regarding a student who scored a 3 on both parts of the exam for a total score of 6.

We are also concerned about the lack of fit between an assessment instrument that looks only at product and composition courses that emphasize process. Though we assign two related writing tasks, one serving as a prewriting exercise for the other, we cannot claim that the time allotted for completing them is adequate to accommodate the deep revision implied by the writing process; the quality of time is stressful, its quantity limited. Nothing like real revision can take place. So students are receiving conflicting messages: composition teachers tell them that what matters is the writing they produce after much thought, work, and feedback; the testing system tells them that the real measure of their writing ability is a quickly written, once-edited expository essay.

Finally, we have had to recognize an apparent conflict with the philosophy of our writing-across-the-curriculum program. A leading argument of writing-across-the-curriculum is that writing is a complex task that varies in character from context to context. All faculty should be concerned with student writing not only because students need more practice writing but also because separate disciplines often constitute distinct discourse communities. Faculty should not expect direct and complete transfer of skills from composition courses to coursework across the disciplines. Yet we do not assess writing proficiency on the basis of how students write in their chosen disciplines.

The writing portfolio option is intended to address these problems. If the writing that students produce for their regular coursework meets minimal standards of proficiency, we should not deny them graduation, regardless of their performance on the impromptu exam. Because students may submit writing completed for credit in a variety of courses, the portfolio option recognizes the decisive importance of writing in the disciplines. It also allows us to look at samples of writing that reflect students' actual academic writing experiences. And since the submissions may be the product of much planning, revision, and editing, the portfolio option, while not measuring process, recognizes that it plays a legitimate role.

The proposal to add a portfolio option was submitted for evaluation to a subcommittee of the Writing Assessment Committee—a Writing Outcomes Program committee including representatives from ESL, the Center for Teaching and Learning, minority affairs, composition faculty, and the faculty at large. Although the subcommittee had reservations about various aspects of the portfolio option—namely, ensuring authenticity of the student's work and evaluating with consistency the diverse types of writing—it recommended piloting the option and set forth the following guidelines for the preparation of portfolios.

The portfolio must contain four samples of writing totalling a minimum of eight typed pages (at approximately three hundred words per page). One sample must be an argumentative/persuasive essay; another, more generally, may be any form of expository essay. The remaining two samples may include research papers, extended lab reports, book reviews, essay test responses, business reports, or any kind of course-related expository essay. Personal letters, poetry, and short stories are not acceptable; in the opinion of the portfolio subcommittee, these types of writing do not reflect the intent of the proficiency requirement. Only the original graded copy of each submission, including the instructor's comments, is acceptable. Transcribed or xeroxed copies are not acceptable. Although some might feel that portfolio evaluators might be influenced by instructors' grades and comments, we have not found that to be so. Instructors evaluate many factors other than writing (mastery of content, for example), and in some cases papers that have been passed by the instructor have been judged inadequate by portfolio evaluators. Each entry must be accompanied by a certification sheet signed by the instructor for whom the paper was written.

The portfolio must also contain a one-page analysis of the four writing samples just described. This analysis is written when the samples are submitted to the coordinator of writing assessment at the Writing Center. Students are informed of this requirement at the time they choose the portfolio option. The analysis must describe each writing assignment and identify the class and instructor for which each sample was written. It should also indicate what processes were involved in preparing the writing samples, including research procedures, rough drafts, feedback from instructors, and any revision or prewriting activities. The portfolio subcommittee views the one-page analysis as an introduction to the portfolio and an internal check on the authenticity of the student's writing.

In addition to creating the above guidelines, the subcommittee acted as a trouble-shooting group. Several problems required immediate attention. The subcommittee foresaw that certification would be one of the biggest problems to overcome before the portfolio could function as a viable option. How could we guarantee that the writing samples truly belong to the students who submit them? At first some members of the portfolio subcommittee vehemently opposed the portfolio option—even if only on a pilot basis—because they believed that this issue was irresolvable. They proposed in its place a set of three essays produced with ample time for revision under the watchful eye of Testing Services. After much discussion it was agreed to pilot the original portfolio proposal along with the controlled sitting option—both of which were to be reviewed after a two-year period.

On the recommendation of the subcommittee, each portfolio entry must be accompanied by a certification sheet similar to one used at the University of Massachusetts-Boston. The certification sheet asks for the course title, title of writing sample, and semester in which the sample was produced. The student must sign the sheet, testifying that the sample is not plagiarized. The instructor signs, vouching that the sample was submitted in the course indicated on the form and that to the best of his or her knowledge (based on acquaintance with prior drafts or other samples of the student's writing) the work is the student's own. Instructors are asked to keep a section of this form in their files for one year. Personnel in the Writing Outcomes Program contact instructors personally in order to verify that their signatures have not been forged. So far we have not encountered any overt faculty hostility to the collection and certification process.

Instructors have helped students prepare their portfolios and have called us at the Writing Center with a variety of questions ranging from requests for guidance in commenting on students' drafts, to clarifying the criteria used for evaluating specific portfolio entries, to soliciting help with writing samples that instructors viewed as nonproficient. As a result, faculty have sent students working on portfolio entries to our writing tutors in the Writing Center for help with focusing a topic, organizing information, or addressing a specific audience. This suggests a positive long-term effect of the portfolio option: if we can make the option work, faculty from across campus will have another opportunity to play an intimate role in the assessment process, not only by assigning and grading written work, but by becoming mentors and facilitators in the preparation of writing portfolios.

An unanticipated problem with certification occurred when an instructor who was not convinced that the student wrote a paper signed its certification sheet anyway. Because the paper was the only one required in the class and no rough drafts, outlines, or notes were reviewed by the instructor, the certification was guess-work at best. In this instance we had no choice but to accept the signature because the signed form had already been collected by the student, and the instructor was not willing to withdraw it on the sole basis of gnawing suspicion. All of us have probably accepted papers partially written by someone other than the primary author — not from any intention on the student's part to deceive, but as a consequence of help in revision and editing. This problem is of less concern in the portfolio course offered in the English Department, where a single instructor monitors the production of all samples, provides opportunity for drafting, revision, and editing, and interacts regularly with the student. But until we have portfolio courses like this one across the curriculum, we feel obligated to allow students to take their samples from a variety of courses.

If authentication is problematic, so, too, is evaluation. The portfolio subcommittee and other participants in the program have raised a host of questions. Can the scoring criteria applied to the proficiency exam be applied to the writing portfolio? Can we develop scoring rubrics tailored to the various kinds of writing that are likely to be found in portfolios? And can we maintain consistency of standards? Since the one-page analysis is written in a restricted environment with limited opportunity for revision, does it not contradict the spirit of portfolio preparation? Can we make a holistic assessment of the portfolio itself, as distinct from the individual pieces of writing it contains? How are the scores assigned to individual submissions to be related to the score of the portfolio?

The subcommittee proposed that all five pieces of the portfolio be individually evaluated. The persuasive and expository essays, as well as any other essays included in the portfolio, are passed or failed based on the criteria used in scoring the written proficiency exam. The individual essays are holistically scored using a 6-point scale. A score of 3 or below is considered failing while a score of 4 or above is considered passing. Other types of writing (e.g., summaries, book reviews, research papers) are to be evaluated with reference to criteria developed by the Writing Outcomes Program staff specifically for that type of discourse. If the instructor has allowed ample opportunity for revision, samples should be held to generally higher standards than pieces, such as essay exams or the portfolio analysis, which are written in situations that do not permit significant revision. Three of the five writing samples must be judged as passing by both readers. If one reader passes at least three of the five samples but another reader does not, a third member of the evaluation committee resolves the disagreement.

We have only begun to work on developing specific criteria for the various types of writing assignments most likely to be found in a portfolio. We want to acknowledge the specific characteristics of particular kinds of writing assignments—in effect, developing a primary-trait scoring system as described by Faigley et al. in *Assessing Writers' Knowledge and Processes of Composing*—and yet continue to apply the more generic criteria of the proficiency exam, insofar as that is possible.

When scoring the impromptu exam, readers base their holistic evaluations on five criteria: focus, organization, development, style, and correctness. An additional criterion, use of source materials, is invoked in assessing the second part of the exam. These criteria govern the assignment of a single score although readers do not assign an individual score for each criterion. A detailed discussion of these criteria, including scoring rubrics and essays exemplifying each of the six scoring levels, is contained in a booklet distributed to all scorers and available to students at the campus bookstore.

Portfolio evaluators relate their assessment of writing samples to the criteria used in scoring impromptu essays. However, these criteria cannot be rigidly applied given the different demands of various discourse types. And so we have begun to develop scoring guides specific to different kinds of writing assignments — extended lab reports, article reviews, and so on. For example, in evaluating the assignment analysis, which all portfolios must contain, we ask readers to consider the following questions: Does the assignment analysis discuss each of the samples included in the portfolio? Does the analysis identify the class and instructor for which each sample was written? Does the analysis contain a description of each sample? Does the analysis discuss the processes involved in producing each sample, including research, revision, and nature of feedback from outside readers? In evaluating article summaries, readers are expected to consider these questions: Does the summary reflect the contents of the summarized text? Does the summary identify the main thesis of the summarized text? Does the summary identify assertions in the summarized text essential to the development and support of its main thesis? Is the summary in the author's own words?

We want to emphasize just how tentative this component of our project is. We believe that the evaluation of individual samples of portfolios should be clearly related to the criteria of the proficiency exam (for the sake of students, faculty, and readers); but we also believe that we should explicitly recognize the special demands of different types of writing assignments. Finding a satisfactory response to these commitments is a major goal of the portfolio project.

Two final but not insignificant problems with portfolio evaluation are cost and time. A quick reader will usually need an hour to evaluate one student portfolio. Because each packet receives two readings, if we were to pay $15 per hour (as we do for scoring the impromptu exam) each portfolio would cost at least $30 to score — and more when a third reader is required. In order to reduce the cost and to maintain consistency in scoring, a cadre of six to eight portfolio readers is selected for each academic year. Each reader is paid a fixed stipend and expected to evaluate no more than one dozen portfolios. Readers are chosen from a cross-disciplinary pool of faculty who have been trained to score the writing proficiency exam.

We estimate that when our writing proficiency program is testing its full capacity of 1,750 students per year, roughly 35 to 50 students will complete portfolios annually. Currently, 10 percent of those students who fail the written exam are opting for the portfolio alternative. Assuming a 20-percent failure rate on the written exam (which we believe may be high considering our current failure rate of 11 percent), we've arrived at the above estimate. We realize that if significantly more students opt for preparing a portfolio, then the cost of the option in both money and faculty time may prove to be prohibitive.

As we enter into the final pilot year of our writing proficiency program, it is necessary for those of us in the Writing Outcomes Program to review writing assessment at our institution. Major issues have yet to be adequately addressed by our current testing program. Foremost, we are concerned that the present writing exam tests for minimal competency only. Students who pass with only marginal scores probably need further writing instruction, and yet the impromptu test seems to certify them as competent writers. Would they not benefit more from the experience of preparing a portfolio of writing in a certified course? As we plan the future direction of writing assessment on our campus, we envision the establishment of writing portfolio courses taught by faculty in departments across the campus. While these writing intensive courses in the students' major fields of study may never completely replace the current assessment instrument, we believe that they would serve the purpose of teaching as well as assessing writing.

# 4

# Implementing a Portfolio System

David Smit, Patricia Kolonosky, and Kathryn Seltzer
*Kansas State University*

In the late spring and early summer of 1988, those of us responsible for training and supervising instructors in the Composition Program at Kansas State University — the director of composition and four advisors — decided to implement a portfolio system of evaluating student writing. Our primary concern was to establish uniform grading standards among our 130 sections of Composition I and II.

Although we had always provided sample grading criteria to our instructors, conducted large- and small-group grading sessions, and given additional information in the *Instructor's Guide to the Composition Program at K-State*, individual teachers were the final judges of what was acceptable and unacceptable writing, of who should pass and who should fail their composition classes. We had to confront the fact that instructors graded papers using a wide variety of criteria and points of view. Some students complained, for example, that they might have passed their writing course if they had enrolled in Professor Jones's class rather than Professor Smith's. Further, we were aware that some teachers passed students who would have otherwise failed their composition classes because they yielded to student pressures for higher grades. In addition, we felt that our traditional final examination, an essay written in two hours, placed too much stress on students to perform at their best. To continue such a procedure, we concluded, was not in keeping with the process approach we endorsed and employed in the Composition Program.

Other concerns also led us to seek a new approach. For years we had wanted our teachers to be perceived as "coaches," enabling their students to reach the goal of improving their writing skills. Most teachers wanted their students to view them as such, but found themselves perceived as adversaries rather than advocates when grades came into the picture. We pondered what could be done to right this situation.

Finally, we wanted to be able to say with confidence to members of the larger community and to faculty members in other departments that students who passed our composition classes were indeed capable of producing clear, correct prose.

After considerable thought and research, we decided to try a portfolio system of evaluation, a system that would not only allow our teachers actually to be coaches, but would also help us move in the direction of establishing uniform standards for passing and failing our composition courses.

Our first step in implementing the portfolio system was to have an explicit set of procedures in place at the beginning of the semester. During our opening orientation session for both new and returning instructors, we discussed the philosophy behind the portfolio system and presented a brief sketch of the procedures, which was also included in the *Instructor's Guide*. Basically, the portfolio system we designed works as follows:

> In order to pass Composition I and Composition II, students must each submit a portfolio of written work to one other instructor, who decides if the work meets the standards of the program. If the second instructor decides that an individual student's portfolio fails, that student must fail the course.
>
> Around midterm, students participate in a trial run of the portfolio examination. They each pick one paper they have written up to that point to submit to another instructor, the outside reader. Students must produce good clean copies of their papers, either typed or handwritten in ink on unlined 8 ½-by-11 paper. They must put their names in the upper right-hand corners, but the papers should contain no grades or comments from the original instructors. Each paper must be accompanied by a copy of the original assignment and all the notes, drafts, and comments the student produced or received while writing the paper. The outside reader decides if the submitted papers pass or fail. The reader returns the passing papers without comment but provides a written explanation of why any other papers failed. If a paper passes, the student may also submit it in the final portfolio.
>
> The last week of every semester is devoted to preparing portfolios. Students each pick four examples of their writings during the semester that fit the requirements of the portfolio. One sample must be an in-class writing. For each piece of writing in the portfolio, students follow the same procedure they did at midterm: they gather all of their notes, drafts, and comments from other readers, as well as copies of the

original assignments. Then they make good clean copies of the final drafts, either typed or neatly handwritten in ink on unlined 8 ½-by-11 paper. Students' names go in the upper right-hand corners of these writings, but there should be no grades or comments by the original instructors on the papers. A different outside reader from the trial run decides if individual portfolios pass or fail. As at midterm the portfolio reader need not comment on passing portfolios, but provides written comment for each portfolio that fails.

Upon receiving the results of the portfolio reader, the original instructor has a number of options. If the instructor accepts the judgment of the reader, the instructor must fail for the course those students who did not pass the portfolio examination. Of course, the instructor may also fail students for other reasons, such as not handing in enough work or insufficient attendance. If the instructor questions a particular judgment by the portfolio reader, the instructor may appeal to the director of composition, who will give the portfolio to another instructor who will in turn act as a second outside reader. In every case, the decision of the second outside reader is final.

All of the papers in the portfolio must meet the minimum standards of the Composition Program in order for the student to pass the portfolio examination. If, however, in the judgment of the outside reader, only one paper is below standard, the student may revise the one failing paper and resubmit the portfolio. If the student cannot be reached during the final examination period or is otherwise unable to rewrite the one failing paper during that semester, that student will receive an Incomplete and be allowed to resubmit the portfolio during the next semester.

In addition to the *Instructor's Guide*, we prepared a two-page "Guide to Students" in which we explained the system as we had done for the instructors. In particular we elaborated on the kinds of papers the students had to submit. For Composition I, we required an expressive essay, a factual report that conveys information, and a documented research report or critical analysis that summarizes and analyzes sources of information and uses an appropriate form of documentation to quote and cite those sources. For Composition II, we required two persuasive pieces, one with appropriate documentation, and a response to literature, also with appropriate documentation. For both courses students also had to submit a piece written in class.

We next explained why students had to submit previous notes, drafts, and comments: to help the outside reader see how much their writing improved during the writing process and how well they responded to other people's suggestions. Such material would also help ensure that the work they submitted was their own. We especially warned the students that they might fail the portfolio if they could not supply this material.

We ended the "Guide to Students" with a statement of what portfolio readers would look for: how well the student writers fulfilled the demands of the assignment; whether their purposes were clear; whether their detail, from concrete description to factual evidence, was appropriate for their purpose and audience; whether their organization was easy to follow; whether their tone was appropriate for the audience they were addressing. We were especially emphatic that the portfolio papers had to be almost completely free of mistakes in grammar, punctuation, and spelling; and that the meaning should be relatively clear on first reading.

The first few weeks of the semester went by without incident, although rumors of student dissatisfaction bubbled up occasionally, and a number of students called individually on the director of composition to express their concerns or ask for clarification. One student wanted to withdraw from Composition II because he had to take the course for a grade and was under the impression that in the portfolio system he could only receive a grade of pass/fail. The director assured him that he would receive a letter grade for the course. Several other students were concerned that they weren't going to be graded by their own instructor and wanted to know why the Composition Program didn't trust their instructor. The director assured these students that they would in fact be graded by their own instructor and that the portfolio system was concerned primarily with establishing a common standard of judgment about college-level work, that if the outside reader determined that they were doing college-level work their own instructor would assign them the grade he or she judged appropriate. All of these students, after they had the chance to voice their concerns and learn more about the system, seemed less upset and even accepting of the system. We were concerned, however, that their individual instructors had not managed to explain the system sufficiently to allay their students' anxieties.

As the trial run approached, it also became clear that we had not anticipated a number of important issues and that our introductory guidelines did not provide enough information for either students or instructors. Instructors came to their advisory group meetings frustrated and annoyed about a number of matters:

*Could an in-class paper be revised?* Our original explanation in the *Instructor's Guide* stated that the in-class piece, like the other three required papers, should be accompanied by previous notes, drafts, and comments — which strongly implied that it too could be revised. Since we had also stated that the point of the in-class piece was to see what students could write on their own with only their notes and a rough plan or outline, some of our instructors told their classes that the in-class paper could be revised; others told their classes that it could not be.

A corollary problem was that some students wanted to submit in-class papers for the trial run because they were more worried about these papers passing than the other pieces that could be revised. If, however, an in-class piece failed the trial run and we did not allow it to be revised, the student could not pass the final portfolio exam unless that student submitted a different in-class piece. Many of our instructors were in favor of allowing in-class pieces to be submitted for the trial run; others were equally adamant that they didn't have the time to schedule additional writing if the in-class writing failed.

In addition, several instructors were told by an advisor in the program that since the nature of the in-class piece was not defined in the guidelines, it need not be the kind of discourse required for the rest of the course but any kind of writing the instructor wished — another interpretation at odds with our original intention. It seemed that even as a group we couldn't interpret our own guidelines in similar ways.

*What standards should we use in judging mechanics?* More than any other issue, this question plagued us. Our original notes to instructors about mechanics were as follows:

> In reading for mechanics, you should look to see whether the writer has consistent control of his or her sentences. An occasional error is tolerable; consistent mistakes are not. If the papers consistently contain more than one or two serious errors per page in grammar, punctuation, spelling, and usage, or if they contain more than three or four minor errors per page, you may fail the portfolio.

In our grading sessions in which we ranked sample portfolio papers together and discussed our rankings, we were severely divided on those papers that seemed to be clearly passing in all categories except mechanics. Many of our instructors argued heatedly that the portfolio exam was becoming entirely a test of mechanics. One instructor threatened to resign because he thought his students were being treated unfairly.

During several brief ad-hoc meetings of the advisory staff, we tried to hash out more specific policies on these matters. We decided that in-class papers could not be revised; students who submitted an in-class piece for the trial run and failed would need to be given the chance to write another in-class piece.

Regarding mechanics, we let the issue simmer until late in the semester when the director managed to publish a revision of the notes to instructors on how to read portfolios. To the section on how to read for mechanics he added the following:

### Some guidelines for noting mechanics

In reading for mechanics, you should exercise your good judgment. Do not read the papers through the first time like a corrupt Puritan searching for wrong-doing. Read first for content. Only if you are constantly struck by the severity or obviousness of various mechanical errors should you look for errors at all.

Use the following guidelines as suggestions only. Your common sense will be more reliable and accurate than trying to mechanically interpret a set of rules.

A. Look to see whether the writer has consistent control of grammar, punctuation, spelling, and usage. That is, note whether the mistakes continue page after page after page. If half of the pages in the portfolio consistently contain more than one or two serious errors in grammar, punctuation, spelling, and usage, or if half of the pages contain more than three or four minor errors per page, you may fail the portfolio. (Serious errors are those such as run-ons, fragments, lack of agreement, unclear pronoun reference, faulty parallelism, and misspelling. Minor errors are such things as omitted commas after introductory adverbials or misplaced quotation marks.) On the other hand, if three or four pages are so loaded with error, say five or six serious errors or eleven or twelve minor errors, that they signal a breakdown in control, you may also fail the portfolio.

B. Distinguish between fundamental errors, which may be counted each time they occur, and errors of transcription, which are the same error repeated again and again. Most of the serious errors noted above are fundamental errors which should be counted each time they occur. However, spelling errors and certain misplaced or omitted punctuation should only be counted once. For example, if the student misspells the same word nine times, you should only count it as one error. Or if the student consistently reverses a period and quotation marks, you may count all such reversals as one error.

In the middle of the trial run, another problem quickly became apparent: despite what we thought were explicit instructions in how to submit the portfolios, many of the portfolios were highly disorganized jumbles of assignments, drafts, notes, and reader-response forms that didn't match with final drafts; a number of instructors complained bitterly that they spent more time organizing the portfolios than reading them. The question also arose: if a portfolio was missing something as simple as an assignment sheet, should it be failed automatically because the student had not followed instructions? It didn't take much of a meeting for us to answer this one. Since the trial run was just that, a trial run, we decided to show no mercy. All portfolios should fail the trial run for the slightest deviation from our stated policies, if for no other reason than to convince students that this was a serious business. When lives were on the line during the final exam, we would decide such matters on a case-to-case basis. And we vowed to make our instructions for how to submit papers with notes, drafts, and reader responses much more explicit in future guidelines.

The trial run itself seemed to go smoothly enough. The director posted a list of pairs of raters several days before the portfolios were collected, giving the partners time to arrange their schedules. Instructors reported few hitches in the logistics of trading portfolios. And a survey of instructors after the trial run indicated that 16 percent of the portfolios submitted had failed; only 5 percent were "surprises" for the original instructors, a percentage of disagreement that gave us a certain amount of satisfaction after all the problems we had dealt with up to that point.

Still, we heard ominous rumors of student discontent and occasional stories of how particular students harbored the most fantastic misconceptions about the exam. We grinned and shook our heads, but our hilarity felt hollow. None of our students had formally protested, perhaps because a number of instructors with a class of discontents asked them for comments on the procedures thus far. The comments were generally negative, but we felt that they often reflected the fact that the instructors reporting these comments were among our most disgruntled with the new system, which they thought required much more work of them than in previous years. However, the comments did indicate that a significant number of students still didn't have a clear understanding of the purpose of the portfolio system or how it worked. Here are some of the comments:

> We believe the idea of having someone read a student's papers to
> decide whether or not he-she passes when they [sic] have, in fact,
> already passed, is completely asinine. This person (the grader) has had
> absolutely no contact with the student and had no idea of how the
> student thinks, writes, or acts. We also believe that the portfolio exam
> is a lousy idea because not all the graders grade alike. Some are
> extremely lenient and others are extremely harsh in their grading. We
> also believe that the Director of Composition, if anyone, should be the
> one to be burdened with reading all these papers.
> —Signed by 11 students
> The final portfolio exam, in my opinion, is a total rip-off! If one goes
> through the whole year making As and Bs on his paper and someone

finds *one* thing wrong in the portfolio then they [sic] fail. I think the English dept. [sic] needs to find a better way to teach their [sic] subject.

The portfolio exam is one of the most worthless evaluations I have ever heard of. It is full of inconsistencies and seems very unfair. Some instructors grade much harder than others, and having one fault in a paper certainly isn't worth flunking someone.

We also asked our instructors for comments and received a raft of concerns:

- Despite our grading sessions, our standards for pass/fail were still radically different.
- Too many readers were using mechanics as the only basis for passing or failing portfolios.
- Failing the trial run caused some weaker students to give up.
- Some rating pairs were being studiously neutral and objective, talking together not at all except to arrange for the exchange of portfolios, while others were going over papers together and "negotiating" the final ratings.
- Above all, encouraging and accepting revisions as well as reading a trial run of portfolios was simply too time consuming; instructors felt harried and overworked; even the Writing Lab was booked solid for the last month of class and some of their students who needed the most help just couldn't get in.

Generally, new instructors were more positive than the second- and third-year instructors, who found the system to be more work than in previous years.

In response to these concerns we decided to expand both the student guidelines and the notes to instructors on how to read portfolios. After an editorial meeting to agree on the additions, we produced a five-page version of the student guidelines just before Thanksgiving and an expanded set of notes to help instructors read the portfolios. We made the student guidelines available at two campus copy centers for a quarter each, and we put two copies on reserve in the library. We discussed the notes for instructors in our advisory groups. As a result of what we hoped was a clarification of our overall purpose and procedures, things seemed to settle down for the rest of the semester.

Nevertheless, we anticipated the worst for the final exam. We scheduled two advisors to be on call throughout the exam period to handle questions and concerns, much as if we were operating an emergency room. We brought in coffee and doughnuts and scheduled extra "quiet rooms" for reading because most of our instructors have desks in large converted classrooms with twenty or so of their colleagues. Much to our surprise we might have overreacted: things seemed to go very smoothly. Indeed, morale seemed high. Most of the time we had nothing to do but read our own portfolios. The quiet rooms were used only by a handful of instructors. Only the instructors who taught four sections complained at all: they had to cart around ninety-odd portfolios. One instructor resorted to using a little red wagon.

When we analyzed the results of the portfolio system in the weeks that followed, we were greatly encouraged. First and foremost, the portfolio system did seem to make our program more rigorous. We wound up failing outright abotu 3.5 to 4 percent of the portfolios; another 1 percent were given incompletes for having only one paper with severe problems. Instructors appealed the judgments on sixteen folders, about 23 percent of the failures. Of those sixteen, five passed on second reading, nine of the original judgments were sustained, and two were given incompletes. However, an astonishing additional 4 percent of our students failed composition for other reasons — not handing in a portfolio at all, lack of attendance, missing work, or not withdrawing from the class before the official date to do so. Students who might have formerly received "gentleperson's Cs" for incomplete or insufficient work could no longer sneak by. Our second-semester figures demonstrated similar results: the failure rate for portfolios was 3.9 percent and an additional 5.5 percent failed for other reasons. Incompletes were 2 percent of the total, and appeals were 1 percent (or 20 percent of the failures). In comparison with previous years, these figures demonstrate an increased failure rate of about four percentage points, an indication that the portfolio exam may have made our courses more rigorous but not by a great deal. In fact, one associate dean suggested that we may still be too lenient, although he had no idea of what a reasonable rate of failure ought to be.

In addition, despite a few rough spots, our instructors were nearly unanimous in the belief that the portfolio system had helped us to achieve our goals for the system: in response to a questionnaire at the end of the year, 88.5 percent of the instructors agreed that the portfolio system had helped establish minimum standards. Instructors seemed to take greater care in assessing student papers, a natural reaction considering that other instructors would peruse the grades they assigned. And we observed increased collaboration among instructors in designing assignments and in deciding on appropriate grades for student papers. Instructors strongly encouraged students to revise in order to improve their chances of passing the portfolio. In advocating revision, instructors came to perceive themselves and were viewed by students not merely as graders looking for errors, but as writing coaches eager to help students through their composition courses. And instructors reported as well that they felt much less student pressure to raise grades; apparently, students came to realize that the independent readers played significant roles in determining who passed and who failed.

Although our instructors were generally pleased, they were concerned with time. An informal survey of the time they had spent reading the portfolio exam indicated a range from two to eight hours per section, for an average of about four. This was more, our experienced instructors said, than they spent grading their own final exams. In response, we pointed out that four hours per section to read a set of final exams did not seem excessive to us, and we wondered whether our regular final exams had become perfunctory.

Students also seemed to appreciate the new system. In questionnaires at the end of the year, 93 percent of Composition I and II students who participated in the portfolio exam during at least one of the previous semesters reported that they were encouraged to revise. Eighty-seven percent responded that they were encouraged to consult with their instructors. And they preferred the portfolio exam over a regular final exam by a four-to-one margin. These results initially surprised us until we realized that many of the problems we experienced were isolated incidents often centering on what we might call "shattered expectations."

Most of the complaints we received about the portfolio exam from students, parents, and academic advisors were, in fact, direct results of these shattered expectations. At midterm, for instance, one parent, a faculty member at the University, complained because his daughter had failed the trial run despite her alleged "solid B average" in Composition II. His daughter had reported that her reader was "getting back" at her own instructor for failing two good students of the reader, and the father was understandably concerned. After final grades came out several weeks later, three additional sets of parents registered complaints, two because their children said they had been getting Cs going into the portfolio examination. In all three cases, the students involved had either not carefully followed their instructors' suggestions for revision or had submitted material that clearly did not fit the stated requirements for the portfolio. One set of parents fully understood the circumstances of their child's failure; another angrily vowed that their child would complete the composition requirements at another institution.

Nevertheless, a number of students who received Cs on their

assigned writings during the course of the semester were rightfully resentful when they discovered they had failed their composition classes "only because of the portfolio." Quite simply, we discovered that instructors operating under a portfolio system need to be much more careful, even cautious, about assigning grades: C papers — and perhaps occasional B work — with obvious weaknesses in explicitness, structure, level of detail or evidence, or mechanics might conceivably fail the portfolio examination.

Regrettably, these complaints indicate problems we cannot easily resolve. Some of our instructors, however, have experimented with not assigning specific grades to individual papers. This strategy obviously dampens specific expectations, but without seeing the grades they have come to depend on to "know where they stand" in their classes, many students become unduly anxious. Some instructors report relative success penning tentative designations such as "above average," "average," "below average," or "unacceptable" on student writings. This grading scheme does seem to alleviate some of the nervousness students exhibit when they do not receive more specific bench marks. We are continuing to explore ways to encourage serious revisions without seeming to be excessively threatening, inappropriately harsh, or merely wishy-washy.

The portfolio system's arrival and implementation at Kansas State University brought with it a certain serendipity. As our surveys demonstrate, instructor and student attitudes improved, expectations and commitments increased, and student writings typically became more worth reading than ever before.

# 5

# Evaluation for Empowerment
## *A Portfolio Proposal for Alaska*

Joan K. Wauters
*University of Alaska Southeast*

"I just don't get it," said Ruby, a senior at a major state university in the Lower 48. "In the writing classes, they tell you how important it is to do all this prewriting and revision stuff. Then they give you an exit test where you can't use any of it."

Ruby has a right to be concerned: her failure to pass the state writing proficiency exam is the only thing holding her back from receiving her baccalaureate in education. She has completed all required university coursework, passing her writing classes with Bs and Cs. She has also received outstanding recommendations for her work as a classroom aide in an elementary school. However, when under pressure to write on an assigned topic in a limited period of time, she froze. "I know I can write," Ruby said. "But," she added in frustration, "I'll never be able to prove it on that test."

Ruby's problem is not unique to her university or state. In this age of academic accountability, about two thirds of all colleges assess students' basic skills (Hexter and Lippincott 3), and an estimated ten million students are evaluated in writing annually (Purves v). But what are we achieving through these assessments? Are they valid measures of student ability, or are we unintentionally setting up more bureaucratic hurdles over which students must jump?

Alaska's geographical remoteness has not removed it from the pressures for assessment that have swept the rest of the nation. The costs of university education in Alaska are the highest per capita in the country, and taxpayers want to be assured that they are getting their money's worth. When state legislators and university administrators began to raise the issue of proficiency testing several years ago, my colleagues and I were concerned that the abuses of testing we had seen elsewhere might be implemented in Alaska. Rather than wait for an assessment system to be imposed upon us, the Communications Department of the University of Alaska Southeast (UAS) decided to design its own proposal for writing evaluation, a proposal that was subsequently modified by a universitywide committee on assessment appointed by the Chancellor. The purpose of assessment as we saw it was to develop a rigorous system that would challenge but also benefit students rather than block their academic progress.

UAS, the smallest regional branch of the University of Alaska system, has a student population of approximately 3,500, and our facilities and students are distributed among three campuses in isolated locations: Juneau, Ketchikan, and Sitka. Since these campuses are not connected by roads, development and revision of the concepts for this proposal took place via mail, audio-conferences, and several on-site meetings in Juneau, to which colleagues from the two smaller campuses were flown. This paper describes the development of the assessment proposal, current pilot projects and faculty training activities, and future plans for assessment at UAS.

## Assessment Goals

Our first concern was to determine what we hoped to accomplish through the assessment process. Only by defining our expectations at the outset could we determine a testing method that would meet these needs. When faculty realized that assessment, rather than a necessary evil, could actually spur improvement of teaching and learning, they gained enthusiasm for the planning process. This proactive perspective resulted in the formulation of four major goals that we saw as integral to any student assessment system we designed:

1.  *To encourage a greater quantity and higher quality of student writing throughout the student's college career.* Our most important rationale for assessment was to improve the educational process itself through placing a higher institutional value on the cognitive skills of reasoning and writing. We have found that our traditional two-semester freshman English requirement has the

unfortunate effect of raising minimalist expectations on the part of students concerning the overall role of writing in college and in their lives. Too many undergraduates view English as a six-credit subject to be survived and then safely forgotten. The implementation of an assessment in writing near the end of their college years would place a clear emphasis on the import-ance of writing for graduates in all disciplines. Knowing this across-the-curriculum priority on writing in advance would encourage students to keep a continuing focus on these skills beyond the usual lower-division English requirements.

2. *To evaluate student writing in a representative range of writing assignments through assessment based on universitywide standards of achievement.* While "competency" exams often focus on ascer-taining minimum literacy levels, we wanted to design a true "achievement" exam for our potential college graduates, a measure that would aim higher than satisfactory or perfunctory performance. We wanted to gain an accurate picture of students' achievement in a number of writing assignments utilizing differ-ent rhetorical strategies and writing styles. Since such a compre-hensive approach would include writing in a variety of disciplines, it calls for standards of writing achievement jointly established by faculty from different departments. Setting uni-versitywide criteria can have a beneficial effect on student, many of whom believe that only English instructors care about how they write as well as what they write. When students view the criteria for successful writing as universal rather than idio-syncratic, they can more easily be persuaded to aim for and meet the high standards required to demonstrate college-level writing ability.

3. *To improve departmental communications and consistency of writing standards and English course requirements.* One unexpected benefit of our preliminary discussions regarding assessment was that it brought us closer as a tricampus department. Due to our geo-graphical isolation, these meetings provided the first format in which some of us had ever discussed with each other our priorities in the teaching of writing. Despite marked differences in teaching styles, we discovered that we agreed on what consti-tutes high-quality undergraduate writing. We still have far to go, however; despite consensus on how writing can best be measured, these planning sessions only began to address con-cerns such as the need for standardized requirements in writing courses. While some faculty may fear a resulting loss of individ-ual freedom within their composition classroom, most of us

agree that further articulation and coordination of standards in writing instruction will benefit our students and strengthen our department as a whole.

4. *To tie student assessment to a long-term program of faculty development in writing across the curriculum.* One key element of success in any assessment program is participation of the faculty as a whole. If evaluation of writing skills is a concern only of English faculty, assessment will fail to impact on the rest of the curriculum and will thus be less effective. We also saw the potential that a universitywide exam in writing could have in motivating other faculty to increase research and writing requirements in their own courses. Some of our faculty hesitate to require substantial written projects because they have not been pleased in the past with the quality of student work. However, if standards in writing at the university as a whole are raised through a proficiency requirement, individual professors will have the needed support to set and maintain their own requirements at realistic undergraduate levels.

Using interdepartmental teams of faculty to evaluate writing proficiency was one suggested method of including our colleagues in the assessment process. By having faculty in other disciplines assess student writing side by side with English faculty, we could encourage them to become more involved with examining the writing process and determining appropriate writing criteria for their courses and academic programs. Because faculty from other disciplines cannot be expected to be instant experts in writing instruction and evaluation, we realized that a major component of any writing assessment program for students must involve ongoing training for faculty across the curriculum.

## Comparing Methods of Assessment

Standardized tests were the first vehicles proposed for assessment by some university administrators as well as a few faculty from other disciplines. From their perspective, the advantages of such exams are clear: they are quick to administer, easy to score, and produce statistics that can be compared to national norms. Our department was united in its opposition to this approach. Since standardized tests can measure knowledge of grammatical and punctuation rules but not demonstrate actual writing ability, we rejected them on the basis that they would not provide as valid a measure of language proficiency as holistically scored writing samples (Cooper

4). Furthermore, because of factors such as cultural bias, norm-referenced tests of literacy skills put minority students at a disadvantage (E. White 72−83; Roscoe Brown 98−102). A reliance on such a measure for a proficiency exam would clearly be inappropriate for a state university that has a special mission to serve the needs of various minorities, particularly Alaska Native students ("UA Six-Year Plan" 15). The convenience of standardized tests may make them helpful for purposes such as course placement, but to deny students their college degree on such a basis could have serious cultural and political repercussions.

We not only felt that to examine actual student writing would be mandatory for any achievement test, but we also wanted to ensure that writing samples would be elicited in a method consistent with the process-oriented theory of writing on which we base our pedagogy. We wished to avoid the disparity that Ruby, the senior in education, discovered between sound classroom practices and testing procedures that contradict these practices. This concern caused us to question the common model of a writing-proficiency test, one which requires only a single writing sample. Research in rhetoric shows that student writing ability varies according to the type of text that writers are asked to produce (Lloyd-Jones 37; E. White 117−18); thus, to require any one mode of writing will automatically discriminate against some students. Low reliability of ratings by readers is another problem with using a single sample of student writing (Cooper 19; Lauer and Asher 139). To measure student writing ability with reliability and validity, several different types of texts should be judged (Odell 115).

The time constraints imposed by most writing-proficiency assessments pose further disadvantages. A rigid time frame for writing assessment undermines the notion that writing is a highly individualistic activity in which writers work at different paces. It also introduces extraneous elements into the evaluation process such as test anxiety, which may have a particularly adverse effect on minority student performance (Roscoe Brown 101). Time limits are especially difficult for bidialectical and bilingual students (Ruiz and Diaz 5), a vital consideration in test selection for a student population that includes Alaska Natives.

Another factor that may contribute to student success or failure on timed essay tests is the choice, or lack, of writing topics. Topic assignments are necessarily limited by the constraints of a timed test; students are often assigned to write on general subjects such as childhood experiences or the value of education. Writers given such topics, when denied time for traditional prewriting activities such as reading and research, tend to rely on platitudes and personal biases — hardly valid indicators of the type of college-level writing that we would like to see demonstrated. In addition, assigned topics may be unwittingly biased against students from economic or ethnic backgrounds other than the majority culture (Brick 32).

These reservations about timed writing tests, both multiple-choice and essays, led us to adopt the idea of portfolio assessment: the evaluation of a varied collection of the student's college writings. Our faculty was impressed by this evaluation system since it would enable us to assess the student's efforts in a number of rhetorical modes written for different purposes. Although the examples of portfolio use we encountered in the literature dealt primarily with portfolios as an evaluation device for individual English courses (Burnham; Elbow and Belanoff; Ford and Larkin), we felt that this method is ideally suited for assessment of collegiate writers for a broader purpose. While encouraging students to develop a wider range of writing strengths, portfolio assessment would allow us to evaluate higher-order concerns such as reasoning, analysis of read-ings, and library research techniques as well as organizational and syntactical skills.

Another advantage we saw to portfolio assessment is the ability to set high performance standards in writing for both the students exhibiting these skills and the faculty teaching them. Since these pieces of writing would be generated in a realistic writing context with revision opportunities, they could be judged much more rigor-ously than timed writing samples. Such expectations of writing achievement would encourange classroom practice in writing, thus benefiting both teacher and students. If teaching to the test is an inevitable result of any evaluation program, we want to make sure our "test" (i.e., assessment process) is worth teaching to. Rather than giving faculty the message that they should help their students to excel in multiple-choice exams or produce instantaneous texts on artificial topics, we want a procedure that urges them to require high-quality, full-length writing assignments in their disciplines.

As strong writing ability can make the difference between ac-ceptance and rejection in both graduate programs and jobs, certifi-cation of such achievement through an external evaluation process may increase students' opportunities for success beyond their undergraduate years. This method of assessment provides all students with a tangible demonstration of writing ability, a portfolio of accomplishment similar to those of professionals such as artists and architects. In an era when a college diploma is no longer con-sidered a guarantee of literacy, giving graduates this opportunity to document their writing ability can indeed empower them in the pursuit of their post baccalaureate goals.

## Portfolio Assessment Proposal for UAS

After determining the purposes of assessment and the method we felt would best fulfill those goals, we wrote a proposal for assessment of student writing, describing how portfolios could be used to fulfill a writing proficiency requirement at our university.

A major issue was the timing of the requirement: When should students be required to submit their portfolios for evaluation? While a proficiency requirement is often viewed as an exit exam for graduating seniors, we saw a risk in waiting until the end of a student's college career for submission of the portfolio. If the portfolio did not pass, the student would be left in the untenable situation in which Ruby now finds herself—finished with coursework but unable to graduate. On the other hand, if required within the first two years in a baccalaureate program, the portfolio would not reflect a student's ability to handle upper-division writing assignments, especially work in the major.

Our solution was to propose the portfolio as a requirement to be fulfilled during the junior year. Rather than serving as an entrance test prior to upper-division work, this proficiency would be required as an early exit assessment for graduation. In this way, students would have work in their major already underway and could be expected to demonstrate upper-division writing abilities. This system would also provide a period of time as a safety net for those who did not pass the portfolio assessment; they would still have a year in which to improve writing skills and resubmit a revised portfolio before graduation. Another benefit of requiring the portfolio in the junior year is the ability to evaluate the writing of upper-division transfer students shortly after arrival.

We did not specify the precise contents of the portfolio since we thought these could best be determined at a later date in conjunction with faculty from other disciplines. The process of setting writing standards together is essential for faculty to have a feeling of ownership in the evaluation system (E. White 164). However, we did make a general recommendation to include samples that cover the discourse triangle of explanatory, expressive, and persuasive modes (Lloyd-Jones 39). We also proposed that students include a cover letter for the pieces in the portfolio, a meta-analysis of their writing purposes and processes (Camp, "The Writing Folder," 97–98). This requirement would involve students personally in assessing not only their writing, but also the overall educative process of their college curriculum.

As long as certain standards in length and variety in rhetorical styles are met, portfolio requirements may vary slightly according to academic program. We believe in a system flexible enough to reflect different personal interests and career-related assignments yet still showing a mastery of general college writing skills. Students may include some writing from lower-division courses as well as upper-division work; however, a project involving library research in their major will be necessary for all students. In addition to presenting several required types of writings, students will be able to choose the mode of at least one of the pieces themselves. A minimum of twenty-five typed, double-spaced pages of final drafts would be required; these pages might include a lab report for a science major, a short story for an English major, or a feasibility study for a business major.

While portfolio assessment is often used as an evaluation technique by individual instructors within a class, we decided that for our purposes a jury of interdepartmental faculty would be necessary. The portfolio of a student would be read and evaluated by both a writing faculty member and a faculty member from the student's degree program. If they disagreed on whether the portfolio passed or failed, a third reader would be used. A juried system of assessing portfolios requires more faculty time and coordination than a single reading, but it ensures students a fair evaluation since standards of good academic writing can vary from discipline to discipline. A juried evaluation also may carry greater weight in the eyes of outside authorities such as graduate schools and potential employers.

The compilation and evaluation of the student's portfolio in the junior year would occur not as a sudden or isolated test, but as the culmination of several years of writing activities and support during the student's undergraduate education. Listed below are specific features of our proposal designed to provide students with continual practice in writing and critical thinking starting in the freshman year:

1. *Writing advisors.* Each student admitted to a baccalaureate program will be assigned a joint academic/writing advisor from the faculty who will oversee that student's progress in writing as well as help the student develop his or her overall educational plan. The writing advisor will make sure the student takes literacy placement tests, enrolls for appropriate reading and writing coursework, and receives tutorial assistance as needed.

As the student reaches the junior year, this faculty member will also advise the student on preparing his or her portfolio for the external assessment. This one-on-one contact is especially important for minority students such as Native Americans, who respond well in an academic atmosphere of interpersonal warmth and individualized attention (Kleinfeld; Wauters et al.). Since this type of advising is time-intensive and requires expertise in writing instruction, faculty advisors will be trained and given time for their advising duties.

2. *Writing-intensive courses across the curriculum.* Students will be required to include papers from different disciplines in their writing portfolio; thus, it is essential that they write regularly in all academic courses. In order to ensure that students receive ongoing practice in writing beginning in the freshman year, a number of general education requirements (e.g., introductory psychology, biology, and history) will be redesigned as writing-intensive courses. Faculty who volunteer to teach large sections of courses in a writing-intensive format will be provided with teaching assistants to help handle the heavier reading load and need for increased attention to student writing.

3. *Portfolio-based English courses.* To introduce students to the practice of compiling a portfolio of their written work, this evaluation procedure will be incorporated into as many English courses as possible, from basic writing to fiction workshops. Although these portfolios will not be graded by external readers, the process of portfolio building will familiarize students with the need to revise repeatedly in order to produce a collection of high-quality writings.

   In addition to our two standard lower-division English courses required of all degree students, an upper-division elective course in essay writing is being developed for students in their junior year. This advanced composition course focuses on the styles of writing for different disciplines and will require an extensive research project in the student's major. This class will provide additional writing instruction for students who need English coursework beyond the lower-division level, as well as serve as a helpful bridge for transfer students who have not been exposed to the writing portfolio concept. This course will be voluntary except for students who do not pass the portfolio assessment on their first try.

4. *Tutorial support.* Students needing intensive writing tutorials will be referred to the UAS Learning Center, where they will work with a trained peer tutor on their papers. Peer tutoring

provides a cost-effective means of delivering the individualized instruction necessary to retain many high-risk students. In addition, Native American students show a positive orientation to peer support and collaborative learning (see Philips), a special concern for our student population.

## Current and Planned Assessment Activities

Both faculty and student responses to this proposal have been generally supportive. Despite reluctance by some individual faculty members, particularly those in business and the sciences, the faculty as a whole has shown positive responses to portfolio assessment, perhaps because this proposal has been developed by the faculty. Some of the initial concerns our faculty had about portfolio assessment have been addressed through the process of our preliminary planning. Fears of a test-driven curriculum have paled since the measure of student ability chosen (the portfolio) reflects the entire learning process rather than being a single, final examination. While definition of consistent standards in writing courses will be an ongoing issue, the portfolio system of evaluation promises toleration of different teaching styles to a much greater degree than other current systems of writing assessment. Many faculty also have proven themselves generally receptive to our goal of incorporating more writing into academic courses. At a recent, voluntary writing-across-the-curriculum workshop, faculty from all disciplines were represented, and the UAS Faculty Senate voted to allocate all of its staff development funds this year to further training in this area for faculty on all three campuses.

Students are naturally wary of any new requirements for graduation, but the general consensus seems to be that if writing assessment in inevitable, portfolio assessment is preferable to other types. Having student representation on the assessment committee during the planning process proved to be an essential element in gaining student support for an idea that originally appeared threatening. At faculty convocation this year, one student spoke eloquently of several benefits students see in this proposal: first, the portfolio will provide them with a meaningful external measure of their academic accomplishments; second, they view a universitywide writing requirement as a needed check on consistency and quality in course and degree standards at UAS because such assessment reflects faculty priorites and performance as well as the achievement of individual students.

Administrative reactions to our proposal have been surprisingly favorable at both regional and statewide levels. Since portfolio assessment involves a more lengthy and costly process than standardized testing, we anticipated opposition from administrators. However, after examining the proposal, the President of the University of Alaska system wrote:

> The University of Alaska Southeast has developed an assessment system that does more than assess student abilities. The program promotes the incorporation of writing and reasoning into the student's college experience at all levels. ... Most importantly, the program addresses the problem of cultural bias in testing our diverse student population. ... This program will strengthen the institution as well as the student. It has my full support and encouragement. (O'Dowd).

President O'Dowd has provided statewide funds to continue assessment-planning activities at UAS, including research on different portfolio-assessment programs, faculty training in writing calibration, and grant writing. With the assistance of the School of Education, Liberal Arts and Sciences, portfolios are being used in two special projects at UAS: an exit portfolio for all Basic Writing students and an entrance portfolio for all students applying for admission to professional education programs. The purpose of the Basic Writing portfolio is to ensure consistent, high standards in a course taught by many different approaches. After its first year of implementation, this intercampus assessment has already led to increased effort by students, higher course standards, and improved communications among faculty at regional campuses, without inhibiting instructor freedom to determine classroom methodology.

The entrance portfolio for School of Education students extends this system of evaluation across the curriculum. For this portfolio, students submit papers from at least four different academic courses taken in their first two years of college work. Portfolios are judged by an interdisciplinary committee; students not passing must complete additional work in writing prior to admission to the program and student teaching. By exploring the uses of writing evaluation through these two projects, we are gaining insights into the problems and potential of portfolio assessment at the departmental and school levels before using it as a proficiency requirement for all degrees.

Securing funds for the full assessment program, including writing advisors and tutorial assistance, is the next challenge. Outside funding sources are being investigated, but there is strong sentiment among our faculty that a legislative appropriation must be allocated to this project if a long-range, quality program of student assessment is an important priority. In these days of wavering oil revenues and budget cuts within Alaska, financial commitment for new university projects is difficult to obtain. Nevertheless, if our state officials are interested in qualitative proof of our graduates' skills and corresponding support for such skills throughout the college curricula, they must be realistic about the cost of such outcomes. Legislators are currently considering an allocation to fund further assessment activities within the University of Alaska system.

What will exit assessment in writing ultimately look like in universities on the last frontier? It is too early to project the final design of our assessment system at UAS, but we hope our present efforts will lead to the adoption of an evaluation process that is intellectually challenging yet humane. Rather than asking students to generalize about arbitrary writing topics within a prescribed number of minutes, we are trying to design a measure of the types of in-depth discourse that writers create in real academic and professional contexts. As Lee Odell wrote, "The surest way to get rid of invalid assessment procedures is to replace them with something better" (134), and we believe that portfolios offer the best alternative to current proficiency exams in writing.

By the end of their undergraduate years, we would like to find our students reflecting with pride on a portfolio of valued writings instead of despairing like Ruby over the incongruity between writing classes and writing tests. We certainly do not envision a form of writing assessment that will force students to the same tactic Ruby has been reduced to in order to overcome her final collegiate obstacle. Being coached to produce quick prose on any assigned topic, Ruby is practicing the lockstep of formulaic writing: the five-paragraph essay. "Maybe I'll pass next time," said Ruby recently, "now that I know what they really want."

# 6

# Using the Portfolio to Meet State-Mandated Assessment
## *A Case Study*

Roberta Rosenberg
*Christopher Newport College*

## Inception of the Christopher Newport Assessment Program

During the 1986–87 academic year, the English department[1] of Christopher Newport College began to formulate plans for assessing its two programs: the Freshman Writing sequence and the B.A. in English. The impetus behind this action was essentially twofold: (1) the goals of the Writing Program and the three tracks leading to the B.A. in English (literature, writing, and language arts–education) had not been reviewed or revised in over five years; and (2) the English department would soon be required to make a formal assessment of its programs to the state of Virginia.

On February 20, 1985, the state of Virginia's House of Delegates passed Joint Senate Resolution no. 125, which required the State Council of Higher Education of Virginia (SCHEV) to "conduct a study of Virginia's public higher education system, and to investigate means by which student achievement may be measured to assure the citizens of Virginia of the continuing high quality of higher education in the Commonwealth." SCHEV conducted the study and reported its results to the legislature, which then passed Joint Resolution no. 83, requiring all state-supported colleges and universities to formulate assessment plans. In order to help the schools in their efforts, SCHEV drafted guidelines that were published as "Recommendations for Measuring Student Achievement at Virginia Public Colleges and Universities."[2]

The English department, therefore, had a difficult, twofold project before it: to improve its own programs in ways that would actually lead to quality curriculum reform and, at the same time, would satisfy the state's assessment guidelines and requirements. The English department, however, was aided in its task by the state's enlightened and flexible attitude toward assessment. SCHEV did not wish to institute minimum competency testing (as in Florida or Georgia) or the standardization of assessment instruments; it nevertheless instructed its colleges and universities to implement cost-effective measures of student learning such as "adopting standardized tests of achievement where feasible" (SCHEV "Recommendations"). The English department, however, did not want to utilize one of the GRE or ACT writing or literature standardized tests since several assessment consultants, including Peter Gray of Syracuse University, had cautioned that information from these national tests often does not translate into curriculum reform. Instead, two departmental committees, the Freshman Composition Committee and the Majors Assessment Committee, began to formulate alternative assessment instruments that would satisfy the state mandate and the department. The result was the creation of two different portfolio systems one for the Freshman Writing Program and the other for the three tracks leading to the B.A. in English.

## Benefits in Using the Portfolio to Meet State-Mandated Assessment

In its "Recommendations for Measuring Student Achievement at Virginia's Public Colleges and Universities," SCHEV required its state-supported schools to "submit annual reports of progress in developing their assessment programs and *concrete, non-anecdotal* and *quantifiable* information on student achievement" [my italics]. Thus, the assessment of the writing and English major programs could not be purely descriptive, but rather "concrete, non-anecdotal" and, even more problematic, "quantifiable." With this in mind, the members of the two departmental assessment committees adapted the portfolio so that it provided both concrete and quantifiable measures of student achievement and served as the basis for program revision and improvement.

The portfolio system would provide students and faculty with a record of student learning; more importantly, however, the portfolio would keep the assessment process where it belongs—in the hands of faculty members who create and revise the curriculum. The state council, which has approved our assessment program, also concurs with this opinion. It specifically states that the assessment program should enable faculty "to use the results to address student deficiencies, evaluate and improve the curriculum, and develop better teaching techniques" (SCHEV "Recommendation 1").

Although portfolio assessment is not without its frustrations, it has already produced positive curriculum revisions for both the freshman writing student and the English major. For this reason, I would like to describe, in a step-by-step fashion, the process of creating the portfolio as an assessment measure.

## Creating a Portfolio Assessment Program in Writing

### Writing Program Goals

In its "Recommendations," SCHEV advised that all measurements of student achievement should "derive from institutional initiatives [and] bear a direct relationship to teaching and learning in the classroom" ("Recommendation 2"). Before selecting papers or tests to be placed in the student's portfolio, therefore, the Freshman Composition Committee drafted a series of departmental goals for all five of the writing courses. Since the five freshman writing courses encompass a variety of subjects and student abilities, from remedial English to an honors course in writing about literature, it was necessary to draft separate goals and complementary individual portfolio requirements for each course. The drafting of these course-specific goals was essential to meeting the state mandate in Virginia, which asked colleges to "involve faculty in setting the standards of achievement, selecting the measurement instruments and analyzing the results" (SCHEV).

The initial faculty response to departmental goals, however, was less than enthusiastic. It was extremely important to differentiate between course goals and methods. Once writing instructors realized that the program called for neither a uniform syllabus nor departmental adoption of texts, their responses were favorable. Course goals set desired levels of student skills in writing, research, and literary analysis while methods (books, specific assignments, tests) reflect particular instructors' means of meeting those departmental goals.[3]

In drafting goals and then portfolio requirements for the first college-level course in the Christopher Newport College writing program (English 101), the committee emphasized eight areas of achievement that students should reach upon the completion of the course:

1. Generate ideas, plan, draft, revise, and edit original writing independently.

2. Formulate a thesis and support it with logical, well-detailed evidence.

3. Select appropriate rhetorical modes and use them effectively in expository prose for a wide variety of audiences.

4. Develop and express ideas in unified, coherent paragraphs and demonstrate proficiency in the conventions of edited American English.

5. Read carefully and interpret the meaning of a wide variety of texts from the academic disciplines and popular literature.

6. Become familiar with the research process.

7. Write a short informative research paper or report with acceptable documentation and format.

8. Use basic word processing programs to complete academic work. (Christopher Newport College, "Student Guide" 1–2)

## Selecting Appropriate Materials for the Portfolio

After instructors agreed on the goals for all five courses, it was possible to select specific kinds of assignments that would reflect student achievement. The portfolio requirements for English 101 as well as the four other courses in the freshman sequence were chosen because they would demonstrate the level of student learning at the conclusion of a particular course. The English 101 portfolio includes the following: a writing placement sample, an expressive essay, a descriptive essay, an expository essay, one completely revised essay and a documented, informative essay (Christopher Newport College, "Student Guide" 4–5).

The writing placement essay marks the student's writing level at the beginning of the course and the other assignments chart his or her progress throughout the term. The instructor, or an external writing consultant, should therefore be able to review a portfolio in order to evaluate the student's success or failure in attaining departmental course goals. Is the student able to develop a thesis, organize ideas, draft, edit, and revise original essays? Does the student have the ability to do library research and write an informative paper complete with documentation? These goals can be quickly assessed by reviewing the portfolio.

## Formulating Summary Evaluation Sheets

Although a scientifically done random sampling of portfolios by either the writing program administrator or an external consultant would provide sufficient feedback on student learning, that alone would not fulfill Virginia's requirement for "quantifiable" evidence. For this reason, we adopted a holistic grading instrument, which all instructors complete and place in each student portfolio. The summary evaluation is also included in the "Student Guide: The Writing Program" in order to give students a clear idea of how their portfolios will be evaluated at the end of the term.

The summary evaluation takes a holistic approach to writing and includes the following categories: ideas, organization, paragraphs, audience, research skill, wording, sentence structure, and punctuation/correctness. Students are given scores of 5 (complete mastery) to 1 (poor). The summary evaluation provides a uniform, consistent measure that makes it possible to report data on all the courses and levels in the freshman writing program. Regardless of the differing assignments and texts in a course, student skills can be evaluated and quantified using this method, which also makes it possible to do a random sampling of portfolios and calculate student learning in specific courses or sequences of courses.

Since the summary evaluation sheet is used for all freshman writing courses, it is also possible to compare the remedial students' relative abilities in ideas, organization, or punctuation/correctness with the average student in English 101 or the advanced English 103 writer.[4] In addition, the writing program administrator, as well as an outside consultant, can compare holistic scores and actual course grades in order to detect discrepancies. If a student receives high marks in ideas, organization, and grammar, the evaluator may want to speculate about why the student received a C for the course. Or conversely, why would a portfolio that received low/average holistic scores merit an A or B? This analysis should shed light on our evaluation procedures and grading practices.

## Evaluating and Reporting Portfolio Results

In order to utilize the portfolio information more fully, we created a portfolio evaluation sheet, which summarizes the information from the sampled portfolios and juxtaposes it with the student's general abilities and the achievements in high school and college thus far. In this way, the department can assess the degree to which successful writing predicts or reflects success in other academic areas. In order to accomplish this final analysis of the portfolios, we do a random sampling of all students who have completed portfolios during a given academic year. Information from the student's college transcript (college GPA, verbal SAT, and Test of Standard Written English — TSWE) is then collated with the portfolio data. The portfolio evaluation sheet, therefore, provides a "history" of a particular student or of an entire group of students taking a course in the writing sequence during a specific year.[5]

The most promising aspect of using portfolios to meet state and departmental assessment, however, comes at the conclusion of this process. At that point instructors, writing directors, and other college administrators can evaluate student strengths and weaknesses and make suggestions for curricular changes: are students lacking in organizational skills (the formation of a thesis and evidence to support main ideas)? After reading several representative portfolios, summary evaluation sheets, and the results of the portfolio evaluation sheet, instructors or curriculum committees can make some program revisions based on reliable evidence. If only 10 percent of students receive a 2 (needs improvement) in punctuation and correctness, and an analysis of the portfolios provides secondary validation, then an instructor may concentrate his or her energies elsewhere. Since the portfolio evaluation analysis is done course by course, it is also possible to do a "value-added" assessment, which analyzes the relative ability level of students at the beginning and conclusion of a learning experience.

Furthermore, portfolio evaluation is superior to one-time testing because the assessment instrument is the student's course work itself; thus, the information received from portfolio analysis translates directly into curriculum revision and reform. If one compares results from other assessment tests, particularly standardized tests that may not share the department's goals, the difference is evident. How does one make specific curricular changes based on a score of 150 or 400 on a standardized test?

### Preparing for External Consultation

The Christopher Newport College Department of English keeps all assessed student portfolios for one year and returns all others to the students. After two or three years of in-house assessment, we plan to have an external consultant evaluate both the portfolios and our assessment process. External validation will provide the department with impartial criticism of the goals, standards, and assignments in the writing program; a consultant can then determine whether we test our students in the areas we acknowledge as important in our statement of goals. He or she will also satisfy the state requirement that colleges seek outside validation of their pedagogical methods.

Our first assessment of the writing program took place in the spring of 1989 and produced some interesting results, not only for the department, but for the college as well. Mean scores of 3 (acceptable) were achieved in 95 percent of the categories measuring students' skills in credit-bearing courses (English 101–104); however, students in remedial English (English 020) scored 3 or better in only one holistic category (organization). We have also discovered that many students who begin in the remedial course have not completed either of the college-level writing courses two years later. Although these findings will need to be validated by several more assessments, we have already gleaned some interesting information that can be translated into curricula modification and better student placement and counseling. In addition, SCHEV was so pleased with the results that it suggested that other departments in the college think about adopting some form of portfolio analysis in their assessment measures.

## Creating a Portfolio Assessment Program in the Major

After the initial success with the writing portfolio, the department decided to use the portfolio once again in its assessment of majors who will graduate with a B.A. in English and a concentration in literature, writing, or language arts/education. Our previous experience with the portfolio helped in the initial stages; however, using the portfolio for major assessment proved more problematic. How does a committee write goals for courses as disparate as Shakespeare, Modern World Literature, or Advanced Grammar? Does one concentrate on process skills (careful reading, thinking, and writing) as we did in the writing program? How do we assess substantive knowledge, the depth and scope of literary understanding, without including every student test and paper? The problem of substantive knowledge proved the most perplexing to the Major Assessment Committee, and there were several moments when, in frustration and exhaustion, we felt like abandoning the entire process and requiring students to take a standardized test like the GRE.

Reliance on the GRE, however, would have ultimately proved disappointing. Despite the allure of the "quick fix" nature of a standardized test, the GRE's emphasis on literary knowledge would not assess what our students in the writing or language arts/education track had learned. What would high or low GRE scores mean to our department, students, or the state of Virginia? How would the scores translate into program revision and curriculum improvement? For these reasons, we opted for the more complicated, but eventually more beneficial, route of drafting separate goals, portfolio requirements, and summary evaluation sheets for the three majors.

## Writing Goals for the B.A. in English

In order to arrive at a consensus about the goals for English majors, the Major Assessment Committee asked faculty to draft goals for particular courses. After collecting, analyzing, and synthesizing the results, one committee member presented goals for the three tracks to the entire department. There were, needless to say, numerous revisions until faculty members were satisfied. In many cases, goals for the three major tracks overlapped or were identical; at other times, the relative importance of one skill or substantive area predominated over another. Although all English majors are expected to have a knowledge of literature, students with a Writing concentration will have special skills in professional writing and journalism, while students in the Language Arts/Education track will need additional coursework in composition, language studies, and curriculum development.

Despite the initial complexity of the task, the process of writing goals was extremely beneficial, since it stimulated faculty to discuss how individual courses fit into the overall program. Committee members discussed the lack of certain areas of study (history of the language and literary analysis) and the need for curriculum revision. As a result of this process, new courses were written into the English major. In addition, the traditional English/secondary education major was expanded into a "language arts/education" track, which in 1991 will bring elementary and middle school education majors into the department as English majors.

## Selecting Appropriate Materials for the Portfolio

In order to use the portfolio to assess substantive knowledge, the committee divided the curriculum for all majors into nine areas: (1) Medieval and Renaissance British Literature, including Shakespeare; (2) Eighteenth-Century British Literature; (3) Romantic and Victorian British Literature; (4) American Literature to 1900; (5) Twentieth-Century British, World, and American Literature; (6) World Literature in Translation; (7) Language and Literature Studies: History,

Grammar, and Criticism; (8) Cultural Studies in Literature: Minority, Women's, and Young Adult; and (9) Composition Theory and Advanced Writing. Each student has to include in the portfolio at least one test and syllabus from at least six of the nine areas. This system provides evaluators with a clear sense of the student's scope and depth of knowledge, and yet it will be flexible enough to account for different concentrations in the English B.A. (literature, writing, or language arts/education).

### Formulating a Major's Summary Evaluation Sheet

The major's summary evaluation sheets for the three B.A. programs in English provide concise but specific information on the scope and depth of student learning in a concrete, nonanecdotal, and quantifiable manner. Each summary evaluation sheet requires students to list at least one course and grade in at least six of the nine curriculum areas in English. After reviewing a senior's portfolio (which includes syllabi, tests, grades, and representative papers), a faculty evaluator gives a numerical assessment (5, excellent, to 1, poor) of a student's skills in literary explication, writing, research, and/or curriculum development.

### Evaluating and Reporting Portfolio Results

The English department graduates between ten and twenty English majors a year; thus, it is feasible to include the complete data on all graduates in its assessment report. Larger schools may need to do a scientific random sampling of graduates, utilizing the format we designed to report data on the freshman writing program.

After the Major Assessment Committee has completed its evaluation, the department will retain the portfolio in order to allow for a consultant to do a five-year review of the program. Since the consultant has access to goals, tests, papers, as well as departmental holistic evaluations and course grades, the external assessment has the optimal chance of providing impartial feedback on student learning and the quality of instruction.

## Conclusion

Using the portfolio as the basis for state-mandated assessment is a good alternative to standardized tests that may not reflect the goals or curriculum of the department. The portfolio is not, however, a panacea that solves all the problems or reveals all answers about student achievement and learning. In particularly large schools, the physical problem of storing portfolios would be more critical than it is at smaller institutions like Christopher Newport College.

Yet, at present, the portfolio system seems an ideal way of evaluating the quality of student achievement and the effectiveness of instruction. It can provide valuable information that is not available from mass-produced, multiple-choice tests. John Harris, an expert in assessment in higher education, believes that "improvements in instruction begin with feedback on student achievement. Such feedback is dependent on assessment, and the occasional use of outside, commercial tests is not enough. The best hope lies in encouraging faculty to improve their assessment procedures and to relate assessed student performance to program and instructional improvement" (23). Since portfolio assessment leads to curriculum reform and faculty awareness, it satisfies not only a state mandate, but any one who is concerned with the quality education of college students.

## Notes

1. I would like to thank the members of the Christopher Newport English department who have served on the Freshman Composition Committee and the Majors Assessment Committee with me: Professors Jane Chambers, James Cornette, Douglas Gordon, Burnam MacLeod, Albert Millar, Jay Paul, Madeline Smith, and Barry Wood.

2. The State Mandated Assessment Plan, referred to as the Virginia Plan, was not a regulation to be taken lightly by either faculty or administrators. An unpublished memorandum sent to the Christopher Newport faculty from the College's Ad Hoc Steering Committee on Student Assessment cautioned that "failure to meet this challenge can result in level funding or reductions in funding from Richmond." In fact, Virginia's decision to undertake a serious, in-depth assessment of its college students is part of a national trend, according to Terry W. Hartle: "Post-secondary student testing has risen in popularity partly because of the states' experience with minimum competency tests for elementary and secondary school students. A decade ago, few states had such testing programs in place; today, virtually every state does" (3).

3. Copies of the goals for courses, summary evaluation sheets, as well as completed assessment reports are available from the author: Professor Roberta Rosenberg, Department of English, Christopher Newport College, Newport News, Virginia 23606.

4. Students enroll in one of three freshman writing sequences: English 020 (Strategies for College Reading and Writing), English 101 (Informative

and Analytical Writing), English 102 (Interpretive and Argumentative Writing); English 101 and 102; English 103 (Rhetoric and Analytical Writing), English 104 (Argumentative and Interpretive Writing About Literature).

5. Thus far, I have completed three statistical analyses for 1987–88, 1988–89, and 1989–90. Interested individuals may write to the author (see note 3) for sample results.

# 7

# Step by Step
## *The Development in British Schools of Assessment by Portfolio*

Patrick Scott
*English Adviser for Cleveland Local Education Authority,*
*United Kingdom*

It is 1963. You are sixteen, British, and still at school because you were one of a minority of fifteen year olds who opted to remain in full-time education. You are about to take the General Certificate of Education (GCE)[1] in English, which happens to be one of your favorite subjects. You enjoy reading, get real pleasure from writing, and have a reputation for being talkative. Even if you make a mess of all the other subjects, you should do well in this one. Nonetheless, you can't help feeling nervous. The examination will start when you are given permission to turn over the paper lying face downward on the desk in front of you. "You have sixty minutes, starting from now." You begin reading:

> English Language 1: Choose one of the following subjects for composition. About one hour should be spent on this question:
>
> 1. The importance of the wheel.

You swallow hard as your eye runs quickly down the page to see what else might be offered.

> 2. Describe the attractions of your favourite month of the year or your favourite county or your favourite Sunday newspaper.
> 3. You have investigated the leisure activities of the boys or girls in your age group. Write out your report.

The sense of impending panic grows stronger.

4. Science in the service of agriculture or building or aviation.
5. Show that the running of a home efficiently is a skilled operation. (from an O-level English language examination, see Burgess 129).

In the entire paper, there is nothing whatever that interests you or fires your imagination, nothing that offers you any clue about what to do next.

With little enthusiasm, but spurred on by a lifetime's habit of doing what you are told however inexplicable it may be, you select one of the questions and make a start. What comes to your aid are all the tips provided by the teacher before you went in to the exam: "introduction, four paragraphs, conclusion": "the first sentence of the paragraph should tell the reader what the rest of the paragraph is going to be about"; "never use *nice*"; and so on. The fact that you have never before written anything in which you found this advice helpful only serves to illustrate that the kind of writing that you do in school is not only different but superior to the kind of writing you actually use in your daily life — stories, letters to friends, your journal, notes, messages, records, poems, lists, explanations, thoughts. It is not a problem; you long ago became used to the failure of what you do in school to correspond to anything that happens outside it.

At the same time as you were sweating it out in that British examination room in the early sixties, the system that had put you there was itself under scrutiny. A committee established by the government of the day to look at the "examining of English language" was about to report that "we have considered most seriously whether we should advise the cessation of these examinations for educational reasons . . . we have come very near that conclusion" ("The Examining of English Language," The Lockwood Report, as quoted in "A Language for Life," The Bullock Report, 176). It would be hard to imagine a more dramatic vindication of what innumerable candidates had instinctively sensed. The judgment of the Lockwood Report, however, was not an isolated case. Ten years later it was repeated in the influential Bullock Report (1975): "English requires a wider and more flexible range of assessment than most other areas of the curriculum. We believe that rigid syllabuses are not the best means of achieving this and that there should be an increase in school based assessment with external moderation" (180).[2] Even this was not the end of the story. Some three or four years later the school inspectors nailed their colors to the mast: "The schools and the boards responsible for conducting examinations might consider

jointly whether exam requirements could be framed so as to encourage more effective learning and use of language," ("Aspects of
Secondary Education" 108). Almost all reputable opinion was critical
of the status quo.

There is no single reason for this remarkable display of unanimity.
By 1965, disenchantment with the status quo had become so wide-
spread that the introduction of a new level of examining (the Certificate of Secondary Education or C.S.E.)[3] could be exploited as an
opportunity for reform. The fourteen Regional Examination Boards
established to run the new system all, for the first time, involved
teachers in the assessment and moderation of the examinations they
were teaching and even made space for them in the boardrooms
and council chambers where policy was agreed. Nothing could ever
be quite the same again. The hallowed institutions, dominated by
the universities, that had traditionally run the British examination
system, were assailed by a new, more aggressive breed of teacher
who expected open government, had some insight into how the
system worked, and was willing, if necessary, to take its custom
elsewhere. Few examination boards were willing to swim against
the tide.

These, however, were opportunities provided by the happy
coincidence of local circumstances. Of more interest outside Britain
are the arguments that were used to provide a theoretical under-
pinning for the changes that, by the early 1970s, were allowing
"coursework assessment"[4] to become increasingly popular as an
alternative to the conventional examination. As the British education
system wound itself up to another reform of the examination system
in the mid-1980s, the case was put in the educational press with
increasing frequency. Here are three different voices, all writing in
the *Times Educational Supplement*. The first, John Dixon, is well
known to an international audience as the author of *Growth Through
English*: "Think of the difficulties of the examiner; how to obtain
evidence in a 2 hour paper on both writing and reading for four
major functions (speaking, listening, writing and reading) *at least*?
. . . It is a tall order, even in class, and in the exam room impossible
to achieve for every candidate on the given day" (October 28, 1977).
Three years later, Mike Raleigh explored some of the same issues by
focusing on the work of Marita, a sixteen year-old who had just sat
O-level English language:

> The first—and most important—thing is that the examination in which
> she achieved her grade was (some 14 years after Lockwood) an
> inadequate test of her competence in language. It could tell us nothing
> about her ability to use the written language in a variety of real
> circumstances and for different purposes, to read and make use of a

variety of material in different ways, to use and understand oral language (1980).

The third extract is taken from an article by the chief examiner for one of the pilot schemes that, by 1982, had been running for a number of years in anticipation of a reform that was constantly being postponed. He was urging the government to follow the advice that was being given by the profession:

> The Schools Council report on English is surely right to see course work as the only way to deal with the range of work needed to assess a candidate who at "O" level has been judged on one or two pieces of writing: "a higher grade should be awarded to pupils who show that they can undertake a wide variety of writing." Today, an "O" level candidate can gain grade C if he can write a story and (in some cases) a letter. But can he set out an argument? Can he describe, explain, give instructions? "O" level papers set their sights too low (Hopwood 1982).[5]

All three make the same point, that only by reference to a portfolio is it possible to assess a sufficient variety of work to provide a reliable verdict.

This may appear to be exactly the kind of debate about fairness and accuracy that examiners might be expected to enjoy. But if it is dismissed in this way, as a technical matter about different kinds of assessment, then an important point is missed. For all three the issue is as much about the nature of language as it is about the nature of examinations. The reason why they lay such stress on the need to look at how pupils use language in a variety of situations is because they are aware that language does not exist in a vacuum. It is not something inert, some kind of appliance that has been attached to people and can be unhooked for regular inspections. Language is more intimate than that, even when it is being used in formal or public ways. What Dixon, Raleigh, and Hopwood are agreeing is that the success with which we use language depends upon a great deal more than whether we know a lot of words, or are skillful in organizing them in complex or original ways. It depends upon how we feel about what we are trying to say, and the people we are trying to say it to.

That may seem a matter of common sense, but it is not. The common-sense view, constrained by the values of Western industrial culture and the metaphors that it provides (however inadequate they may be), will tell you that mastery of language depends upon a knowledge of how it works, so that all the bits of the machine can be kept well greased and in good working order. Repudiation of this view is not a simple matter, particularly since it has some currency within the education system itself.

The route from this to assessment of coursework is fairly direct. The starting point is what the Bullock Report calls "the concept of the inseparability of language and the human situation" (p. 174). That is crucial because it draws attention to the problem of trying to assess language without knowing something about the circumstances under which it has been used. What is more, a single instance of how language has been used, such as a 450-word essay, begins to look like pretty flimsy evidence if performance can change significantly according to context. The simplest solution to both of these problems is teacher assessment of the kind of extended sample that can be provided only in a portfolio.

The best way to illustrate how, in practice, this alters what is required of teachers and examiners is by going back to that English O level set in 1963. What, on reflection, is most striking about the examination paper is how relentlessly uninteresting the questions are. It prompts the suspicion that the examiner was not just having an off day. Perhaps that is how it was meant to be.

This view is not as perverse as it may at first appear. There are good reasons why the subjects chosen are remote, and the language pitched at a daunting level of abstraction. Don't forget that the examiner has a responsibility to ensure fair play, and nobody should have an unfair advantage by virtue of prior knowledge. More important than this, however, is the question of standards. Implicit in a question paper of this kind is a kind of veiled linguistic hierarchy that does not just have standard English at the top, but a very specific use of it. What is most highly valued is the ability to remain coolly detached, to generalize, to hypothesize without commitment. What will be rewarded is elegance of expression, wit, the kind of rationalizing intelligence that can construct a hundred plausible solutions and burst each one of them with an unexpected logic. Never mind that writing is turned into a kind of circus trick, like balancing bricks on a six-foot pole or juggling knives, while the examiners applaud. That's all part of the game. What impresses is whether the candidates manage to keep their balance, and so there is little incentive for providing tasks with any intrinsic value of their own. Indeed, the quest for "challenging" questions in which "able" candidates are "stretched" by being encouraged to perform ever more unlikely tricks is almost guaranteed to ensure that what they are required to write is increasingly removed from anything likely to be encountered in situations where language is used for real purposes.

When the final assessment is on the basis of a portfolio of work, the whole business of developing children's language can be tackled in a quite different way. Writing ceases to be about applying a set of rules, or about conforming to some kind of ideal, unvarying pattern. On the contrary, instead of training children to apply pre-determined formulae, the teacher has to find a way of encouraging them to see writing as a dynamic process, one that not only allows but requires them to make decisions. This means putting pupils in charge of their own writing. The skill demanded of the teacher is not a knack for providing memorable tips about what to do next in a crisis but the ability to create an environment in which children can use their initiative.

The implications of this are far-reaching. Pupils need to have some kind of working awareness of language variety so that they know what options are available to them, and teachers not only have to devise tasks that allow children to use their judgment, but also have to create the kind of classroom environment that makes it possible for them to do so. Bearing in mind what the Assessment of Performance Unit (APU)[6] had to say — "the mastery of language will also involve the mastery of a variety of language modes" (Dept. of Education and Science 10) — there is some point in exploring these issues in greater detail.

The problem of conventional practice was tartly summarized in the 1979 survey by the Schools Inspectorate:

> [Despite visiting] nearly 400 schools, the lasting impression was of a general uniformity of demand. There were considerable differences of format and custom among subjects as there always have been. But the pattern most frequently found could be described as essentially one of "notes" and "essays," interspersed with the practice of answering examination questions alongside the drills of exercises and tests. ("Aspects of Secondary Education" 83)[7]

With the advent of GCSE[8] in 1986, portfolio assessment was officially acknowledged as one of the most effective ways of remedying this problem. The new examination created a flurry of interest in the numerous attempts that had been made over the previous fifteen years to identify what a "range of writing" ought to cover. Writing had been variously categorized, sometimes according to its formal properties, sometimes by reference to the circumstances under which it was produced, and sometimes with an eye to the purposes for which it was being used. Fortunately, no single taxonomy was successful in cornering the market and becoming the universal model for all examination syllabuses. Had it done so, we would probably, by now, have codified "writing" into a set of uniform procedures from which pupils depart at their peril.

Although provision was made for centralized control over the GCSE, and each syllabus was required to meet "national criteria," this control was exercised with an encouraging recognition that there can be a variety of good practice. It is interesting to see how little the rubric provided by one examination board actually changed in the transition from experimental scheme to pilot syllabus to the fully fledged GCSE. The first examination syllabus in Britain to be assessed exclusively by coursework was an O level in English language devised by the Joint Matriculation Board[9] in the early 1970s. It included the following:

> VARIED RANGE OF WORK. All English teachers will realise that the potential range of work is infinite and that individual teachers are in the best position to determine the limits within which their own candidates work. The following suggestions might be borne in mind, however: the candidate should be given the opportunity to produce and sustain argument, both subjective and objective; to offer a wide variety of descriptive writing; to order and express factual information; and to exercise the imagination. (Scott, "Coursework in English," 1980, 10)

By 1989, the tone had changed:

> To meet the assessment objectives, the selection must include work that shows the candidate's ability:
>
> a.  to produce and sustain argument, to handle and present ideas, and to persuade;
>
> b.  to write imaginatively and expressively and to recount real or imagined experience in any appropriate form such as narrative, description or drama;
>
> c.  to order and present factual information, such as an account of an event or process, a report of a visit or interview or a piece of research. (GCSE, 4)

Although, in keeping with the times, this version dispenses with the reassuring preamble of the original, it effectively leaves the teacher in exactly the same position. The definitions provided are sufficiently broad to give the writer some autonomy, and the teacher some responsibility. Perhaps more important than this, however, is their pragmatism. They smack of the classroom, of explanations provided under pressure that are instantly recognizable as what pupils actually do. This lack of sophistication is a strength. It ensures that the writing will not be dominated by the way in which it is defined.

Although a great deal of attention was focused on the question of how it might be possible to legislate for a range of writing, the real challenge was about how, within this kind of agreed framework, to devise the kind of assignments that would put pupils firmly in charge of their own writing. If pupils were to be given a menu rather than a set meal, then they also had to be offered some guidance about how to make sensible choices. The solution lay in the notion of "real" writing tasks with some kind of identifiable purpose. The significance of this was that the purpose provided a yardstick by which to judge the effectiveness of what had been written. It freed pupils from the tyranny of the teacher's opinion about what was right and wrong, and allowed them to make judgements for themselves about what *worked*.

There was an initial rush of enthusiasm for attaching to every assignment some kind of real or imagined *audience*.[10] But as teachers became more familiar with the new ways of working, they also began to arrive at a less literal understanding of what it means for a piece of writing to have a purpose. There was increasing interest in the kind of journal writing that might be described as *expressive*, for example, and renewed efforts to think about how pupils could be introduced to narrative in ways that did not simply invite the retelling of a film seen last night on television. There was also a growing understanding that for some pupils in the right circumstances, there could be a sense of purpose in exploring the potential of a particular written form for its own sake.

Two examples should suffice to illustrate what happens when pupils are allowed to take charge of their own writing. Both are fragments from much longer pieces of work. The first is from Paul's "Guide to Salt Water Fishing." Here he is dealing with the baits that anglers use:

> There are five main types of sea bait used to catch fish in British waters. These are; Lugworms; Ragworms; Crabs; Mussels, and strips of fish. This bait can be found along most coastlines with the exception of Rocky Coasts. If for some reason the bait cannot be found along the beaches, it can be ordered from most of the better Tackle Shops. (Scott, *Countdown* 22)

The suggestion that Paul might want to produce a guide had arisen directly from his interest in fishing. He revealed an impressive level of expertise and there was no doubt that he was in the driving seat and that the teacher was simply a consultant. As a direct result, Paul grew in confidence and his work assumed a new authority. Even in this brief extract, it is possible to see the way in which the writer has distanced himself from the material in order to gauge how it might be received. As well as the careful classification of "types of

sea bait" in the first sentence, there is the telling reference to
"British waters," a clear sign that he is operating within the fiction
that his guide would be published and read by an audience who
might need that kind of explanation. By the third sentence, he is
handing out good advice in exactly the right tone because the
constraints of writing for an audience have forced him to anticipate
the kind of problem that might be encountered by somebody trying
to do as he has suggested.

A sharp contrast is provided by the second example, written by
Wendy, though the lesson to be learned is very similar:

**The Ballad of Spit Nolan**

Spit Nolan was a bony lad
His face was pale and thin,
But put him in a trolley race
And he would always win.

Ducker Smith he challenged Spit
To race him down the hill,
Spit Nolan knew he was the champ
And said, "Of course I will."

They both agreed the time and place
On top of Cemetery Brew,
They gathered there on Sunday morn
With all the friends they knew.

(Quoted in Scott, *Coursework*, 1983, 49)

The ballad continues for another twenty-nine verses, retelling the
tale of Spit Nolan from the original short story by Bill Naughton.
What is not evident from this extract is the skill with which Wendy
captures the feeling at the end when Spit veers out of control under
a bus and is killed. Nonetheless, it is clear, even from these three
stanzas, that she is able to handle the verse with real flair. Part of
the purpose of the writing for Wendy was to submit herself to the
disciplines of the ballad form in order to see whether she could
make it work. In the process she also demonstrates how well she is
able to capture the attention of an audience in telling her story. The
dramatic emphasis at the beginning of the second verse, for example,
is no accident. She knows that if Ducker Smith is to be viewed as a
real threat to Spit's preeminence, the line needs to start by using his
name like a declaration of intent.

The point about both of these pieces of writing is that they
could not have been produced under examination conditions. Work
of this kind, and length, needs time for research, reflection, drafting,
and redrafting. When this is available, it is evident from the piece

itself that something quite fresh is happening, that the writing has been tackled in ways that are quite different from the days of external examinations and 450-word essays.

It would be a mistake to imagine that these writing habits develop in some magical way once the teacher has embraced portfolio assessment and put the pupils in charge. Research needs to be carefully guided, reflection is often most valuable when it is undertaken collaboratively, and drafting is a difficult and painful process, even when the writer has ready access to a word processor. The teacher has a key role to play in helping pupils come to terms with the process as well as the product.

In an attempt to be precise about the kind of support that pupils need, it is easy to underestimate the importance of the relationship between teacher and taught. Because it is elusive, it is sometimes hard to be sure what it contributes to the development of the pupil as a writer. One final example, however, from Jane's autobiography, suggests that the support of a trusted adult can be of crucial importance:

> My cousin David died when I was sixteen. He got knocked down by a car. He was only twelve. At the funeral I sat next to my cousin Sandra. She cried openly, whilst I was ashamed of my tears, and although they were streaming down my face, my breathing was regular and if my face had been covered no one would have known that I was crying. It was a small church. To tell the truth, I did not take in much of my surroundings, but I do remember some things. The interior of the church was cold. The air felt moist, the whole place had a feeling of being submerged in water for hundreds of years. There was silence except for the vicar's voice, the rain, and quiet, muffled sobs.
>
> All in all, it was not a nice experience, but I have a craving for the morbid and a strange excitement is aroused in me by death. I feel happy when I am unhappy. Sometimes my own strange feelings send shivers down my spine. I have secret fantacies of being burned, screaming as a witch or to be hanged for something I did not do. It seems that I have got carried away with myself. A little of myself, that perhaps no one else knows about has been written on paper for all to see. Including me, and it is me that most of all does not want to see it. (Quoted in Scott, *Coursework*, 1980, 10)

The extract makes explicit the confessional nature of the entire work. What is moving about this piece are the contradictions within it. The language is quite unusual. Jane is able to move effortlessly from the figurative — "the feeling of being submerged in water for hundreds of years" — to the expressive — "it seems that I have got carried away with myself" — in an engagingly naive way. She is also able to resist the temptation to edit out the unwelcome perceptions about herself. Neither of these things would be possible unless the relationship with her teacher was capable of acting as some kind of catalyst. Significantly, Jane had started her autobiography with a disclaimer: "If I said that I was going to write an autobiography I suspect that most people would laugh. In my seventeen years and three months I have done nothing outstandingly brilliant or unusual" (Quoted in Scott, *Coursework* 1980, 10). It is hardly surprising that she is diffident about her own credentials as a writer and keenly aware of the reaction she might provoke. But her self-doubt is more deeply rooted. Even as she writes her opening sentence, she remains unsure whether her experience really warrants such attention. The disclaimer is designed to preempt the accusation that she is being presumptuous. The teacher is important as a kind of privileged reader, able, by earning her trust, to allay these fears. It would be difficult to imagine any other way in which Jane might experience the sense of being valued that people need if they are to write like this.

It would be wrong to conclude without saying something, however brief, about the way in which events have been nudged and steered one way or another by government. The account provided here has stressed the part that portfolio assessment has played in giving pupils control over their own writing. The way in which it has been written might suggest that the introduction of new forms of assessment in Britain has been politically uncomplicated. Nothing could be further from the truth. In the model of language development that coursework promotes, the pupil has to be active, thinking, critical, aware, and, above all, capable of making choices. That view of the English curriculum is put neatly into its wider perspective by the following passage:

> James Moffett raised the question of whether or not society truly wants the schools to create students who are literate in the fullest and best sense. More than one study group suggested that society seems to want students who clearly can function at a minimum skills level—who can, say, read and obey commands—but does not crave to have them raised to higher levels of skill, where their literacy might disrupt the political status quo through articulate criticism. (Tchudi)

Much of the writing about portfolio assessment over the last ten years has been preoccupied with the need to empower pupils, to give them the power through language to alter the circumstances in which they find themselves. As the government in Britain has taken more control over the education system through the National Curriculum, it has also sought to sponsor other, less threatening, definitions of language. The most significant example of this is in the recently published Kingman Report on the "teaching of English language." The Kingman committee, established to enquire into the teaching of English language in the schools, was asked to recommend a model of the English language that would "inform professional discussion of all aspects of English teaching" (73). The model managed to discuss language variety without making reference to social class, something of an achievement in contemporary Britain. Instead, it included a section on "Communication," which focused on the way in which "speakers and writers adapt their language to the context in which the language is being used" (23). More than anything else, this refusal to acknowledge a social or cultural dimension to language betrayed the committee's real intentions. It allowed them to conclude that children's language development was simply a matter of learning how to conform ("adapt") to the linguistic demands of the society in which they find themselves. They were thus able to ignore the inconvenient fact that children also have rights, that in the democracy of language everybody has a vote. It should come as no surprise that the government that sponsored the Kingman Report is also seeking ways of limiting and constraining the role of portfolio assessment.

## Notes

1. The General Certificate of Education (GCE) examinations are taken at age sixteen (O level) and eighteen (A level); they were originally designed to meet the needs of children in grammar schools (roughly 20 percent of the total school population).

2. The Bullock Report was prepared by a committee of inquiry established by the Conservative government of 1970 to 1973 in order to investigate the teaching of English in schools and to suggest ways of monitoring attainment.

3. The Certificate of Secondary Education examination was introduced in 1965 to cater to the majority of children in British schools who were not entered for the GCE.

4. The term *coursework assessment* is commonly used in Britain to refer to assessment of a folder of writing produced by the pupil over the duration of a course. The folder, or portfolio, characteristically includes a selection of between five and eight pieces written over a two-year period. It should be distinguished from *continuous assessment*.

5. The Schools Council is a body representative of the teaching profession with advisory, and some limited statutory, power over curriculum and examinations. It was replaced by the current Conservative government

in 1984 with the Schools Curriculum Development Council (SCDC), and the Secondary Examinations Council (SEC), both appointed bodies. These have now become the National Curriculum Council (NCC) and the Schools Examinations and Assessment Council (SEAC).

6. The Assessment of Performance Unit was a unit attached to the Dept. of Education and Science with responsibility for monitoring standards in schools.

7. Her Majesty's Inspectorate (HMI) is a group of officials attached to, but independent from the Department of Education and Science, which inspects all schools in Britain.

8. The General Certificate of Secondary Education is a system of examining that combines GCE O level and CSE. It was introduced in 1986.

9. The Joint Matriculation Board is one of the largest of the nine GCE examination boards that serve England, Wales, and Northern Ireland.

10. The significance of *audience* and *purpose* in writing can be directly traced back to the work of James Britton and the Schools Council project "Writing Across the Curriculum 11–16," led by Nancy Martin. It has recently been developed and extended in Britain by the work of the National Writing Project.

11. *Language, Schooling, and Society* is an account of an international seminar run by IFTE at Michigan State University in November 1984.

# 8

# Portfolios and the M.A. in English

Bonnie Hain
*Southeastern Louisiana University*

- Two weeks prior to the M.A. competency test, a professor is asked to make up two or three questions in her area of expertise for the exam. She writes the questions in fifteen minutes, hands them to the secretary to type, and the exam is ready.

- As a student begins to read the questions for her M.A. competency exam, she realizes that she will have to think and write quickly. She has studied more than three hundred texts of primary and secondary materials on the English Renaissance, including the complete works of Shakespeare and Milton. She now has two hours to write an essay that answers these questions: Was there a "Renaissance" in England? If so, when did it occur? What movements in literature, music, art, and architecture reveal the nature of this "Renaissance"? The instructions tell the student to remember to be specific.

- There are fifteen students ready to begin their second year of graduate study. Each one must write and revise a thesis under the supervision of a full-time faculty advisor. There are only fifteen full-time faculty members in the English department. Each professor teaches four classes a semester and there is no extra remuneration for the directing of theses. Of the fifteen students who need advisors, only ten can find professors willing to direct their theses, and only seven of those students have directors whose teaching and research is directly related to their theses projects.

The M.A. competency exam is the most prevalent means used by departments of English to evaluate the readiness of its students to graduate and to receive the M.A. degree. Many of the programs that do not require an exam require a thesis instead. For some departments these measures work well; for others, as in the above scenarios, the M.A. exam and the thesis prove to be problematic. For these departments, a portfolio system of evaluation offers an excellent alternative to the M.A. exam or thesis.

The wonderful thing about portfolio systems of evaluation is also what makes it most difficult to write about them in a generic way: they are valid, reliable, and usable precisely because they are designed to meet the needs of specific departments with specific goals. The purpose of this essay is not to prescribe a particular set of rules to follow to establish a portfolio system of measurement for all English departments, but to describe some of the possibilities portfolios offer for measuring graduate student achievement.

Art programs have long evaluated the proficiency of their students through using portfolios. Young artists produce many artworks, from which they select the best pieces to be evaluated at the end of their term of study. This system teaches the student-artist the process of the professional artist, who might start many pieces, but shows only the best pieces in an art show. Though professional writers and literary critics don't always collect their most finished pieces like the artist, many draft several pieces before publishing one work. The English M.A. student, then, in producing a portfolio of writing samples, can integrate the professional writing/critical practices of developing ideas, drafting, and redrafting writings.

Most M.A. programs in English teach two identifiable competencies, reading and writing. On the graduate level, these competencies extend beyond the minimal expectations of traditional definitions of "reading or writing competence," of "saying aloud" a text or physically producing a script. When speaking of what we expect of our graduate students, we might define reading competence as the ability to discover and interpret the complex theoretical, historical, philosophical, literary,and aesthetic concerns revealed in the language of literary and metaliterary texts.[1] The traditional M.A. competency exams and theses, as written products, test this reading knowledge/ability as writing competence. That is to say, the measures we choose to evaluate our graduate students' reading abilities are usually also reflections of their writing abilities. Since we do test our students' learning most directly through evaluative measures of their writing competency, the writing portfolio seems a logical evaluative measure.

In "Defining and Assessing Competence in Writing," Lee Odell defines writing competence as "the ability to discover what one wishes to say and to convey one's message through language, syntax, and content that are appropriate for one's audience and purpose" (103). In "Changing the Model for 'Examining' Achievements in Writing," John Dixon and Leslie Stratta suggest that the best way to evaluate this type of writing competence is through a collection of several samples of a student's writing. Similarly, Gertrude Conlan writes:

> If we had but money enough and time, we would measure writing ability by collecting, over a period of several months, a number of samples of a student's writing, produced in reaction to various stimuli and written under various conditions — some impromptu exercises strictly timed and some untimed essays done at home, for example. This collection would then be evaluated by as many different trained evaluators as we could manage, and the score achieved might then provide, if all goes well, an extremely accurate picture of that student's writing ability. But since we have neither enough money nor enough time to do that kind of extended evaluation, we usually compromise . . . Which sort of compromise is best? The answer lies in our priorities, our concerns, and, sad to say, our budgets. (116)

The portfolio approach seems a likely compromise, since as an evaluative measure, the writing portfolio can be easily designed to be valid, reliable, and usable (the three significant measures of good tests). Validity is the

> degree to which an instrument measures what it is supposed to measure . . . Validity refers to the care that is taken to include, in a test, items of prime importance and to exclude items of trivial nature; validity refers to the degree to which an instrument parallels the material which has been taught and the way in which it has been taught; validity refers to the degree to which an observational tool provides for objective appraisal of that which is observed; validity refers to the specificity of results obtained by means of a measuring device. (Lien 79)

Every graduate program in English teaches critical thinking and writing skills, but the language theories and ideological foundations (literary, rhetorical, aesthetic) of thought used to teach those skills vary from department to department. In designing a portfolio system, each school might ask its students to produce different genres of reading/writing samples, in accordance with these theories and ideologies. For example, programs that had previously asked students to study an author, a genre, and a literary/historical period for the M.A. exam, might ask the student to provide three analytical papers of fifteen to twenty pages, each focused on one of those three traditional topics. A program that stresses the importance of current literary and composition theories might ask its students to provide at least one essay devoted strictly to theory. Still another program, one that asked its students to study creative writing as well as literature, might demand a collection of ten poems, a short story, a chapter of a novel, or one act of a drama, along with an essay explaining the most significant ideological concerns of a particular literary/historical period. A quick review of the important concepts or bodies of knowledge stressed by the required courses in the department and a corresponding requirement of genres of writing samples for the portfolio would help ensure the validity of the portfolio as an evaluative measure.

The reliability could also be designed into the system developed. Reliability is defined as the "degree to which an instrument consistently measures what it does measure" (Lien 83). The means used to evaluate the portfolios may vary slightly from department to department, but for the portfolio approach to work well, at least three readers are usually required. The simplest system calls for each portfolio to be read by two readers, with only pass/fail options. Each reader grades the portfolio without knowledge of the other reader's opinion. If the two readers independently reach the same decision, the portfolio is given the grade agreed upon. If the two readers give different grades, a third reader makes the final decision. Before grading the set of portfolios, the graders meet to discuss the grading of sample portfolios, in order that a consensus on grading procedures and practices can be drawn. This "calibration" can ensure that the testing procedure is reliable. After the first set of portfolios has been graded, the department will have "real" sample portfolios to practice with and, as readers grade together and compare notes on these "real" exams, the reliability will be near perfect.

The best thing about a portfolio system of evaluation is that it is highly usable. Since the system is geared to the needs and belief systems of each department, after the initial tussling about the design of the requirements of the portfolio, the system will require little time and money of the participants. For example, those departments with limited budgets might ask for students to sit for four timed exams. The students could then be asked to choose two of the four exams and to revise their writings into full-blown essays. The students might also need to choose one of the remaining two essays to include in their portfolio as an example of how the student writes a timed essay. A group of three professors (with two readings for each essay, and a third reading to break a tie) could grade the exams. This system would require little time to devise the essay questions, since the questions would serve mainly as jumping-off points for the student's thoughts, not as "essay exam questions" meant to determine all the student knows about a certain subject. This system would also require the time of one professor to proctor the exam, and the same, or less, time for grading than that generally devoted to the traditional M.A. exam (since two of the three essays would be typed neatly unlike most current M.A. exams, and therefore might be easier to read). The program would require funds to compensate the person who types the exam questions, the proctor, and the graders, as well as monies for the xeroxing costs of the tests. Clearly, the funds required are no more, and perhaps less than those required for traditional M.A. competency exams or M.A. theses.

This program has additional advantages that make it usable. It allows the student to demonstrate knowledge and writing skills in various contexts (both timed and untimed essays). The graders can see the way a student takes a draft (the timed exam) to completion (the completed paper in the portfolio). Additionally, the design of the program tells the student that the English department recognizes the need for both a fine product as well as a developed writing/ thinking process.

In an alternative scenario that is equally budget and time conscious, the portfolio contains essays started in courses. As the student progresses through courses, the student will surely be required to produce essays (either as seminar papers or as essays for midterm or final exams). The program could ask the student to revise a few of these works and to compile a portfolio of writing to demonstrate the knowledge gained through the M.A. program. This system eliminates the need for typing and xeroxing exams and paying a proctor, while retaining the majority of the advantages outlined above. In addition, this system allows the student to see the final evaluative measure as a natural part of the work done previously in the program. A disadvantage of this type of program is that students may not have written papers in previous courses that will meet the genre/historical-period constraints that departments may wish to build into the portfolio requirements. A similar disadvantage is that professors may feel pressured to "teach to the test," to require papers that would fit the requisites of the portfolio, but that are not necessary to the specific course content.

A way around the disadvantages of this second model is for a department to designate a required course in advanced composition for all graduate students, in which the students initiate papers and/or revise and expand on written work produced in previous courses. The completion of an adequate portfolio of writing for this course could serve as the pass/fail measure of the graduate student's competence. One advantage of this type of measurement is that it builds well-deserved remuneration for the work of the professor into the system. As with the second model presented, it nicely integrates the final evaluative measure and previous coursework. In addition, this type of portfolio system allows for a student to receive educational assistance in developing skills as a writer.

All three of these models may be usable, but not all of them will work for every department. Yet, the unique qualities of each portfolio system are, in the end, what make the portfolio approach worth the effort, because it allows each department to assess fairly the knowledge students have gained through its M.A program. Furthermore, as more departments begin to develop portfolio systems, to publish and share these evaluative measures with other institutions, to discuss the standards by which we judge our students and ourselves, the usability of the portfolio will increase. Indeed, the most important aspect of the development of a portfolio system of evaluation for a department is that such a system brings to bear a knowledge of the assumptions that guide our judgments, and thereby lets us see who and why we are.

## Note

1. Because they emphasize different strains of thought within the discipline, English departments might define the notions of reading and writing competence in unique ways. Nonetheless, English as a discipline has always been associated with the two Rs of reading and writing, and reading competence on the graduate level has most often been tested through written measures.

# II

# Program Assessment

# 9

# Metacognition and the Use of Portfolios

Karen Mills-Courts and Minda Rae Amiran
*State University of New York College at Fredonia*

> True learning can't be defined by an opscan sheet or by memorization. The only real way to learn, I believe, is through experience. Classroom lectures and information lay the groundwork for learning, but it all comes down to whether or not you can do what you've supposedly learned.
>
> —from an anonymous college student's test response

The State University of New York College at Fredonia's portfolio plan resulted from a careful assessment, funded by FIPSE, of its general education program, the General College Program (GCP). Our faculty were eager to discover whether or not students were actually learning those things that the program was designed to teach. This is always the basic question and the only one, finally, that matters. Concerned teachers are, too often, made painfully aware of the gap between teaching and "real" learning, which lies behind the criticism of memorization and opscan forms in the epigraph above. Most of us would agree, vehemently, that "it all comes down to whether or not you can do what you've supposedly learned."

The focus of the GCP assessment was on student *progress* in three major areas: reading, writing, and reflexive thinking; scientific reasoning and numerical problem solving; socioethical understanding. The emphasis was on development rather than on criterion- or norm-determined competence in a subject area. The process and results of the assessment are fascinating in themselves, but the most important outcome for our purposes was the recommendation that the activities of the GCP directed toward developing analytical and reflexive thinking be enhanced. The assessment committee asked for a plan to develop students' metacognitive skills, one that would help them achieve an awareness of how they "do" intellectual work.

The GCP assessment showed that our students were not approaching their own learning consciously enough and were operating much too often on unexamined basic assumptions about both the learning process and the content involved in that process. We found them to be too disengaged and passive to use information in analytical, creative, and productive ways. We believe that those weaknesses are not confined only to our program, but are typical of postsecondary education in general. In fact, the control group from another college that participated in our assessment exhibited the same problems in metacognition, critical thinking, and socioethical development as were demonstrated by our own students. The assessment exposed what D. N. Perkins has identified as the failure of higher education to develop "informal reasoning," the sort of reasoning meant when we claim that education does not just convey information and basic skills, but also teaches our students "to think." As Perkins points out, our failures in this area betray the "higher mission" implied by the often-articulated, but rather vague, claim that we teach students to think. His "informal reasoning" resembles what most of us mean when we talk about "critical thinking." This is the thought process that comes into play when "you can do what you've supposedly learned"; it must involve awareness of one's own thinking processes, at least at the beginning.

To the extent that students are asked to select and justify their contents, the first, most obvious advantage of portfolios is that they require a "doing" of learning that demands this intellectual self-consciousness. Portfolios can take many different forms; since Fredonia's is designed to meet the needs of our rather unique GCP, a word about its structure is in order. The GCP is purposefully constructed as a loosely integrated series of courses intended to develop a student's ability to "do" thinking—not just to absorb information but to learn to use it, to put it to work. Beginning with an introduction to the ways in which people think, write, read, and "use numbers" in various areas, the program is divided into three developmental sections; each part is designed to develop competencies learned in the previous one. Part two develops further the skills introduced in part one, through the study of specific fields. Part three offers courses that are designed to teach students to identify and to question basic assumptions and to help them develop cross-cultural and historical perspectives as well as the ability to examine biases, ethnocentric viewpoints, and stereotypes. Composition is required of all students, as are one course in mathematics, two in the natural sciences, two in the social and behavioral sciences, and two in the arts and humanities.

While every discipline may offer courses in each part, it is not course content but the method of teaching, the structure, and the goals of the course that qualify it for acceptance into the program by the GCP Committee. Wisely, the campus coupled the implementation of the program with an intensive focus on faculty development, emphasizing writing across the curriculum. For the link that holds all of the program together is the focus on writing as the appropriate method for "doing" intellectual work—whether that work be mathematics or philosophy, music or art, physics or English. The centrality of writing in the program makes it possible for us to use portfolios as both a pedagogical and an assessment tool.

Portfolios offer an ideal site for the exercise of the kind of reflexive, critical thought that the GCP intends to develop. Most of the best research on cognitive development suggests that it is extremely important to create situations in which students must think about their own thinking, reflect on the ways in which they learn and why they fail to learn (see Flavell; Flower; and Sternberg). It's clear that the more students are aware of their own learning processes, the more likely they are to establish goals for their education and the more deeply *engaged* they are in those processes. This focus on process should not suggest that we undervalue content or see information and product as opposed to process. As the GCP Assessment Report says: "It is a *false opposition* that sets these matters at odds: process versus product, reasoning versus content, coverage versus the development of understanding. Rather, content is learned by reasoning, understanding is developed as students interact with information that covers the field, students who have understood and can use previous information in an active and critical way are those who acquire further knowledge."

Whatever the anonymous student quoted in the epigraph means by "true learning," most of us would agree that it is not defined by opscan sheets or memorization. The definition of "true learning" remains the muddiest and yet most crucial issue in our profession; the goals of our GCP are an attempt at a definition, though they make no claim to being a final answer. To fulfill those goals, students must be able to engage in reflexive thinking, that is, they must consciously understand their own assumptions, they must be able to analyze their assumptions as well as those of others, and they must be able to evaluate them in order to act on them. They must learn to synthesize information gained from this analytic and evaluative process into a meaningful understanding of the subject at hand. In addition, and importantly, they must be able to transfer that process from one discrete area of thought into others. If we expect students to integrate their learning experiences into a focused whole, we need to develop their ability to reflect upon their own thinking—not just as college students but as lifetime learners, as citizens of the world.

It's important to understand that our plan was designed to address the problems we identified in our students' intellectual development. It is not formulated to address all the problems facing postsecondary education or all the weaknesses we find in students' learning processes. Such a plan may be much desired, but it is most certainly a pipedream. It also seems important to point out that the portfolio committee that developed the plan consisted of students and faculty representatives from a wide range of disciplines. Every member knew that no single plan could solve the problems of teaching and learning in all those disciplines. On the contrary, for GCP purposes, the committee sought a plan that would not be discipline specific and that would encourage the integration of learning derived from all aspects of the program, leaving individual departments to address learning development in specific content areas. However, since the GCP goals for analytic- and reflexive-thinking goals are applicable to all disciplines, many departments on campus have used the portfolio structure as a model to develop more content-specific plans of their own—plans that are motivated by the same needs that generated the GCP portfolio plan.

That writing is the most effective tool for encouraging reflective and analytical "critical thinking" is an assumption most English teachers automatically make (often *too* automatically). The effectiveness of writing for promoting "true learning" in other disciplines is just beginning to emerge in current research, however. What we loosely call "problem solving" is at the heart of all studies and it is becoming clear that writing promotes a self-consciousness about this endeavor that enables students to understand rather than merely to memorize and repeat by rote formulaic responses (always an ephemeral act). The results of our own assessment demonstrate clearly that we need to give students more practice in solving quantitative and nonquantitative word problems, in solving nonformulaic problems, and especially in explaining the mode of reasoning they use in their solutions. This emphasis on explanation is suggested not only by our findings, but by current thought in the American

Mathematical Society on the use of writing in mathematics. Explanation promotes understanding whether the subjects under consideration are physics, the social sciences, music, or English literature. And explanation means using, *through writing*, all of the skills we wish to foster in our GCP.

Given this set of theoretical beliefs, concrete needs, and available structures, our turn to writing portfolios as a pedagogical tool was nearly as inevitable as it was logical. We should emphasize the "nearly" in that last sentence. Because most members of the portfolio committee had participated in faculty development workshops and those who had not were reading literature on the uses of writing in their own fields, the committee itself understood quickly and in depth the value and goals of the enterprise. In our presentation of the idea to individual departments, however, we discovered that the ways in which writing can encourage students to analyze and synthesize their thinking, the ways in which it can be used to demand metacognition as well as focus on subject matter, were not immediately self-evident. Those of us who deal with writing all the time are too sanguine about others' understanding of its potentials. In order to explain, we turned to many years experience with portfolios in creative writing classes.

Creative writing on this campus is not confined to a small group of talented English majors and has few of the "cult" aspects that sometimes accompany such programs. In fact, the introductory course is one of those GCP courses that any incoming freshman may choose toward satisfying the requirements of part one. As a result, those classes are eclectic in the extreme, consisting of twenty-five students from nearly every discipline possible. Courses in creative writing do not produce great professional poets and novelists nor should that be their intent. We are delighted with the number of our students who have gone on for graduate work in creative writing; we're proud and pleased when their work is published and we're most elated when we speak to them years after they've completed their studies and discover that they are still writing or, at least, that they remain passionate readers. But our courses, from first to last, are designed to encourage students' sensitivity to language, to develop their ability to articulate their thinking and feelings as precisely and powerfully as possible, and to increase their analytical skills and their ability to be self-conscious, reflective thinkers. Certainly such aims will make a talented poet a better poet, maybe even help that student become an extraordinary poet, but the aims are designed primarily to teach all students, not just the gifted.

Creative writers begin to build their portfolios immediately and they continue the process throughout the entire course. They are asked to keep every draft of every piece of work, from their first to their last. None of the drafts are graded, but all are read, heavily commented on by both the teacher and peers, and returned to the writer for further work. Since the purpose of the course is to *develop* the writers' skills, they are expected to be engaged in a continual process of revision, returning over and over again to even the earliest work as their competence expands. Students, then, are constantly engaged in a double process: creating new work and revising old work at the same time. And there is a third element involved here: since they read professional writers and also read for each other, they are also constantly behaving as analytic thinkers who must interpret meaning; seek out weaknesses in logic, development, and expression; and offer suggestions for improvement in each work that they read. They are, then, being asked to think critically at all times, whether their subject is their own work, the work of professional poets, or that of their peers. They must, in the process, analyze, evaluate, synthesize, reach conclusions, and act on those conclusions. They must become "problem solvers."

Throughout the semester, the teacher meets individually with the students to discuss the progress of the portfolio in terms of the revisions that have been made. During each conference, the students explain their process of revision. The teacher tries to elicit specific goals that the writer has for each work and guides the discussion so that the student articulates his or her reason for each change made toward fulfilling those goals. Finally, students are asked to select their five best pieces and to write a brief introduction to their work, explaining the grounds for their choices and the aspects of each work that they believe make it exceptional. The portfolio is then submitted for evaluation during the last week of classes. Every student is given the opportunity to retrieve the portfolio and discuss with the teacher, in detail, the evaluation that has been made. In that conference, the focus is as much on the process demonstrated in the portfolio as it is on the product, final drafts.

While all of this sounds rather cool and distanced in the telling, the fact is that the portfolio process generates excitement, commitment, and a warm, relaxed sense of community in the classroom. It also builds confidence; even the weakest writer can experience success when the focus is kept steadily on improvement rather than on evaluating the product. The students readily discern the differences between first and last drafts and, importantly, they *take ownership of their own work*. The work *belongs* to them, matters to them, in ways that rarely occur in typical classroom situations. They feel empowered by this collection that clearly demonstrates how far they have come, that is concrete evidence of their own growth as learners. They often laugh with chagrin at the earliest drafts, delight in later versions, and quietly take pride in the final products. Few students fail to retrieve their portfolios and many pursue their teachers around campus eager to talk about their work, sometimes even wanting to discuss further revisions that they want to make. This is the kind of active learning that we all desire in our classrooms and it is the kind that students want too. We underestimate who they are as well as what they can do when we allow them to take exams and turn in papers that are purely passive responses to what "the teacher wants to hear." Such work is quickly, and we think properly, mentally discarded once the students know their grades; it is simply a by-product of a structure that erroneously focuses attention on the teacher's response to their responses — which were originally the teacher's anyway. In addition to the fact that this is a situation that requires blank passivity, the circularity of the process creates learners who are entirely dispossessed.

The importance of all this from a teacher's perspective also has something to do with *ownership*. Nowhere else can teachers see with such clarity the effects of their efforts in the classroom. It's all there, from awkward first draft to the clear demonstration of the growth of analytical, evaluative, and decision-making skills evidenced by the students' selections and reasoning in the introduction, the process of revision, and in the final drafts. Every portfolio demonstrates in concrete ways the *growth* in students' abilities to think reflexively and critically and to act on the results of such thinking. Some portfolios show developmental leaps that are breathtaking, most show slow but steady progress, very few show no change at all in the students' metacognitive skills.

The kind of energy and commitment generated by portfolios in which students reflect on their own work is much desired by our colleagues. Once the structure of the creative-writing portfolio is explained, most seem to understand readily that, regardless of subject matter, the structure of the portfolio system can be translated into their own disciplines. They have suggested that videotapes, lab reports, musical compositions, evaluations of field trips and research, traditional essays, and a wide variety of other things can evoke the same self-reflective processes that poetry does. It's clear that the portfolio does demand the exercise of the aptitudes and skills that are the goals of SUNY Fredonia's General College Program, but, in addition to that, many faculty have come to see how those goals are embedded in their own disciplinary studies.

The pragmatic aspects of implementing a campus wide portfolio program are very complex, of course. On a campus where every department is already working at near capacity in terms of student load and research demands, we had to devise ways of using structures already in place. That meant surrendering ideal versions of GCP portfolios to less-demanding requirements that could still help our students to develop reflexive and critical thinking. The plan finally proposed does not require the focus on revision or the number of student contact hours involved in a creative-writing portfolio: it uses papers already written for courses taken in the GCP. However, since those courses focus on the writing process, including revision, and students have access to their teachers as a result, this loss is not as devastating as it might appear. Further, we decided to use the existing advising system on campus, wherein students *must* make contact with advisors at least once every semester and may contact them much more often, as the need arises. Given this one-to-one relationship, the advisor is the logical person to direct the development of each student's portfolio.

The plan that follows, then, is integrated into the already existing proceedings of the campus. It has been devised to use advising time that had already been designated but had remained rather unfocused. The formerly rather loose and sometimes uncomfortable discussions about course selection ("What do I *have* to take?") and academic problems ("I hate math, I've never been good at it!") now allow students to engage actively in their own learning processes. We believe that the plan not only encourages students to discuss what they *want* to take in order to fulfill their intellectual needs and goals but also allows them to understand *why* they might hate math and to do something about it. The sort of critical analysis and reflexive thinking which the portfolio requires invites genuine engagement. It is designed to help them create goals, to assess their own progress toward those goals and to help them understand the decisions they need to make in order to reach them. This process encourages students to take ownership of their own education, to become active participants in their own intellectual growth. Perhaps most importantly, it exercises the intellectual abilities needed for students to learn "to think." The plan that follows, then, is our attempt to answer the student who believes that "it all comes down to whether or not you can do what you've supposedly learned." We've created a mode of "doing" that we hope will become an integrated part of lifetime thinking.

## Description of Portfolio Process

1. All freshmen write a brief paper that explores their past history as learners, evaluates that history, and projects their intellectual goals. The history should reveal something of the students' learn-

ing processes and, in a general and highly speculative way, should suggest goals. This is the first entry in the portfolio, presented in the fall before course selection for the spring semester, freshman year. Advisors do not correct the papers but attend only to the content and are prepared to discuss students' comments.

2. During the first course-selection meeting, students are advised to begin selecting work from GCP courses to add to the portfolio. They attach to each paper a brief explanation of why they believe the paper is representative of their best work, how they perceive their performance in the course, and their assessment of the course's value in relation to the GCP and their goals in choosing it. The students select five papers over the course of their studies in the GCP; these are submitted upon the completion of any given course. The students copy the original papers, including the instructor's grade and comments, and their own explanation of their choice, place the copies in their portfolios and keep the originals for their own reference.

3. All seniors submit a final paper before selecting courses in their seventh semester. This "exit" paper has the same structure as the "entrance" paper. It should be an evaluative history of students' intellectual growth throughout their involvement in the GCP and their studies at Fredonia. It should review the contents of the portfolio as a whole and reconsider students' earlier assessments of papers and courses as well as their freshman papers. The students should discuss the relationships among the courses they have taken in the GCP and the relationship between those courses and their majors. This is the time for a full attempt at integration. Advisors read these papers prior to the last advising session and discuss their implications with the students during their last course-selection meeting or at another time during the advisors' office hours.

### Role of the Advisor

Advisors are not asked to assess the quality of the writing in the portfolio, nor are they asked to grade the papers in the portfolio in any traditional way. Instead, advisors should use the work as a focus for discussion with students about their learning processes and goals. These discussions would constitute an ongoing review of the portfolio and would occur during standard advising meetings. The students' writing should serve as a basis for planning and reflection. Advisors should focus on students' sense of their achievements and of areas that need improvement, using the work as a key indicator of successes and problems. Advisors serve as evaluators only insofar as they accept or reject the portfolio in terms of its completeness. A statement that the portfolio is complete is required in order for the student to be eligible for graduation. A complete portfolio would contain all required work, submitted at designated times, and confirmation that the work has been discussed with the advisor at proper times over the span of the student's college career. An incomplete portfolio lacks required papers or self-evaluations or has not been discussed with the advisor in a substantive way. If advisors believe that the student has not taken the reflective essays seriously or that the portfolio is incomplete, they will not endorse it. A student who feels mistreated can appeal the advisor's decision. However, since students and advisors will have met for discussion over a span of three years, it is highly unlikely that any student would reach the senior year with no indication that the portfolio needs work. If such a case occurs, careful attention must be paid both to the advisor's and the student's failure to meet responsibilities.

### Instructions for Students

The following are instructions we have prepared for students.

#### Description of "Entry" Paper

This is an informal, conversational, and personal paper: there are no "right" or "wrong" answers. You should focus on your own history as a learner and on your own desires for your future educational experiences. You probably can't take a thorough look at those things in less than 3 pages, but the paper can be as long as you like. Think of it as an informative letter to your advisor — one that lets her or him know who you are as a student. Begin by looking back at your experiences in high school and try to judge which courses were most and least valuable to you. Then try to explain *why* they affected you as they did. After you've said all you need to about your past, noting which sort of study seems to work best for you, have some fun — create your own educational future. Your only limitation is, of course, that you must create it out of the material offered by the GCP. Study its requirements, then make up a "wish-list" and explain your choices — how would they help you to grow intellectually? The content of the paper is up to you, but you might want to consider some of the following questions to help focus your writing:

1.  What were the most valuable learning experiences you had in high school? Why? If there were courses that you think were not valuable, what were they and why did they fail? Were there some you'd like to study in more depth?

2. What qualities do you value in a good teacher? How important is the teacher to the success or failure of a course? What do you think a student should do to benefit from a course?

3. Which courses in the GCP would help you to become an educated person?

4. How do you think the courses on your "wish-list" reflect your ideas and experiences in the answers you've given to any of the above questions?

### Description of Attachment of GCP Papers

Attach a statement of at least one page to each paper you include in your portfolio, answering one or more of the following questions:

1. What problems did you face in writing this paper and what did you do to overcome them?

2. What are the strengths and weaknesses of this paper in your own mind? What do you wish you had added or done differently?

3. How does your thinking, argument, or expression in this paper represent an advance over previous papers? How does it relate to your own educational goals?

4. Were you helped in thinking through this paper by work you have done in another course? If so, how?

### Description of "Exit" Paper

Like your "entry" paper, this one is an informal and conversational reflection on your intellectual history, on your experiences as a learner. Review your experience as a Fredonia student, especially as a participant in the GCP. Using the papers that you've submitted for your portfolio, try to evaluate your own work and your earlier assessments of that work. What do you think of them now? In addition to reconsidering the work in your portfolio, try to evaluate your general experiences in the program. In the process, you might want to consider the following questions as ways of focusing your writing:

1. What were the most valuable learning experiences you have had? Why?

2. How did your "wish-list" affect your final choices in the GCP? Which courses were most valuable? Are there others which you wish you had taken? Why? Which courses failed to meet your expectations? Why?

3. How did the learning experiences provided by your work in the GCP relate to your work in your chosen major?

4. How successful have your combined studies in your major and the GCP been in offering you those qualities of an educated person

which you believe are essential? Has your idea of an "educated person" changed since you first discussed it in your entry paper? Why or why not?

5.  If you could talk to incoming freshmen, what single piece of advice would you give them concerning their intellectual futures?

# 10

# Bridges to Academic Goals
## *A Look at Returning Adult Portfolios*

Anne M. Sheehan and Francine Dempsey, C.S.J.
*College of Saint Rose*

In 1971, the College of Saint Rose inaugurated its Experienced Adult Program (EAP) to serve the growing numbers of older, nontraditional students entering higher education—adults whose histories contain numerous knowledge-bearing experiences that are clearly equivalent to the kinds of learning available in traditional college courses. Students in this program, usually older than the traditional college students, bring with them wide assortments of learning experiences from their varied backgrounds. Some of them have had previous college experience; still others have no prior college background. Despite differences in their ages, races, and life situations, they all bring an accumulation of college-level learning gained through specific life experiences, whether in business, the professions, or community involvement.

## EAP Portfolio

When EAP was initiated, a major task facing both the students and the College was to determine a method for precisely identifying experiential learning and authenticating that learning to the satisfaction of credit-assessing faculty from various disciplines. The chosen assessment method that has been used with success over the years is the EAP portfolio program. This approach enables the student to prepare a collection of pertinent materials: namely, various personal statements of background and intent, as well as direct and indirect documentation of claimed college-level learning acquired outside of college. Direct documentation includes samples of work produced in learning experiences, such as written materials, computer programs, outlines of speeches, and the like—items that provide concrete evidence of the student's mastery of knowledge in one or more academic areas. Indirect evidence, on the other hand, incorporates information about the student's learning experiences, such as verifying letters, job descriptions, certificates, and such.

An essential and governing feature of the portfolio is that it must validate what the student has learned, not merely what the student has done. This obligation to prove learning outcomes from life experiences places great significance on background statements and statements of intent, which the student includes in introductory and credit-request essays in the completed EAP portfolio. These essays, like the samples of work and the indirect documentation, must explain and prove college-level knowledge and ability comparable to that which one would acquire in respective academic courses.

In the introductory essay, the student addresses his or her evaluators, giving them a clear indication of background experience, academic plans, career goals, and the like. Such an essay typically summarizes postsecondary education and experiences, reasons behind various life choices, and an overview of the EAP portfolio as it fits into overall academic and career plans.

In the credit-request essay, the student strives to describe specific experiential learning clearly and to equate that knowledge convincingly with the learning outcomes of one or more college courses. For example, a student who ran a ceramics business for ten years may decide to apply for up to three credits in art (specifically, Ceramics I) if able to prove a college-level knowledge of clay construction techniques, glaze calculations, kiln usage, and similar learning outcomes as cited in the course description and syllabus. This same student may also seek up to three credits in marketing, if able to verify college-level knowledge in principles and functions of marketing as well as other types of learning offered in a business/marketing course. Another student, trained and certified by the Red Cross as a qualified lifesaver may well be qualified for one credit in physical education for mastery of skills and knowledge equivalent to that acquired in an advanced life saving course. Letters and a validated Red Cross certificate would constitute the kinds of documentation required for assessment of credit equivalency; the student's credit-request essay would precisely indicate the correlation between the extracollegiate learning and that presented in the college's comparable physical education course.

Over the years, this method of carefully compiling both direct and indirect documentation has proven to be a reliable means of identifying and authenticating experiential learning; however, despite the success of this fully accredited program, the essential portfolio component has not been without problems. Portfolio preparation has proven to be a most formidable task for many of these adult students. As a rule they tend to be far removed from any previous formal writing courses; typically, they are understandably insecure about their writing abilities, particularly when asked to write in an academic setting. Not uncommon are such apologies as "I've been away from school and writing so long" or "I'm a terrible writer." Actually, over the years most have continued to develop as writers, to varying extents. Still, their writing skills are often rusty indeed, and their experiences with types of writing tend at times to be limited.

In light of these circumstances, the demands of the EAP portfolio often overwhelmed and discouraged students from progressing and succeeding in the program. Despite their conviction that they had indeed gained college-level knowledge in nonacademic settings, the task of precisely identifying and defining such knowledge to the satisfaction of academic appraisers sometimes became discouragingly elusive. Confident that they could provide authenticating documentation to validate the knowledge they had gained, some students faltered at the prospects of conveying precisely how that knowledge matched specific courses and of calculating how much credit such learning was worth. Moreover, even when they were able to sort out such information for themselves, the task of having to prove their cases in informative and persuasive writing to an exacting academic audience often became a major roadblock. This challenging prospect of writing for the EAP portfolio and organizing its contents frequently caused excessive delays in academic advancement and, in some instances, resulted in the student abandoning the program.

## Portfolio-Writing Workshop

To address this problem, the College of Saint Rose instituted a one-credit, pass/fail writing course specifically designed for EAP portfolio development. This course, devised through the combined efforts of the EAP office and the English Department, is now presented as a fifteen-week, portfolio-based writing workshop, which meets one hour per week. The objectives of the course are threefold: to teach the students how to use writing to discover and evaluate their extracollegiate knowledge, to assist them in developing their overall writing abilities, and to guide them toward the production of the informative and convincing writing they will need to include in the EAP portfolios they will later present for credit.

To these ends, the student in the portfolio-writing workshop is required to maintain a preliminary "workshop portfolio," different in design and purpose from the later EAP portfolio, yet intrinsically related to it in very specific ways. The writing portfolio required in the workshop is similar in some respects to those used in other undergraduate writing courses, but it differs in its highly task-oriented nature. In the portfolio workshop, these often tentative writers learn to use writing—in personal journals and portfolios—to identify prior knowledge, to discover relationships between experiential learning and academic learning, and to sharpen their own writing skills. Moreover, the workshop portfolios are far from dead-end productions because samples of the writing produced in them will actually be included in the later, credit-requesting EAP portfolio.

In effect, then, these students produce two portfolios: first the writing portfolio for assessment in the course and ultimately the completed EAP portfolio for credit assessment. The informative and persuasive writing required for the final EAP portfolio is largely transactional in nature; however, the writing in the workshop encompasses expressive and exploratory aims as well. Because the EAP portfolio is assessed not on an individual's actual experiences, but rather on the learning outcomes of those experiences, these writers must be able to make clear distinctions in this regard. Moreover, they need to be able to range their thinking along the abstraction ladder by relating specific examples of experience to the theoretical bases that underlie various academic courses, and by indicating the connections between theory and practice. Preliminary assignments in the workshop, therefore, require types of writing that foster self-discovery and structure reality in valuable ways.

Four main pieces of writing are required for the workshop portfolio by the end of the course. The first is an autobiographical essay with speculative and expressive aims. This essay results from exploration, through journal writing and other means, and presents a retrospective look at past learning experiences and interests, as well as speculation on the future academic and professional possibilities that the past suggests. Being explorative as well as expressive, the essay searches for ways that past experiences and future goals will influence present academic undertakings. This piece need not arrive at clear resolution and, in fact, may result in the posing of new questions. Also incorporated may be expressions of hopes or uncertainties relative to the whole process of returning to school, and to the tasks involved in attempting credit for experiential learning.

The second type of writing required for the workshop portfolio is persuasive and instructional: a validation-request letter to be sent to one or more persons able to provide indirect documentation for the EAP portfolio. This piece of writing prompts specific rhetorical concerns. It must be written in an appreciative, yet confidently assertive, tone. It must also be clear and highly readable, for it is essential that respondents—such as former employers, coworkers, or other associates—realize that their replies must not take the form of personal references or recommendations but must authenticate the student's claims regarding particular learning experiences.

Although neither of these workshop portfolio items is actually included in the subsequent EAP portfolio, they each contribute significantly to successful completion of that later portfolio. The first assignment nurtures the creative and critical thinking so necessary to producing the EAP portfolio, while the latter assignment helps to insure procurement of needed documentation. And of course, both assignments also serve to advance the student's writing skills.

The remaining two pieces of writing required for the workshop portfolio are essays to be eventually included in the EAP portfolio: the informative introductory essay and the persuasive credit-request essay, described above. These essays, like all of the writing for the workshop portfolio, pose very specific rhetorical demands. However, such demands are met with each writer's strong motivation to succeed, for the awarding of college credits depends so greatly on the effectiveness of the speculative, informative, and persuasive writing produced in the workshop.

To aid the students in producing their texts, the portfolio-based writing workshop includes such methods as writing in journals, multidrafting, peer-group response, and teacher-student conferences. The written results of all of these procedures are maintained in the ongoing writing portfolio, which is added to and reviewed throughout the course and which, for final assessment, contains final copies of the four required essays at the end of the semester.

Early in the course, students are shown how to use writing as a discovery procedure, whereby they tap their inner data of memory and imagination through free writing, brainstorming, and journal entries. They are instructed in various approaches to journal writing, including techniques based on Progoff's "life stepping-stones" process and inner "wisdom dialogues" (119–130; 269–284). In a "stepping-stone" exercise, the journal writer is asked first to list significant learning experiences from any period of his or her life. The writer then chooses those that seem most related to academic goals and writes about each of them. This exercise brings to the forefront of the writer's memory key learning experiences and then allows him or her to recall rather quickly various activities within that experience. Later the writer selects from this "raw data" that which is appropriate for further research, elaboration, and documentation.

In a "wisdom figure" exercise, a similar process is used as the writer lists significant "mentors" — people who have been sources of wisdom — from his or her past and, through journal writing, explores particular learning experiences fostered by them. Frequently, the same learning experiences are explored in both exercises, thus allowing the student to recall many details and themes of recent or distant learning experiences. Again, this invention technique provides data for further research, elaboration, and documentation.

The journal writing is produced in loose-leaf notebooks and the students are required to accumulate these pages (with the exception of any especially private entries) in the left side of the pocket-folder portfolio. These journal entries serve the students not only as recollections of learning experiences, but also as revelations for future academic direction. Further, in "discovery workshops" based on their journals, students are able to share personal findings and to interact with and advise one another. The journal entries in the writing portfolio also provide the instructor with a basis for discussion in conferences on how these experiences can best be developed and structured on the academic model, in academic discourse, for the academic audiences in specific disciplines.

The journal writing, then, initiates the creative thinking from which all the writing for the workshop portfolio, and eventually the EAP portfolio, will grow. Throughout the fifteen weeks of the course, students continue to write in their journals for two additional purposes: to practice brainstorming for various writing tasks required and to record the progress of their portfolio preparation. In this way, writing as discovery and writing as story ultimately form the foundation for the informative and persuasive tasks of EAP portfolio preparation.

By tapping memory and imagination in their journals, the students are able to bring into clearer focus, for themselves and others, recollections of experiential learning that formerly may have been vague or unstructured. These recollections, once clarified, provide a rich source for the first two writings required for the workshop portfolio. The first of these, the speculative/expressive essay, is developed in stages, just as are all the essays produced in the workshop. It begins as a rough draft, which is followed by a revised, typed (or legibly handwritten) second draft. This second draft is shared with others in the class in portfolio exchanges and workshop discussions.

Because of its exploratory aim and open-endedness, this first assignment fosters prewriting invention and provides a comfortable starting point for discussion in the first student/teacher conference. Also, this particular piece of writing provides the student with a clarifying review of self as writer. Most importantly, it initiates the kind of thinking needed for making connections between collegiate and extracollegiate learning outcomes, connections essential for successful EAP portfolio presentation.

Following the student's retrieval of information from memory and imagination — through journals, class discussion, and exploratory composition — the class engages in freewriting and discussions to search for ideas for those documentation possibilities that might assist them in identifying and verifying extracollegiate learning experiences. Such sources include, for example, college catalogues, course outlines, interviews with professors and other professionals, library readings, and such. Class discussion also aims at generating suggested lists of types of direct and indirect documentation for inclusion in the EAP portfolio.

As well as providing a forum for brainstorming, the peer-group discussions throughout the semester involve all the students in reading and responding to one another's writing-in-progress as contained in the workshop portfolios. This peer evaluation of portfolios stimulates invention and revision for all writings produced. Silent readings of exchanged portfolios are followed by discussion in order for students to respond to one another's work with evaluative and constructive criticism. Written peer responses on "audience-response" forms are completed by peer readers and given to each writer. These responses, added to the contents of the portfolio, provide the student with specific revision suggestions. As part of the portfolio, these forms also assist the instructor by presenting both a range of evaluative perspectives and an indication of the extent to which each writer incorporates, or rejects, audience response.

Besides collecting evaluations by peers, each writer is required to maintain ongoing "writer's-response" journal entries, logging responses to peer and instructor evaluations as well as indicating plans for improvement in subsequent drafts. Inclusion of continuously updated writer-response journal entries in the workshop portfolio provides both the writer and the instructor with insights into that person's writing process.

Student/teacher conferences for portfolio reviews occur twice during the semester and once at the end of the semester. The student compiles his or her work in a pocket folder, placing essays in progress in the right pocket and all other writing for the course — journal entries, prewriting, rough drafts, peer-response forms, and such — in the left. For the first conference, about five weeks into the course, the student presents his or her best, in-progress versions of the first speculative/expressive essay and the letter of request. The instructor collects and reviews the portfolio prior to the conference and provides a written assessment not only of the essay and letter, but also of the student's writing process and revision skills as indicated in all "rough work" included in the portfolio. The conference gives both the student and the teacher an opportunity to discuss and assess the full content of the workshop portfolio and to arrive at strategies for improvement where needed. The instructor's written comments are added to the portfolio at the end of the conference, but no grade is given at this time.

The second conference, four weeks before the end of the course, consists of additional portfolio review. At this time, the left pocket of the portfolio again includes all journal entries, prewriting, rough drafts, peer-response forms, and instructor recommendations to date. The right pocket contains the prior two assignments, revised as needed, plus two additional assignments: the introductory and credit-request essays aimed for inclusion in the later, EAP portfolio. The student and the instructor review the entire portfolio, with the instructor again providing written assessments and suggestions, but no grade.

One week before the end of the semester, the student resubmits the portfolio, now scaled down to include only his or her final drafts of the four major writing assignments. The instructor assesses these for pass/fail evaluations, using correctness, respective rhetorical effectiveness, and indications of writing growth as major criteria. Ideally, if more than one section of the course is offered, workshop teachers may at this time exchange portfolios for multiple readings and shared assessments. The instructor may also seek informal responses from faculty in those disciplines targeted by the students in their essays. With assessment completed, the last week of the workshop is devoted to final conferences, at which time the student and the instructor review the assessment and the instructor records in writing any particular recommendations.

One of the major advantages of this workshop portfolio method is that it delays submission of works for final grading, thus empowering the student to decide how many drafts are needed. Also, the procedure initiates the students into the process of portfolio preparation, a method they will employ, albeit with variations, in compiling their later EAP portfolios. And finally, through portfolio compilation of in-progress and finished products, along with evaluative responses from several readers (including themselves), the writers gain useful insights into their own writing processes and writing progress.

## Making Connections

It should be emphasized that students producing these two types of portfolios do not receive credit twice for the same work. The single credit earned in the writing workshop is awarded for skills achieved in writing, as evidenced in the final workshop portfolio. Credits gained through EAP portfolio assessment represent college-level learning from prior, extracollegiate experiences, as authenticated in that portfolio. Despite these essential distinctions, the two portfolios are clearly linked in significant ways. The exploratory essay in the workshop portfolio enables the student to focus on possibilities for credit requests as well as on ways to connect those learning experiences with course equivalencies and with long-range personal and career goals. The workshop letter in turn facilitates the attaining of needed documentation for the EAP portfolio. The two assignments that bridge both portfolios, the informative introductory essay and the persuasive credit-request essay, serve different purposes in each. In the one, they are evaluated for skill in writing. In the other, they accompany the material being assessed; and although the essays do not actually earn credit here, they influence assessment to a great extent.

The portfolio process, both in workshop and in EAP presentation, guides students in reassessing their own strengths and weaknesses, teaches them to value revision, and invests them with a sense of control over their work. In preparing and assembling portfolio materials, these adult learners gain fresh insights into their knowledge, skills, and academic goals. By identifying and clarifying experience, and by making appropriate connections between prior learning and current academic programs, they discover how the past and the present converge to give meaningful structure to the future. And when the process is truly successful, their tentative confidence in themselves as writers is reaffirmed, nurtured — and eventually fully restored.

# 11

# An Echo of Genesis
## An Assessment of the Business-Writing Portfolio

Judith Remy Leder
*California State University, Fullerton*

An old *Peanuts* cartoon shows Lucy and Charlie gazing at a huge bank of fluffy clouds. Lucy proceeds to describe the "pictures" she sees in the clouds—a triptych, in which the center element is the four horsemen of the Apocalypse, flanked on the right by the angel of death and on the left by Dante's vision of Dis. Asked for an account of his picture, hapless Charlie mutters, "I was going to say I saw a horsy and a doggie, but I've changed my mind."

This chapter is a Charlie Brown look at one type of writing portfolio: it deals with how we came to use the portfolio in our business-writing classes at Cal State, Fullerton; what we aimed to achieve; what difficulties we encountered; what the response has been, and what our recommendations—built on our experience— are. Since our portfolio assignment was adopted in response to a practical rather than a theoretical need, this essay is a case study of a portfolio that, like Topsy, "just growed." I will leave to minds more theoretically oriented than mine the explanation of why the business-writing portfolio works so well.

## Background

For the past five years I have had the pleasure of running an exceptionally large writing program at California State University, Fullerton. The program consists of many sections (seventy to eighty per year) of one upper-division writing course. Stepsister both to writing and to business classes, our Business Administration 301 course attempts to transform upper-division business majors into competent writers. The students enter this required course fervently hoping that it will turn out to be a cinch, a rehash of junior high school personal journals. Our real challenge as teachers is to convince this uninterested audience that rhetorical strategies are not only important and effective, but also (to be crass) are probably going to save them lots of money.

For my first two years as coordinator, I ran the program as an exercise in deferred gratification. My tacit message to my students: "You'll understand the value of this instruction when you get out into the work force and are given a promotion because you are capable of constructing a clear and intelligible memo." Most of my students, needless to say, were hard put to suspend their disbelief. They came into the course unwillingly; they left it fairly certain that they had been unnecessarily abused. Indeed, since the end product of the class was a sheaf of dog-eared, overcorrected pages, I could sympathize with the general opinion that BA301 papers should be relegated to the circular file.

Then, three years ago, while preparing a portfolio of my own photographs — the culminating assignment of an intermediate photojournalism class — it occurred to me that the project was un-usually satisfying. There were no photos to rival those of Ansel Adams, but I was inordinately proud of the polished final product. The newly printed, properly cropped, nicely mounted photographs showed clearly how much I had profited from instruction. I wondered if my business-writing students would experience a similar rush of delight if they prepared a final portfolio of their best written work. In that Archimedian moment, the business-writing portfolio was conceived.

Hesitant to incorporate the assignment into the basic course syllabus without a trial run, I used my brightest spring 1987 business-writing class as a test case. I required that (1) they revise one letter, one memo, one proposal, and one report (four of eight basic class assignments, most of which had been revised at least once before); and (2) that they present the revised work in a professional binding. The benefits to the students were an opportunity to polish and correct their work for credit (the assignment carried ten points out of one hundred); practice in revising and editing; and an *unmarked* product, which they would not only be able to keep as a pattern for various business forms but could also show to a prospective employer as evidence of literacy.

Because the portfolio nearly doubled the work for the term (especially for those who had no access to computers), I expected many complaints; however, student response was remarkably positive. During an informal assessment of the course, all twenty-three students said that they thought the portfolio was a great idea. Although they found the *process* tedious and anxiety producing, the *end product* was, as one student put it, "a miracle—even my Dad was impressed." Armed with this unanimous student support, I approached my already overworked faculty. I wanted to incorporate the portfolio into the next semester's basic syllabus for all the sections of BA301. That meant that we would be inundated with between eight hundred and one thousand portfolios.

## Faculty Response

Despite apprehensions about "another long assignment to grade," the faculty agreed to "try the portfolio one time." Four faculty members were genuinely unenthusiastic on the grounds that the additional correction was too burdensome; nevertheless, even they were willing to assign the portfolio once.

The results were moderately successful: eight of eleven faculty members were delighted with the portfolios—"It was a real shot in the arm to see how much I'd taught them," said one. "My students acted as if this were a professional assignment," commented another. There were three teachers who remained unconverted: "It took me hours to go over these; isn't there some way of cutting down on correction time?" The most resistant teacher grumbled, "Even the students thought that requesting sixty pages [thirty draft and thirty final] from one hundred students was nutty." There were, then, still problems, but after a good deal of discussion, we decided to have another go at it. We did, however, determine to provide more precise instructions, to initiate a portfolio contest with small cash prizes, and to commit to grading the portfolios holistically.

With 75 percent of the faculty enthusiastic about the assignment, we determined that it was time to poll the students to get their frank opinions and suggestions about the portfolio. The most efficient way to find out what the students thought was to make an assessment of the portfolio part of the common final examination. On May 13, 1988, we asked the students the following question:

Dr. J. Remy Leder, the Coordinator of the Business Writing Program, has asked your instructor to prepare an evaluation of the newest addition to the BA301 assignment list: the portfolio. The assignment is designed to give students experience with final polishing and editing; to provide them with a finished product to show prospective employers; and to send them out of the class with a pattern book which includes samples of the basic types of writing they are likely to do on the job. The portfolio has been somewhat controversial, however. Some people see it as the best part of the syllabus, others dislike it intensely. Your teacher, wanting to provide Dr. Leder with more than a teacher's-eye-view of the portfolio, has asked you to assess the assignment. Be honest, be specific, and be thorough. Address your memo to Dr. Leder.

Of the 952 students originally registered in thirty-four business-writing classes, 822 took the final examination. Seven students either did not answer the question that we asked or failed to do the assessment part of the examination. Out of 815 valid responses, 738 (90 percent) were enthusiastic in their support of the assignment. There was a predictable range of responses (see table 11-1). Positives ranged from 97 percent (66 students of 70) for one faculty member, to 85 percent (60 of 71) for another (who, as a result of illness, fell behind schedule and gave students little time for the portfolio).

The enthusiasm of the response was gratifying; in addition to the 738 students who were predominantly positive about the assignment, 59 of the 77 predominantly negative responses recommended that the assignment be continued in a modified form. Not surprisingly, there was a direct correlation between positive assessments and the excellence of the portfolio the students prepared. It was evident that our students like success.

## Negative Responses

I read the negative assessments with considerable care because I guessed that these 77 students spoke for others—perhaps as many as another 10 percent—who were not brave enough to complain. There were three basic themes in the negative assessments: the lack of time, the uselessness of the course, and the pointlessness of revision.

Almost one-third of the unhappy students (24) complained that they did not have enough time to complete the assignment. This is a puzzling complaint, given that the portfolio was listed on the course syllabus, which must be distributed during the first week of class. It is possible that some of the students planned their time poorly or that, as several alleged, the instructors did not plan the assignments wisely. Whatever the reason for the complaints, the tone is plaintive.[1]

*Table 11−1*  **Student Assessment of Business-Writing Portfolio.**

| Faculty Member | No. of Classes | Enrollment | Invalid Response | Positive Response | | Negative Response | |
|---|---|---|---|---|---|---|---|
| A | 3 | 73 | 1 | 68 | (94%) | 4 | (6%) |
| B | 3 | 74 | 1 | 60 | (82%) | 13 | (18%) |
| C | 4 | 98 | 1 | 89 | (92%) | 8 | (8%) |
| D | 4 | 91 | 0 | 85 | (93%) | 6 | (7%) |
| E | 3 | 70 | 1 | 66 | (97%) | 3 | (3%) |
| F | 4 | 101 | 0 | 95 | (94%) | 6 | (6%) |
| G | 3 | 68 | 0 | 62 | (91%) | 6 | (9%) |
| H | 3 | 71 | 0 | 60 | (85%) | 11 | (15%) |
| I | 4 | 108 | 3 | 91 | (87%) | 14 | (13%) |
| J | 2 | 47 | 0 | 44 | (94%) | 3 | (6%) |
| K | 1 | 21 | 0 | 18 | (86%) | 3 | (14%) |
| Totals | 34 | 822 | 7 | 738 | (90%) | 77 | (10%) |

*Source*: May 1988 business writing final examination, California State University, Fullerton.

> If I would have been free from doing the portfolio assignment, then maybe I wouldn't be so far behind in the calculus class. (Julian G)

> I did not have enough time to concern myself with final polishing and editing. However, I did [learn] how to type fast and stay awake at 3:00 in the morning. (Beth G.)

> Our teacher should give us more than 10 days for an assignment this long. (Yesuko L.)

Ten students (13 percent) revealed their misunderstanding of the nature and purpose of a business-writing course.

> Should a writing class have a project that deals with just correcting the [student's] own mistakes? Since the project mainly deals with the corrections of one's mistakes, I believe that it misses the point of the class, which is to learn how to write in the business world. (Harold B.)

One wonders what Harold B. thinks learning to write in the business world *does* entail.

Nineteen students (25 percent of those offering negative assessments) either loathed or misunderstood the process of revision.

> The portfolio [is] redundant. Students are basically copying the original work. Revisions are for the most part just duplicated from the corrections that were made by the instructor on the original. (Chris B.)

> I dislike [the portfolio] intensely. My boss is not going to tolerate work done in this fashion when I get into the business world. He will want everything completed and polished the first time. I'm sure an employer looks for day to day polishing, not a final surprise every month or so

that the work has been gone over and over again until perfect. Not only is this a waste of time for students, I will waste time and money if the idea is brought into the business world. (Gary G.)

The most comprehensive negative assessment came from a young man whose spelling is poorer than his thinking:

I feel that the portfolio is an unnecessary and extremely burdensome part of the syllabus. The writtings are just a rehash of assignments that we've already turned in. Nothing new was learned that couldn't of been learned by just reading over the corrected paper. It was very tedious to go through and make all of those corrections, plus having to retype the whole thing. This type of schoolwork is taken care of in high-school. As business students, we need to learn to write effectively and efficiently in preparation for the business world. However, we are business students, not writting students, and this assignment took too much time away from classes that should be my main focus. The portfolio seems like it was designed to give future employers samples of our work. My experience with employers, however, has shown me that if they want a sample of my writting, they will ask for it on the spot. They do not ask for something that I've spent a lot of time on trying to make perfect. (Gary S.)[2]

My faculty and I expected some complaints about the cost of producing the portfolio. There were none. One student commented insightfully that the grade on the portfolio was "to some degree influenced not only by the skill of the writer, but also by the tools used by the writer" (Jody B.); Jody's, however, was almost the only comment about how the assignment was structured.

The negative comments were quite valuable. As a result of the criticisms, we resolved the following as a faculty:

1. To make a more active effort to establish a common ground of agreement about what BA301 is attempting to do and why (i.e., convince students that in business they will need to write well, correctly, and coherently).

2. To demonstrate more clearly the importance of process in writing — the typed draft is not necessarily the "final" draft.

3. To remind students occasionally to budget time for the portfolio assignment.

## Positive Assessments

The positive assessments of the portfolio were even more helpful than the negative. Although the students did not come up with practical suggestions about improving the assignment, they revealed

*Table 11-2*  **Positive Responses to Portfolio Assignment**

| Category | Number of Responses | |
|---|---|---|
| "Tangible product" | 58 | (8%) |
| "Made me objective" | 79 | (10%) |
| "Learned time management" | 122 | (16%) |
| "Taught me editing" | 186 | (26%) |
| "Not a waste of time" | 218 | (30%) |

Source: May 1988 business-writing final examination, California State University, Fullerton.

a great deal about what makes an assignment good and what their expectations about writing classes are. Students in this group commonly cited five "benefits" from the portfolio: it gave them a tangible product, it taught them time management, it gave them editing skills, it made it possible for them to be objective, and it was not a waste of time (see table 11-2). Of the 738 students who liked the portfolio, 8 percent celebrated having something tangible to show for their efforts in the course, something that was worth saving.

It is good to leave a college course with some physical evidence of one's work. (Denisha W.)

The portfolio is good tangible evidence showing that I have well developed writing skills. (John H.)

One-fourth of the students (186) mentioned how valuable the experience of final editing was.

I learned to be flexible with my results instead of getting offended that my final paper was not perfect. (Karen G.)

[The portfolio] helped me to recognize my mistakes and review them instead of just looking at the grade and putting the paper away. It made me realize the lucidity that I was lacking in my writing, it gave me a sense of accomplishment, knowing that I did learn something. (Rico B.)

[The portfolio] allowed me to edit my writings and gave me a good idea of the types of problems that I run into a lot in my drafts. In particular, I realize that my thoughts and ideas are good, but that I am usually too calculating in my drafts. (Steven Y.)

Having the opportunity to correct my errors helped me to realize where my strengths were. (Conchita E.)

I could finally see my weaknesses and strengths. This enabled me to polish my work, making each sentence convey the meaning I had intended. (John V.)

The practical experience with the portfolio made the students unusually articulate about the value of revision.

> Revision and polishing are essential in the writing process. Preparing my portfolio, I discovered how much an already decent piece of work can be made even better. (Anna M.)

> While editing, I was learning better, more efficient ways of writing. New ideas came to me: words I could add or delete, phrases I could switch, even whole sentences I could delete. This was a valuable learning experience. I learned that I could have written the same thing with fewer words. (Mario S.)

> At times, the revising felt like busy work, it was challenging to make myself expand on my own work. It is usually easier to see other peoples mistakes and point out how they could improve their own work, but this project made me dig deeper and improve my own. (Lynne R.)

Almost 75 students talked about the importance of the time lapse between initial and final drafts; they were grateful for the opportunity to look at their work objectively.

> It is better to review your writings after you have forgotten about the grade you received. (Susan S.)

> Somewhere in our textbook, it states that a writer should take a day or two off before doing final editing. During the semester, this was difficult to do, because of the shortage of time. The portfolio assignment made me look back to my older papers, thus giving me a new perspective on them. (Mario S.)

The value of working under time pressure was mentioned by 122 students: it was easy to read between the lines and realize that they are not often asked to submit long projects that require detailed planning.

> After not seeing a paper for an extended length of time, the student [can] look at his own work objectively and critically. (Michelle A.)

> The time crush was part of the learning experience. Future employers are not going to give me a month or two to complete a report. I viewed the portfolio as a small taste of the real world. (Scott C.)

> I really learned a valuable lesson in time management and the cost of a rush job. (Ken K.)

For each complaint that the "assignment should be made known at the beginning of the semester," there were several assessments in which students revealed irritation with classmates who didn't budget their time carefully.

It was known throughout the semester that this assignment would be due. So the revision and retyping could have been done during the semester after each graded rough draft was returned. (Jennifer C.)

Many students ignore the fact that they can revise before the assignment is actually handed out, but then, they have only themselves to blame for not being finished earlier. (Michelle S.)

One of the most interesting aspects of the assessments was the revelation of the students' attitudes toward education — their expectations, their desires, and their frustrations. They seem to *expect* assignments that are a waste of time. Fully one-third of the students mentioned "surprise" that the portfolio was not simply "another bit of busy work."

I feel that my time and efforts were not wasted; [the exercise] taught me that people expect the very best from you. (Maruska S.)

Before starting the portfolio I thought it would be a waste of time. However, now that I have completed the work, I feel proud of myself for doing it. The polishing and editing seemed to take a long time, but it was worth it. (Jacqueline R.)

One student asserted that the portfolio was "the most serious type of work I have ever done in my college life." "The portfolio is the best writing assignment I have been given in my four years of college," said another. Given the relative simplicity of the assignment, such admissions from upper-division students are most distressing.

The students' frank comments about how infrequently they have had the opportunity to learn from mistakes are equally disturbing:

[In the portfolio] the students are also allowed to find mistakes in their own work and correct them. *This is rarely done in a learning environment.* (Kenny K.)

Many times when I receive a corrected assignment back, *I never had the chance to learn from my mistakes;* the portfolio provides for this. (Daniel P.)

*In so many other writing programs, I wrote paper after paper without realizing my direction.* (John V.)

*I don't think I have ever before had the chance to see exactly how much I have improved from the first day to the last.* That experience alone is reason enough, I believe, for students to complete this portfolio. (Katrina G.) (emphasis added)

Many writers made candid observations about what students expect of themselves and how much they are willing (or unwilling) to work. For each student who confessed becoming "attached to work I have had to slave over" (Lori S.), there were four taking a more cynical stance.

> Practically, students do not give much attention to the instructors' remarks. The preparation of the portfolio forces us to correct our mistakes and become better editors. (Akbar S.)

> The students' basic tendency is to do as little revision as possible. (Blake R.)

> I enjoyed putting [the portfolio] together because I knew it wouldn't just end up in the trash after the semester was over. (Joel R.)

My staff and I were unprepared for the glowing assessments of the portfolio. After a few hundred papers, the rave list began to sound like a movie review: "I was so proud," "what a sense of accomplishment!" "I'm really grateful for the opportunity," "this was the most meaningful exercise in my college career," "the portfolio is inherently valuable," "two thumbs up," "it will be my ace in the hole," "gratifying," "I was amazed at how good it looked," "I was astonished by my progress." These raves were pervasive, occurring in 65 percent of all the positive assessments.

One of the best comments revealed the sense of creation that the portfolio was able to give students:

> My first thought was—it was hard enough to do the first time, now she wants us to do it all over again. But what I produced was something I could take pride in. If I were not forced, I probably would not have looked over these assignments again. Once the assignment is completed, a sense of pride is felt. I looked back on all my work and was pleased. (Jesus B.)

The echo of Genesis was almost certainly unintentional, but it is thought provoking.

The most interesting of the assessments were written by students with mastery of voice:

> What a sense of accomplishment! When I handed in that big fat portfolio, I felt like I had just written a book. Here was a semester of grind neatly bound with my name on it. I was proud of my work. Looking back, the portfolio didn't have to be that difficult a task. My instructor left valuable remarks on my graded papers; I simply followed her suggestions and corrected my typos. (Ken K.)

> I have something [tangible] to leave this class with. Besides offering knowledge, what is there to gain from most courses at CSUF? Certainly, I could keep my texts, but why not get 1/3 of their value back from the book store? Of course, I have my report card to gaze

upon. And it goes without saying, I will improve my Trivial Pursuit game. But unlike Biology, Psychology, or Political Science, I will leave Business writing with something in my greedy little hands. I will have a portfolio that will serve a purpose. If nothing else, I can hold my portfolio and say, "Look what I did in BA301." (Sharon S.)

The Portfolio assignment will, no doubt, be of value to me for many years. It not only gives me a sense of finality and completion, but it gives me something tangible to show prospective employers. The four assignments all demonstrate problem solving abilities. . . . All in all, however, it would be difficult to interest anyone in looking at [these samples of my work] were it not for the tidy, convenient, and professional-looking package I've constructed. The Business Writing Program is on the right track. (Dave N.)

After reading 822 exams (twice), my faculty and I are inclined to agree with Dave N: the portfolio assignment is the right track for our students. The upshot of the assessment exam is that we are committed to continuing the portfolio, programwide, for the next several years. There are, of course, administrative issues and concerns not addressed by our students that we as a faculty have had to consider with a good deal of care.

## Administrative Issues

### Assignment Specifics

As with all programwide assignments, arriving at a workable and comprehensible basic paradigm has proved a challenge. Our first portfolio was little more than a retype-with-revision assignment. All original work was paper-clipped together and tucked into the back page of the bound portfolio. This has gradually given way to a much more reportlike portfolio, which includes a memo of transmittal, a table of contents, and an assignment-description page for each element. The added bulk makes the portfolio look and read better. The additional work is minimal and student satisfaction is higher. Several students and at least one faculty member have argued in favor of requiring that revised versions of *all* business-writing assignments be included in the portfolio. Since most members of the faculty do not like this suggestion, we have arrived at a compromise: five required assignments (proposal, report, memo, letter, summary) followed by additional revisions at the discretion of the student or faculty member. It was a student's suggestion that persuaded us to discourage inclusion of the job application package in the portfolio (in case the real application bears too close a resemblance to the portfolio application).

## Logistics

The success of the portfolio assignment is dependent in part on having the students type long assignments on a computer disk. Even a good typist is somewhat daunted by retyping twenty-five pages of text; thus, computer access is invaluable. About one-fifth of our business-writing classes have a computer component (MSWord) and weekly computer workshop sessions. That means that the remaining 750 students must fend for themselves. We have discovered that an average of 50 percent of these students either own or have access to a personal computer. How do we help the remaining 400 students? We use several approaches:

1. Familiarize students with available computers on campus.
2. Set aside one class period each semester to give interested students a "quick" intro to word-processing programs available on campus.
3. Make available to the students word-processing programs for which our university has site license.

These efforts have solved most of the logistics problems; we expect that with increased computer literacy the problems will decrease.

## Character and Cost of Portfolios

In an era during which the students believe the medium is the message, the temptation to pay for a glitzy high-tech portfolio is almost irresistible. One of my own students had her portfolio typed professionally — twice — at considerable cost. My faculty and I think that such expense is excessive and have actively encouraged students to hold cost down to $10 or less. That means a few dollars for good-quality paper and a few dollars for binding. We discourage laser printing (unless students have access at home or work to laser printers), and we point out that the best portfolio of 1988 was typewritten. We are presently negotiating with a local printing company to see if we can get a discount rate for printing and binding.

## Portfolio Competition

For the past three semesters, we have run a portfolio contest in conjunction with the portfolio assignment. Each teacher submits his or her best portfolio to the contest committee. Contest winners receive letters of commendation and money prizes: first place, $50; second, $30; and third, $20. A local business has just guaranteed the prize money for the next three years. Students and faculty alike enjoy the added edge of competition.

### Evaluation

The problem of grading the portfolios continues. Eight of my eleven faculty members teach between seventy-five and one hundred business-writing students each semester. That means, of course, that each will receive between two thousand and three thousand pages to review during the last week or two of the semester. Even if we rigorously hold our review of each portfolio to between five and ten minutes (counting the time it takes to write a comment), we are facing a time commitment of between six and sixteen hours. How do we do it?

My faculty members have come up with creative ways of cutting down the time. One professor sits with the portfolios propped up against her computer and types a brief and professional-looking comment for each student. Another professor employs a xeroxed check-sheet to which she adds a brief handwritten note to each student. One instructor concentrates on only one or two small parts of the portfolio (e.g., the memo of transmittal, summary) and bases the holistic grade for the whole portfolio on those parts. A most dedicated instructor matches the original with the revised version of one assignment to make sure that her students have followed revision instructions. Only one instructor continues to dislike the portfolio assignment.

## Conclusion

There is no dearth of research supporting the claim that the portfolio is an invaluable resource in standard expository-writing classes; that the portfolio can be just as effective in business-writing classes has been demonstrated by the three-year experiment that I have described in this essay. The cost of producing the portfolios is moderate; the assignment gives students an opportunity to strengthen their revision skills, to see how much they have learned, and to leave the class with something they value. As an added bonus for business students, the business-writing portfolio is a practical way of showing their writing skills to prospective employers. Although evaluation of the portfolios is almost as onerous as the preparation of the assignment, resourceful faculty members are able to make the task manageable.

Because the business-writing portfolio is such an effective and pedagogically sound assignment, it has become the favorite assignment of students and faculty alike. Anything that can get students to look at their work and see that it is good is an invaluable addition to the syllabus.

## Notes

1. No quotations from student papers have been edited.

2. Interestingly, Gary S., whose portfolio was very poor indeed, was required to resubmit it at the end of the summer. His assessment of his final, excellent portfolio was: "I could not believe how good I felt when the print shop handed this back to me. Thanks for *making* me do a good job."

# 12

# Using Portfolios in the Assessment of Writing in the Academic Disciplines

Richard L. Larson
*Lehman College of the City University of New York*

Portfolios, though they are much discussed these days as tools for teaching and for assessment, are in fact quite familiar as a method for doing both.[1] As a freshman at Harvard, I was required to keep my English A (composition) "themes" in a pigeonhole with my name on it in the English Department office; when I went for an interview with the instructor, I took the collected themes with me, and returned them to the pigeonhole after the interview. Without knowing it, I was compiling a portfolio of my writings in freshman English. When I directed the freshman program in writing at the University of Hawaii in Honolulu, I arranged for the printing up of "theme folders," in which students in all sections could place their writings after the instructor had responded to them. Without knowing it, I was urging that the teaching staff in composition use portfolios to help them in teaching writing and judging students' work. People seeking admission to classes in studio art often have to submit portfolios of their previous work, to convince instructors that they are worthy of admission to the course. People seeking jobs as designers of advertising copy often submit portfolios of their previous designs as part of their applications for employment. In at least one state, teachers seeking employment must offer school administrators portfolios (including sample syllabi, lesson plans, letters of recommendations) as part of their applications for teaching jobs. There is, indeed, nothing new about the notion of compiling an ordered collection of one's work for a teacher or employer to look at. But now we've given these diverse collections an honorific name, *port-folios*, and hence also an identity they may not have had before.

*Portfolio* should designate, at least, an ordered compilation of writings. A casual gathering up of papers one has written over a year or two probably does not deserve to be called a "portfolio." A portfolio ideally should be a deliberate compilation, gathered accord-ing to some plan, for use by an identified reader or readers for specific needs or purposes. A portfolio gathered for the teacher in a writing course may help with the teacher's instruction of a student; if submitted at the end of a course, it may help with a final evaluation of the student. A gathering of writings in chronological order to show a student's development in an academic major program may help demonstrate what the student has accomplished and testify to the student's fitness to receive a degree in that major. Or a portfolio of writings gathered over a student's academic career, from freshman to senior year, may be examined by faculty for evidence of changes in the way the student thinks, reacts to problems, assesses data, or chooses values. In portfolios, students may include their own written reflections on the writings (and or other works)—what they think the writings show about their development, what they have learned in a particular course of study, what they value in their writing, or what they think are the strengths and weaknesses of that writing. Though a portfolio should be ordered and purposeful, it can also be flexible—a tool of value in bringing elements, steps, or parallel tracks in a student's academic career together for examination at the same time by a single reader or group of readers.

Portfolios have, or can have, a further important potential advantage for evaluating a student's education or a program. Because a portfolio is composed of works drafted and completed at different times, possibly in different settings, most likely over a period of time, portfolios resist—though they do not prevent—easy summative evaluation. If it is difficult—and I find increasingly that it *is* difficult, indeed almost impossible—to recognize the complex values in a piece of writing (or any other kind of work) in a single summative grade,[2] it is doubly or trebly difficult to recognize in one summary score the multiple as well as complex values represented by the different pieces in the portfolio. (I use the words *summative* or *summary* here—in preference, for example, to *holistic*—to emphasize the way in which single scores or grades have to *sum up* diverse features and perhaps varying kinds of accomplishments in a piece of writing or group of writings.) Of course, those who are determined to assign a single score to a portfolio can do so if they want, and in a large-scale assessment such persons can probably train readers to assign summative scores that are technically "reliable" (I have not tried such scoring). In particular, those who must, or wish to, determine whether, overall, a given student has completed a major satisfactorily or deserves admission to, say, an advanced course in professional writing, can establish the standards they wish a student to meet and can decide whether those standards are met in a given portfolio. But a portfolio, almost by definition, embodies diversity in subjects and the treatment of subjects. And diversity invites the application of multiple ways of looking at the collection, multiple approaches to identifying the distinctive accomplishments and shortcomings (usually there are both) within the collection. Portfolios invite an effort to identify and describe in at least a little detail what is going on in the compiler's writings: the application, as it were, of multiple filters, employed successively (or sometimes, by good readers, at the same time) to recognize or highlight the many achievements in the works in the portfolio.

At Lehman College in 1986, when we planned to include the gathering and reading of students' portfolios in our project on the evaluation of Lehman's new curriculum for general education and distribution (see the Appendix) we had thought out some, though not all, of these features offered by portfolios. Several of us, including Professor John Richards of chemistry, chair of the Provost's Committee to Evaluate the New Curriculum, were developing an application (eventually approved and funded) to the Fund for the Improvement of Postsecondary Education (FIPSE) for support of our efforts at evaluation. We wanted to do more than track the progress of students working under the new curriculum and compare it with the progress of students who had worked under the previous curriculum. We wanted to do more than survey the faculty and students to learn their views about the curriculum. We wanted to see whether we could learn what effects participating in the new curriculum was having on students' actual *performance* in their studies. We could not, without expending a great deal of time and energy, enter classrooms and observe that performance — when students were not listening to lectures. We could not bring students individually to a kind of oral testing of their ways of responding to questions the curriculum might help them to explore. And, except in Speech Department courses, oral performance was usually not asked of students moving through the new curriculum or through upper-division courses. We could give to a sampling of students a test of their ability to respond to complex academic problems — some problems requiring the addressing of moral issues and some requiring the evaluation of quantitative data — in written essays. (And we did include such testing of ability to write about complex problems in our evaluation plan.) But we knew that a time-limited test of students' abilities at solving problems suddenly placed before them would put students in an artificial situation; it would not be likely to elicit a full indication of what they had learned to do while taking our new curriculum or how they respond in writing to academic issues. Our best opportunity to obtain examples of students' performance, we thought, would come if we obtained from students examples of the writing they had done in their courses — whether general education courses, courses in their academic majors, or courses in their academic minors. Those papers, we thought, would let us see both what students were asked, and/or allowed, to present as writings in our college, and would also let us see how well — on various criteria of "effective" academic writing — they could perform.

Using the term that had just begun to come into prominence to identify ordered gatherings of students' writings, we included in our proposal to FIPSE, then, a plan to gather portfolios of students' writings "across the [general education/major/minor] curriculum" and develop a procedure for reading the writings in these portfolios to see what students in these courses were writing, and how. And after our proposal had been funded, we set about to gather suitable portfolios.

The process of gathering portfolios proved unexpectedly difficult. We asked faculty members who had been identified to us as prominent and committed teachers in the new curriculum to help us by giving us copies of students' writing submitted to them; we learned that many of these faculty required no writing of students, even on examinations. ("Our students write *so* badly," one faculty member in psychology complained "that I often can't understand their writing, and I can't take the time to read it and try to respond to it.") We considered asking faculty who did assign writing to help us elicit papers from students in their classes, only to find that a given faculty member might be the only one on a student's schedule that semester in whose course writing was assigned — and thus could not quite help us get writing from several disciplines. We then obtained the names of a sampling of students at representative points in their college careers and wrote directly to them, asking them to compile portfolios and allow us to read them. The response was minimal; students, we discovered, do not voluntarily do extra work, and many whom we asked had written nothing outside of English composition anyway. Finally, we obtained the consent of our FIPSE program officer to offer students cash payments in return for compiling portfolios and delivering them to us; when we offered $25 per portfolio, we obtained enough writings from students at various levels (upper sophomore, lower junior, etc.) to make the assessment effort work.

Even so, we had to make our stipulations concerning what we wanted in a portfolio minimal: we had to set only those qualifying features absolutely necessary to give us the writings we needed. With the guidance of an interdisciplinary faculty working group — each part of our project is guided by such a group, in this case it was composed of the chief librarian, a faculty member in specialized services in education, a faculty member in recreation, a faculty member from the social sciences, and myself — we decided that a portfolio should consist of the following:

- At least three pieces of writing (more if the student would give more).
- Each piece at least *two* pages in length, longer if possible.
- No piece from a course in English composition.

Papers in English composition were excluded on the assumptions that (1) they might be final drafts completed after extensive conferences with an instructor about earlier drafts, and thus be unrepresentative of papers submitted in regular academic courses; and (2) the assignments on which the student wrote might be untypical of those in regular academic courses. Assignments in composition, at least at Lehman College, often do not invite writings addressed with a serious communicative purpose to readers familiar with, and concerned about, their subjects. With an offer of compensation, and with these minimal specifications, we obtained some seventy portfolios, many of them, indeed, containing more writings, and often longer writings, than what we had specified.

We now confronted the question of how to analyze these "unplanned" portfolios. (We call them "unplanned" because when the students wrote the pieces included in the portfolios, they had not intended or envisaged that the pieces would eventually become parts of portfolios. In many projects that collect portfolios, such as those for assessment of students' work in a major or in, say, freshman English, the students are told that what they write will eventually be placed in a portfolio and reread at the same time all other pieces in the portfolio are reread. Such portfolios might be described as "planned" portfolios.) Our interdisciplinary working group decided to retain the twin foci for reading the portfolios that we had tentatively agreed upon earlier: what sorts of writings are in the portfolio, and what characterizes those writings as pieces written in an academic setting? For reasons discussed earlier, we reaffirmed our policy against attempting summative judgments of the portfolios, preferring instead to try to identify affirmatively (without *negative* description) what is *in* each portfolio. But we also followed that policy because, in a project on evaluation of the effects of a curriculum on students' performance, we were less interested in the perform- ances of individuals than in the performances of groups of students — students who had varying contacts with our curriculum — at various points in their progress through our college. We wanted to aggregate the features of thinking and writing displayed by students at various points in their college careers, so that we can point out to the College what our students are showing that they have practiced and what they are capable of doing — and, by implication, what they have not practiced and may be less well prepared to do.

How, then, to *identify* — designate the identity of — the papers in the portfolio? What system of division/classification to employ? To this task, the customary and familiar groupings of discourse are entirely inadequate. They rely on relatively small numbers of fixed categories (exposition, narration, description, and argumentation make up one famous system) or methods of exposition (definition, analysis, comparison/contrast, and so on), or aims (expressive, refer- ential, and so on). The assignment of writings to such categories is often arbitrary; usually no allowance is made for a piece that does not fit neatly within a category, even if it seems clear that the piece has features characteristic of more than one group. Nothing is gained, in the analysis of the writings within a portfolio, from attempting to locate them in such rigidly conceived categories. Moreover, the categories speak not at all of writers' specific purposes and audiences for writing: few writers, I suspect, ever sit down to a writing desk with the thought that "I am now going to produce a piece of expository writing," nor have very many writers (unless struggling to respond to an assignment from a teacher of writing) set out to produce, by name, some "expressive" writing. For our studies of the writings in our portfolios, we needed a way of identifying writings that respected the reasons why, in each piece, the writer was coming before his or her reader or readers.

To find such a way of talking about such writings, we adapted from philosophers like Austin and Searle the concept of *speech act*[3] and applied it to written texts with the aid of a different phrase, *act of discourse*. We conceived of an act of discourse as a specific kind of action performed by a writer in addressing a reader or readers to meet the specific requests, wishes, interests, or possible needs of those readers: for example, summarizing data, reporting and analyz- ing a sequence of events, defining a problem, setting forth criteria for judging an item and applying them to that item (such as a work of art), analyzing the structure of a text, and so on. With the aid of the readers working with us on the portfolios—graduate students or teaching assistants in academic fields such as English, history, philosophy, even music—we set about to construct, from the first portfolios themselves, a draft list of acts of discourse performed by writers in the writings in the portfolios. We agreed to construct an "open" list of such acts, initially tentative, to which we might add if later papers were clearly performing acts of discourse not already on our list. We agreed that it would be possible within the same writing to find the writer performing two or more acts, successively or even concurrently. We looked for the acts by which writers seek to add to their readers' knowledge, alter readers' beliefs, evoke feelings, change attitudes, prompt judgments, lead their readers to action, encourage readers to follow out a line of inquiry or speculation, assist readers in understanding the personalities or motives of the writer, and so on.

Working, then, from the portfolios themselves, our faculty team and our readers (whose "training" for reading included this work on identifying recurrent acts of discourse in students' writings) developed a list that now numbers some twenty-five "acts" but that probably will grow longer as we examine additional papers. Since our work of analyzing portfolios and identifying acts of discourse continues even as this article is being written, I cannot yet offer a complete list. But the following items fairly illustrate the kinds of acts we are identifying as representative of those assigned, invited, or considered valuable in academic writing in our program:

- Narrative, with or without commentary, of events in the writer's life.
- Descriptive representation (it may include some narrating) of persons, objects, or conditions directly observed by the writer, *not* part of autobiographic writing (where the focus is on the writer's self).
- Analysis of the reporting or argument in a piece or pieces of writing by a person or persons other than the student compiling the portfolio.
- Presentation of the student's own views on a conceptual (e.g., philosophic) or historical issue—a question difficult to resolve and to which there can be two or more possible answers.
- Analysis and recommendation concerning a "problem" in the world outside of college (in the larger society or in a particular institution), on which action must be taken.

- Presentation of essential data about a historical period, social condition, political structure, and so on.

- Analysis of the data presented concerning that historical period, social condition, or political structure, to suggest what the data tell the student (what the data "mean") and whether in those data any interpretive problems or problems requiring action arise.

- Summary of the "research" findings of others, along with evaluation of what subsequent research is needed.

- Analysis/interpretation of all or part of a work of art (literature, music, sculpture, film).

Our procedure for tabulating these acts of discourse in each portfolio is fairly simple: a reader identifies the acts chiefly performed in each writing (there may be two or three, sometimes more) and records in how many pieces of writing within the portfolio each is performed. (Any difference of opinion between readers about what acts of discourse are performed within a portfolio is resolved through discussion.) From this tabulation we learn which acts of discourse our students at various points in their college careers are performing frequently, occasionally, or hardly at all. We will report our findings to the faculty of the college, and ask whether they are satisfied with these (implicit) emphases in the work assigned to/accepted from students. If they are not, curricular change may follow.

At the same time as we learn what students in various courses are doing in their writings, we seek, of course, to learn how well they are doing those things. We resist summative scoring, as explained earlier, and anyway summative scoring would yield only misleading results given the diversity of tasks attempted by students within the portfolio and the varying kinds of demands placed upon writers by those tasks. (The score of 5 or the grade of B, if we somehow *could* assign such grades, would mean altogether different accomplishments from one portfolio to another.) Instead, we have sought to identify characteristics, or qualities of accomplishment, that are valued by persons reading the writings produced within a university, and to determine how frequently we find these qualities in the writings presented to us in portfolios. Again, the goal is not primarily to generalize about a student, but to be able to say what characteristics are displayed by students at particular "levels" in the college — and whether those characteristics change as we move from level to level in college standing (upper sophomore, upper junior, etc.). Probably not many university faculty would dispute the value, indeed the desirability, in students' writing of the characteristics our working group has decided to look for in the portfolios; they are not, we think, idiosyncratic. Here is a partial list of these qualities (our group is still refining the list and the ways of describing the qualities), expressed through affirmative statements about writings.

- Each writing exhibits a clear purpose and is not just a mechanical effort to carry out an assignment. The writer appears to have reasons for coming before a reader and has a point to make.
- In each writing, the writer has a clear subject and makes a clear point about that subject.
- The writer identifies early in the writing the problems and/or issues presented by the subject discussed.
- Writings analyze and evaluate—show the importance, significance, or usefulness of—quantitative data presented to or located by the writer.
- Writings analyze and evaluate nonquantitative data presented to or located by the writer.
- The writer uses clear standards to reach judgments about the value of different kinds of data.
- The writer evaluates general statements, recognizing which are more, and which are less, dependable.
- Where appropriate, the writer clearly explains the bases for choosing a particular course of action for resolving an issue or meeting a need.
- The writer reasons soundly from premises to conclusions.
- Each writing exhibits clear organizational plans (even if the plans are not mechanically marked out).
- The writer makes successful use of metaphor and analogy.

Our procedure for recording the presence of these characteristics is like that for recording the presence of acts of discourse: the reader notes for each portfolio the number of papers about which the particular affirmative statement can be made. Again, if there is disagreement between readers concerning the presence of a feature within a portfolio, the readers discuss the portfolio and resolve the differences.

Some of the features listed here we would expect to find in most papers in most portfolios. The first two listed above, for instance, and the presence of clear organizational plans we would hope to find in almost all writings. Other features—the analysis and evaluation of quantitative data, for example, and the explanation of how the writer chooses among possible courses of action — might appear in only one paper in a given portfolio, and in some portfolios might not appear at all.

As has been explained earlier, our analysis of the findings from study of the portfolios will bring together the descriptions of portfolios from groups of students, particularly groups of students at different points in their progress through the college, and groups divided according to whether they have taken our new curriculum in the sequence planned, or have taken only parts of it. In interpreting the findings, we will focus on the frequency with which the various affirmative statements can be made about the portfolios of the different groups. If fewer than half of the writings we received from a given group of students exhibit the making of a clear point about a clearly identifiable subject, for example, that finding may have substantial implications for the success with which those students are learning, in our writing program and throughout the curriculum, to communicate ideas. And if fewer than half of the writings we receive from a given group display the writers' efforts to evaluate general statements before relying on them to make points, that finding may tell us much about whether those students are learning to think evaluatively about what they read and hear. If on the other hand we find the analysis and evaluation of quantitative data in a relatively small percentage of the writings from a particular group, that finding may tell us only about the interests of students who submitted portfolios or the kinds of writings they elected to submit. An almost total absence of writing about quantitative data in the papers by members of a given group, however, may be much more significant, particularly in view of the College's insistent inclusion in the curriculum of work on quantitative reasoning. Each finding, about the appearance of acts of discourse and about the demonstration of the qualities we value in academic writing, has to be evaluated individually. We cannot, any more than our students, reach quick, broad generalizations, or draw hasty inferences.

From the portfolios, we can make one other group of observations. Since the writings are placed in the portfolios exactly as they are returned to students by faculty members (for *this* kind of portfolio, we do not ask students to revise their work), we can not only observe the kinds of writings faculty invite and/or students submit, but we can also make inferences about the ways in which assignments for writing were given and observe directly how faculty respond to the writings. *How* the assignment was made must, of course, be a matter of inference, though at times a piece of writing that seems uncertain of what it is trying to do, and whom it is addressing, may be responding to an assignment that is unclear — one that does not inform students precisely enough what acts of discourse they are to undertake. (No instructor, obviously, uses or should use that phrase in making assignments for writing.) But what the instructor wrote in response to the student's work is displayed before us. We take note of comments that are nonexistent, cryptic, focused on topics covered or not covered in the writing, focused on the "correctness" of data or ideas in what the student wrote, or nearly uninterpretable. If the comments do not in any way respond to the writings as composed pieces, we take note of that apparent failure. When, as those working on the Curriculum Evaluation Project at Lehman hope will happen, we draw on the findings of our project to substantiate applications for funds for workshops that may help us urge faculty to assign writing as a way of helping students think and learn, we will use the results of observations of faculty comments on students' pieces.

Portfolios of students' writings, of course, are not the only examples of students' performance in their academic study that we use to help us gauge the impact of our curriculum. As discussed earlier, an important part of our project that also looks at students' performance is administering, to a selected sample of students at various levels in the college, time-limited essay tests. In our project, these tests invite students to respond, rather swiftly, to brief problem-posing texts from major writers; students are asked to say whether they agree or disagree with the position taken by the writer of the text and to explain their views. Students' essays are then scored according to a complex rubric that focuses on students' understanding of the quoted text, their reasoning, their use of data from observation and readings, and their ability to compose coherent, focused writings in a short time. Discussion of the test essays is matter for another (longer) paper; we note here only that the tests complement the portfolios by giving us access to writings that are brief, that deal with an assigned subject, that are problem centered (and hence give us access to students' reasoning), and that can easily be compared (as the writings in portfolios usually cannot). Together the portfolios and test essays give us dual perspectives on the performance of students who have and students who have not taken our general education curriculum.

We believe that the intensive reading of students' portfolios to find out what kinds of writings are in them, and what specifically has been accomplished in those writings, contributes significantly to an evaluation of a curriculum concerned with developing in students productive ways of thinking, of evaluating ideas, of responding to issues, and of communicating composed thought. For this project, our goal has not been to present students with comments on their work, because what we are trying to learn about their performance does not necessarily correspond with what *they* were *trying* to demonstrate. But we could easily take the logical next step: to adapt the reading of portfolios so that we give feedback to students about how well they are developing the abilities that they have been trying deliberately to develop. For that step, as well as for the goals sought in our project, the intensive, nonsummative reading of students' texts enacts a humane approach to teaching and learning. Students have the right to have their texts read carefully, understood, and valued, not for what they lack but, affirmatively, for what they achieve.[4]

## Notes

1. A bibliography of writings about the uses of portfolios in recent years appears elsewhere in this collection.

2. Peter Elbow discusses the problems of evaluation at length in his forthcoming report on the English Coalition Conference: *What Is English?*

3. For brief introductions to these concepts, see J. L. Austin, *How to Do Things with Words* (New York: Oxford University Press, 1965 [Galaxy Books]), and J. R. Searle, "What Is a Speech Act?" in *The Philosophy of Language*, ed. J. R. Searle (London: Oxford University Press, 1971 [Oxford Readings in Philosophy]), pp. 39–53.

4. I welcome comments or questions about the evaluation plan discussed in this essay. My address is Institute for Literacy Studies, Lehman College, 250 Bedford Park Boulevard West, Bronx, NY 10468–1589.

## Appendix

The new curriculum at Lehman College that is being evaluated in part by the procedures discussed here consists essentially of five parts.

1. A sequence of courses in academic skills (one of which is a course in basic logic), required *only* of students who score below an established minimum on tests of students' abilities at reading and writing that are given *after* students' admission to the College.

2. A set of five "core" courses (in humanities, social sciences, Origins of the Modern Age, science, and quantitative reasoning) taken by *all* students entering the College as new freshmen.

3. Certain other "qualification" requirements, in English composition, oral communication, a foreign language, and physical education.

4. "Distribution" courses — one in each of seven distribution areas, within each of which the student has a choice of some ten departmental courses.

5. An academic major.

6. An academic minor, required of all students except those majoring in certain fields (e.g, nursing, accounting) where the major requirements are especially heavy.

# III

# Classroom Portfolios

# 13

# Bringing Practice in Line with Theory
## *Using Portfolio Grading in the Composition Classroom*

Jeffrey Sommers
*Miami University—Middletown*

Portfolio assessment in the composition classroom offers not a methodology but a framework for response. Rather than provide definitive answers to questions about grading criteria and standards, the relationship between teacher and student, and increased paper loads, the portfolio approach presents an opportunity for instructors to bring their practice in responding to student writing in line with their theories of composing and pedagogy. My essay proposes to take an exploratory look at how portfolio evaluation compels instructors to address a number of important, and long-lived, issues underlying response to student writing. When an instructor chooses to use a portfolio system, certain other decisions must inevitably follow, and it is the implications of these decisions that I propose to examine most closely.

As the writing process has become the focus of composition classes over the past three decades, it seems an almost natural evolution for portfolio evaluation to have entered the classroom. Emphasizing the importance of revision to the composing process—regardless of which theoretical view of composing one takes—ought to lead to a classroom practice that permits, even encourages, students to revise. While such revision can, of course, occur in a classroom in which the writing portfolio is not in use, the portfolio itself tends to encourage students to revise because it suggests that writing occurs over time, not in a single sitting, just as the portfolio itself grows over time and cannot be created in a single sitting. Elbow and Belanoff argue that a portfolio system evaluates student writing "in ways that better reflect the complexities of the writing process: with time for freewriting, planning, discussion with instructors and peers, revising, and copyediting. It lets students put these activities together in a way most productive for them" (this volume 14).

Additionally, the portfolio approach can help students discover that writing is indeed a form of learning. Janet Emig has argued that writing "provides [a] record of evolution of thought since writing is epigenetic as process-and-product" (128). Portfolios provide a record of that record. Emig also describes writing as "active, engaged, personal — notably, self-rhythmed" (128). The notion that writing occurs over time in response to the rhythms created by the individual writer — a notion that makes eminent sense when one considers that no two writers seem to work at precisely the same pace and that no two pieces of writing seem to take form at the same pace even for the same writer — is another excellent argument for using portfolios. The portfolio approach allows writers to assemble an *oeuvre* at their own pace, within the structure of the writing course and its assignments, of course. Nevertheless, the portfolio by its very nature suggests self-rhythm because some pieces will require more drafts than others, even if explicit deadlines are prompting their composition.

For good cause then have portfolio systems of evaluation become commonplace in composition classrooms. But with these portfolios also come serious issues about grading standards and criteria, about how teachers and students relate to one another, about how teachers handle increased paper loads. Before examining how these issues might be resolved, perhaps it is time to acknowledge that this essay has yet to define *portfolio*. I have deliberately avoided doing so for two reasons: first, *portfolio* is a familiar-enough term and not really all that mysterious, and thus what I have written so far should be comprehensible to my readers; second, no consensus exists about just what a portfolio is or should be, however familiar the concept may seem. In fact, two distinctly different models of portfolios exist, each compelling its adherents to address the central issues of response in very different theoretical ways.

The first model is described well by James E. Ford and Gregory Larkin, who use as an analogy an artist's portfolio. Each student's work is "collected, like the best representative work of an artist, into a 'portfolio'" (951). We are to see students in the role of free-lance commercial artists approaching an art director at an advertising agency with a large portfolio case containing their "best representative work." Such a model is easily transferred into the writing classroom. Students in the writing course produce a certain number of written documents during the term, agreeing in advance that only a specified number of those documents will be graded by the instructor. Commercial artists would never compile a portfolio that consisted of every piece of work they had done and neither do the students; the idea is to select a representative sampling that shows the creators at their best.

This portfolio model most likely grows out of instructors' concern with grading criteria and standards. Ford and Larkin, as the title of their article suggests, came to the portfolio as a means of guaranteeing grading standards. Instructors are justified in upholding rigorous standards of excellence because their students have been able to revise their work and select their best writing for evaluation. As Ford and Larkin comment, "A student can 'blow' an occasional assignment without disastrous effect" (952), suggesting that the instructor is being eminently fair. Elbow and Belanoff, in the context of a programmatic portfolio-assessment project, make a similar argument, one equally applicable to the individual composition classroom. "By giving students a chance to be examined on their best writing — by giving them an opportunity for more help — we are also able to demand their best writing" (this volume 13). This portfolio system "encourages high standards from the start, thereby encouraging maximum development" (Burnham 137).

To Ford and Larkin, Burnham, and Elbow and Belanoff, a portfolio is a sampling of finished products selected by the student for evaluation. Although the instructor using this model may very well be concerned with the students' development as writers, as Burnham's remark indicates, essentially this portfolio model is grade driven and could be accurately labeled a *portfolio grading system*. It is grade driven because the rationale for using the portfolio framework grows out of an understanding that the student's written work will ultimately be evaluated.

However, portfolio grading, paradoxically, not only grows out of a concern for eroding standards, but also out of a concern for the overemphasis upon grades in writing courses. Christopher Burnham calls the students' "obsession" with grades a "major stumbling block" (125) to effective learning in the composition classroom and turns to portfolio grading as a means of mitigating the students' obsession with grades. Burnham concludes that the portfolio system "establishes a writing environment rather than a grading environment in the classroom" (137).

Thus, by addressing the issue of responding to the student's writing, Burnham wants to change the relationship between the student and the instructor. He wants to create a more facilitative role for the instructor, in accordance with suggestions about response from Donald Murray, Nancy Sommers, and Lil Brannon and C. H. Knoblauch. He not only wants to allow students to retain the rights to their own writing, he wants them to assume responsibility for their writing, asserting that portfolio grading "creates independent writers and learners" (136).

The question then of when and what to grade becomes quite significant. Although grading criteria must be established by instructors who employ portfolio grading, new criteria for grading the final drafts do not generally need to be developed. Presumably, instructors will bring to bear an already developed set of criteria for grading, applying these criteria rigorously to designated papers, thus protecting the integrity of their standards.[1] Nonetheless, a crucial question arises: when will student work receive a grade: at midterm, only at the end of the term, with each submission? Some instructors grade every draft and revision as students submit them, some grade only the revisions, some grade only papers designated as final drafts. In some portfolio-grading systems, the students select a specified number of final drafts at midterm and a second set at end of the term, while in other systems, all grading occurs at the end of the term.

Instructors using portfolio grading must decide when to offer grades. Grading every draft keeps the students informed, but, because even a temporary grade has an air of finality to many students simply because it is a grade, this policy may undercut the idea that each draft may potentially develop into a finished product. Grading revisions only may encourage the grade-obsessed student to revise if only to obtain a grade, thus introducing revision to some students who may otherwise lack the motivation to revise, but also reinforcing the primacy of grades.

By deferring grades until the end of the term, instructors can extend the duration of the "writing environment" that Burnham hopes to substitute for the "grading environment" in the course. However, if students are indeed obsessed with grades, as he argues, then it seems likely that for a substantial number of students, or perhaps for all of the students to varying extents, there will always be a grading environment lurking beneath the writing environment of the course. If instructors respond effectively and frequently and confer with students individually, they can keep students informed of their approximate standing in the course, possibly deflecting their grade anxiety, but it is disingenuous to claim that portfolio grading removes grade obsession. If the portfolio ultimately produces an accumulation of individual grades, grade obsession cannot really be eliminated although it certainly can be reduced.

Yet a larger issue arises, an issue related to one's pedagogical assumptions about the significance of grades. Burnham discusses the portfolio system as a means of leading to student development, a development inevitably measured by the final grades earned by the student's portfolio. Inherent in this model is the idea that students can improve the writing, and thus the grade, by revising and selecting their best work. Inevitably, then, instructors using portfolio grading must address the issue of grade inflation. Although one of the motivating forces behind portfolio grading, as we have seen, is protecting grading standards, the system itself is designed to promote better writing by the students, and it stands to reason that many students are going to be submitting portfolios that consist of writing better than they might be able to produce in a classroom employing a traditional grading system. Will instructors raise the standards so high that even the improved writing in the portfolios falls into the usual grading curve? Or, and this seems much more likely, will the grades themselves on the whole be somewhat higher because of the portfolio approach despite higher standards? Should higher grades be of significant concern to instructors? Do higher grades mean "grade inflation"? What is the role of grades in writing courses? Portfolio grading compels instructors to consider these important questions.

Finally, portfolio grading presents problems to instructors in handling the paper load. Since most programs suggest or stipulate a certain number of assignments per term, instructors using the portfolio system must determine how they will count assignments. Will newly revised papers count as new assignments? By doing so, the instructor can keep the paper load from mushrooming. Let's focus on a course that requires seven papers in a semester (the situation at my institution), with the understanding that the portfolio will consist of four final drafts selected by the student. If instructors count revisions of papers 1 and 2 as papers 3 and 4, their paper load will be less because students will still only produce seven drafts for them to read. On the other hand, the students' options at the end of the term will be reduced by this method of counting; they will have to select four final drafts from only five different pieces in progress.

To ensure students the full choice of seven, however, instructors commit themselves to more responding. In our hypothetical case, they will read at least nine drafts, seven first drafts, and revisions of the first two papers. Thus a routine decision actually has important pedagogical implications.

Several methods of controlling the paper load do exist. One is to divide the term in half, asking students to produce two miniportfolios. At midterm, for instance, in the situation already described, students are required to submit two final drafts for grading out of the first four assigned papers. At the end of the term, students must select two of the final three assigned papers for grading. Thus the paper load is under greater control because the students cannot continue work on the first four papers after midterm. On the other hand, Burnham's desire to create a writing environment rather than a grading environment will be affected because grades will become of primary concern not once but twice during the term.

Another method for controlling the paper load is to limit the number of drafts students may write of individual papers. Without such a limit, some students will rewrite and resubmit papers almost weekly, adding greatly to the paper load; of course, one can argue that such students are developing as writers in an important way. Deadlines for revisions of papers can also be used to control the paper load since "real" writers always work under deadlines. They may revise and revise and revise, but ultimately they must conclude. Instructors may allow students to revise a given assignment as often as they wish but within a designated period of time. Another method of controlling the paper load is to limit the number of revisions students may submit at one time or to designate specific times when revisions may be submitted. Late in the term, industrious students may have revisions of three or four different assignments ready to be submitted; some limit on the number they may hand in at one time can help instructors manage the course more effectively. Stipulating that revisions can be handed in only on certain days can allow instructors to plan their time for responding more efficiently.

Eventually, the end of the term arrives, and for many instructors using portfolio grading, the paper load explodes. Portfolios of four papers or more per student come in at the end of the term and must be graded quickly in order to submit final grades on time. Holistic grading can make the paper load manageable as instructors offer no comments but just a letter grade on each final draft. Grading portfolios at the end of the term undeniably requires more time than grading a single final exam or final paper would. However mundane these questions of handling the paper load may seem, the answers one supplies affect the entire portfolio grading system because many of these decisions may influence the relationship between students and their instructors, and some may influence, or be influenced by, instructors' grading criteria and standards.

To sum up then, a portfolio grading system defines a portfolio as a sampling of students' finished writing selected by the students for evaluation. Portfolio grading offers instructors a means of keeping their grading standards high while employing their usual grading criteria, it presents one potential method for reducing students' obsession with grades and transforming the classroom environment into one more engaged with writing than grading, and it increases instructors' paper loads. Instructors' decisions about when to grade and how to manage the paper load raise complications because they affect the relationship between instructors and their students. Thus, teachers planning on implementing portfolio grading need to consider carefully how they will do so in a way that will keep their practice in line with their own theoretical assumptions about writing and about composition pedagogy.

The second, newer, portfolio system model I will call the "holistic portfolio." The holistic portfolio is a response to continued theorizing about the nature of the composing process. Louise Wetherbee Phelps argues that theories underlying teaching practices evolve toward greater depth, and she sketches a hierarchy of response models to student writing beginning with one she labels "evaluative attitude, closed text" (49). In this model, the instructor treats the student text as "self-contained, complete in itself . . . a discrete discourse episode to be experienced more or less decontextually" (50). This concept of response to a text views reading as evaluation; instructors responding in this model may speak of "grading a stack of papers." The next response model described by Phelps is one she calls "formative attitude, evolving text" (51). Instructors read students' drafts as part of a process of evolution, thus entering into and influencing the students' composing process. In this model of response, instructors locate "learning largely in the actual composing process" (53).

Phelps describes a third model of response as "developmental attitude, portfolio of work": "Whereas the first group of teachers reads a 'stack' of papers and the second reads collected bits, scraps, and drafts of the composing process, the third reads a 'portfolio' of work by one student" (53). Phelps elaborates on two ways to work with portfolios, describing first the portfolio grading model we have already examined, which she dubs "the weak form." In this approach, she writes, "teachers continue to read and grade individual papers, attempting to help students perfect each one" (53). As Phelps has described the models of response, we can see that she has first described portfolio assessment used in a programmatic approach to large-scale decision making about student proficiency and placement. Her second model fairly accurately describes the portfolio-grading approach of Ford and Larkin and Burnham, elaborated upon somewhat in her depiction of "the weak form" of her third response model.

In the second method of using portfolios, Phelps also describes a different portfolio system. Some instructors employ portfolios because they wish to respond from a *"developmental* perspective." From this perspective, the student writing "blurs as an individual entity" and is treated as a sample "excerpted from a stream of writing stimulated by the writing class, part of the 'life text' each literate person continually produces" (53). Phelps concludes:

> The reader's function is [to read] through the text to the writer's developing cognitive, linguistic, and social capacities as they bear on writing activities. The set of a single writer's texts to which the reader has access, either literally or through memory, is the corpus from which the reader tries to construct a speculative profile of the writer's developmental history and current maturity. (53)

This definition of portfolio no longer serves as an analogy to the commercial artist's carefully assembled portfolio of a representative sampling of her best work. Instead it more closely resembles an archivist's collection of a writer's entire *oeuvre*. Instructors do not deal with selected writings but evaluate the entire output of the student writer. The implications of such a definition are quite different from those of the portfolio grading model defined by Ford and Larkin, Burnham, and Elbow and Belanoff.

While portfolio grading systems are driven by pedagogical concerns with fair grading as well as with composing process theory, the holistic portfolio system is primarily driven by a pedagogical concern with composing process theory. Although Knoblauch and Brannon's polemic *Rhetorical Traditions and the Teaching of Writing* does not discuss portfolio evaluation, its view of the composing process might very readily lead to it. Knoblauch and Brannon describe the "myth of improvement" that has stifled writing instruction by focusing on the kind of evaluation Phelps details in her first model of response (evaluative attitude, closed text). Knoblauch and Brannon suggest that "the most debilitating illusion associated with writing instruction is the belief that teachers can, or at least ought to be able to, control writers' maturation, causing it to occur as the explicit consequence of something they do or ought to do" (165). This illusion is reductionist, leading to a view of the writing course "in minimal functionalist terms" (165). This "myth of improvement" has produced a definition of teaching and curricular success that stresses "trivial but readily demonstrable short-term 'skill' acquisitions" and has led some teachers "to imagine it is fair to 'grade on improvement,' mistaking a willingness to follow orders for real development" (165).

While Knoblauch and Brannon's book remains controversial, their critique of "the myth of improvement" cogently articulates many instructors' reservations about grading practices based on the artificial academic calendar, a system that demands students learn at a given pace, defined by a ten-week quarter, a fourteen-week trimester, or a sixteen-week semester. Knoblauch and Brannon conclude by arguing that "symptoms of growth—the willingness to take risks, to profit from advice, to revise, to make recommendations to others—may appear quickly, even if improved *performance* takes longer" (169).

For instructors whose conception of the composing process is compatible with the developmental schemes underlying Knoblauch and Brannon's book and Phelps's third model of response, the holistic portfolio should have great appeal. It presents these instructors with difficult decisions, however, in the same areas that the portfolio grading system presented its practitioners: grading criteria and standards, the teacher-student relationship, and handling the paper load.

While upholding grading standards was the catalyst for portfolio grading, holistic portfolio systems appear to be less concerned with the notion of grading standards, at least in traditional terms. Because the holistic portfolio system does not focus instructors' attention on specific final drafts, it does present instructors with some major decisions about criteria for the final evaluation.

Several possibilities exist. Instructors may create a grading system that weights final drafts but also grades draft materials, notes, peer commentary, and so on. Counting the number of drafts or the variety of included materials is a way to "grade" preliminary materials. However, any counting method might distort the course's emphasis on development by encouraging students to create "phony" drafts, drafts written after the fact simply to pad the portfolio (just as many of us used to compose outlines *after* completing high school term papers as a way of meeting a course requirement).

Another way to grade the final portfolio is more holistic, and thus probably "purer" in the sense that it avoids treating individual drafts as "collected bits, scraps, and drafts" and treats portfolios as part of "the life text" (Phelps 53). The instructor looks for "symptoms of growth," to borrow Knoblauch and Brannon's phrase — "the willingness to take risks, to profit from advice, to revise, to make recommendations to others." Those students who demonstrate the greatest growth receive the highest grades, assuming that the instructor has developed a scale that measures growth — no small assumption.

While the holistic portfolio can fit very nicely into a developmental view of the composing process, it presents great difficulties in fitting at all into a traditional academic grading system and poses serious questions for instructors about how they see their writing courses fitting into the academy. This method of evaluation works most readily in a pass/no pass grading situation, indeed is an argument for such a grading system. But pass/no pass writing courses are the exception rather than the rule. Unfortunately, neither Knoblauch and Brannon nor Phelps really addresses the issue of how to grade in a writing course that emphasizes a developmental perspective on writing. It is conceivable that an instructor holistically evaluating a set of portfolios could assign an entire class of industrious students grades of A, having developed grading criteria that emphasize "symptoms of growth"; such an instructor can have rigorous standards in that only those students who have made the effort and demonstrated the growth receive the As. However, one suspects this instructor would face a one-to-one meeting with a concerned writing program administrator or department chair sometime after submitting the final grades.

Some compromise or accommodation must undoubtedly be made by instructors, perhaps along the lines discussed earlier of weighting final drafts. The important point to make here is that instructors should be aware of how the grading criteria they develop correlate with the theory underlying their use of portfolio evaluation.

Given the problematic nature of grading holistic portfolios, why would instructors adopt this model of the portfolio system? The holistic portfolio system offers distinct advantages in defining a healthy teacher-student relationship. Burnham's hopes of creating a writing environment rather than a grading environment are more readily realized in the holistic portfolio system. Because the final portfolio will not be graded in any traditional sense, because individual grades on drafts do not occur, in theory the classroom using the holistic portfolio can indeed become a writing environment, since there is no reason for it to become a grading environment, and the instructor can truly doff the evaluator's role and don instead the facilitator's role.

Burnham praises portfolio grading for encouraging students to assume responsibility for their learning; portfolio grading "creates independent writers and learners," he concludes (137). His point is that when students know that they can control their grades through extra effort in revising and through the selection process available to them prior to final evaluation, they become more responsible and more independent; in today's terminology, they become "empowered." However, the motivation comes from a concern with grades.

In the holistic portfolio system, the students are also afforded the opportunity to become more responsible, not for their grades so much as for their development. They can indeed become independent learners, independent of traditional grading obsessions as well. The teacher and student can become "co-writers," in Phelps's phrase. The emphasis in the course falls not on improving texts as a means of improving a grade but instead falls on developing as a writer, understanding that this development is more important than grades on individual texts.

Both models of portfolios, then, hope to free students of the tyranny of the grade. The portfolio grading system does so temporarily, but also readily accommodates the traditional institutional need for grades. The holistic portfolio system can indeed free students to become learners and writers for the duration of a writing course but only if instructors have resolved the essential conflict between their course and the institution's demand for traditionally meaningful grades.

In the final area of paper load, it seems most likely that the holistic portfolio system will produce a heavier paper load than the portfolio grading system will. Any schemes to limit students' output would likely conflict with the theoretical assumptions that lead to using the holistic portfolio system. Thus students' portfolios are likely to grow in length as well as in the hoped-for depth of development. At the end of the term, instructors must read not merely a specific number of selected final drafts, but entire portfolios, certainly a slower process. Periodic reading of the growing portfolios — which instructors taking such a developmental perspective will probably wish to do — may reduce the paper load at the end of the course since instructors can scan the familiar materials in the portfolio, but it will not significantly reduce the paper load so much as spread it out over the course of the term.

Instructors contemplating a portfolio system of either sort, or a hybrid version of the two models described, are faced with the need to answer some important questions for themselves before incorporating the system into their writing classes. Louise Wetherbee Phelps concludes her discussion by commenting that her depiction of response models represents an increasing growth on the part of instructors. She argues that "experience itself presses teachers toward increasingly generous and flexible conceptions of the text and the reading task" (59). If she is correct, as I think she is, then the movement in composition classrooms toward portfolio systems of one sort or another will accelerate as the emphasis on the composing process as central to writing courses continues.

As the profession continues to refine its thinking about composition pedagogy, portfolio systems seem destined to proliferate in use and to grow in significance. The portfolio system of evaluation has tremendous advantages, which are described throughout the rest of this book, but it also requires great thought on the part of instructors because a portfolio system implemented in a scattershot manner may well undercut the goals of a writing course. The portfolio offers instructors wonderful opportunities to bring their teaching practice in line with their theoretical assumptions about writing and about teaching, but that convergence can only occur if instructors ask themselves the right—and the tough—questions and work out the answers that best provide what both instructors and students need in the writing course.

## Note

1. I am assuming that instructors themselves will grade the papers. Ford and Larkin describe a programmatic use of portfolio grading wherein the portfolios are graded by a team of graders not including the students' instructor. My interest in this essay, however, is in the issues faced by individual instructors who do not have the power to implement such grading practice but must conduct their own evaluations.

# 14

# Portfolios
## *Solution to a Problem*

Kathy McClelland
*University of California, Santa Barbara*

I confess right now—I used to hate grading. It was the one aspect of teaching that methods classes hadn't prepared me for or I hadn't figured out for myself. I could always get papers graded and back to the students quickly enough, and I felt I was being fair—I always based my evaluations on the rubric that we'd discussed in class. But I was puzzled (and sometimes hurt) by some students' responses to their grades: "I worked for three hours on this paper! Why isn't it an *A*?" or "There's nothing wrong with it! I should get an *A*!" I hated having to justify a grade to a student and trying to explain that three hours of work or mechanical and grammatical correctness weren't enough to insure an *A*. But I really resented the office hours I spent talking with a student about why the paper wasn't an *A* instead of working together on a draft of the next assignment.

I finally admitted to myself that I had let grading force me into a situation I didn't like: I had to be an authority, telling students what to do and how to do it, instead of someone who could work with and guide students as they learned to write. Students wanted me to teach in terms of how to write an *A* paper because I let it happen—and that was my problem.

As I tried to work through this dilemma, I realized something: Students needed grades (or so they thought) because they came from a system that had taught them that grades indicate "How I'm doing." What that really meant, I finally figured out, was that grades told them how close they were to the right answer, to the *A*. And grades told them how well they were doing in comparison to the rest of the class, how much harder they had to work to be the best, how close they were to "doing what the teacher wanted," how close they were to "getting it right."

But their ideas about what I "wanted" and "getting it right" didn't have anything to do with how I wanted to teach writing. What I really wanted was to change that attitude and have students focus on texts, readers, revision, development, and potential—not on grades. I realized that as long as I bought into the perspective that grades were the most important aspect of learning to write by grading individual papers, telling students why each wasn't a B or an A, I could never really teach them anything about writing. I decided I had to put evaluation in a different place, a more appropriate place—at the end of the term when we were done with the work we wanted and needed to do.

So, I took a risk—I decided to try portfolio evaluation. I didn't know that much about it, but I had the perfect opportunity to experiment since the classes I was teaching were small and designed to be workshops. I made up my own rules, ones I thought I'd be comfortable with: nothing the students wrote would get a grade, but I would keep track of whether or not they did the homework and drafts, their attendance, conferences, class participation, etc.

## Portfolios—The Early Days

On the first day of the next term, I presented my students with a choice: we could work under a traditional grading method—each paper having a specific due date and getting one, final grade (no rewriting for a higher one)—or we could focus on writing by using the artist's portfolio idea, working together on five papers that I would grade at the end of the term. I described the rules I'd follow and told them I would ask for a self-evaluation at the end of the term; we would meet to review the portfolio and discuss their final grades then.

My arguments against writing to a grade must have been convincing (either that or *my* choice was obvious) for both classes I was teaching agreed to portfolio evaluation. We made a deal to not even mention grades throughout the term and just carry on as usual. And amazingly enough, it was that simple.

"As usual" meant that we did all the same things we had done before in my classes—learning to write by writing, reading, and talking. We examined what worked and what didn't and why in both the texts the students were working on and the ones we read;

we examined demands that texts and rhetorical situations made on us as writers and that we as readers made on texts. And we wrote and responded and revised and wrote some more. But something happened because we didn't talk about grades and papers weren't "due" for a few weeks—a real workshop atmosphere developed quickly. Our talk focused on texts and our concerns were with choices—the ones that helped texts be successful, not which one was "right" or which would get the writer an *A*.

I decided to let the students self-select into response groups after they had gotten to know each other and we had practiced responding and figured out what kinds of responses writers really need. I kept track of their work through letters, checking with them in class or in conferences. I tried to help them keep up by assigning "first draft days" every couple of weeks as a reminder that they should go ahead and start another paper. Other days were "response group days," class periods set aside for them to work with their group members on revisions that they wanted more response to.

I was excited to realize the students were learning something about writing when they began to value working with each other, getting and giving response to their work. Response group sessions became intense; I often had to ask a group to stop because another class was waiting for the room. And, towards the end of the term the requests for extra "group days" became numerous, so some lessons got condensed or cut. (This still happens; I've learned to leave the last few class periods free so we can add group days if we need them.) The students seemed to revel in the fact that they got to make the decision about which paper they worked on for any group session; they reported feeling in complete control of their own writing. I began to suspect that having so much control over their writing gave the students a sense that what they were doing was real; they began to talk and think as writers.

My suspicions were confirmed whenever I'd eavesdrop as they worked in groups; I'd hear them say, "I really need response to this draft; it's really rough. I'm not sure which way I want it to go. I want to know what you guys think," or "I tried to add examples in that part you couldn't see last time; tell if it works now." I liked that; they were thinking about their audience, thinking of their writing as their own, and wanting it to be good in and of itself— not for an *A*.

This control that they adopted allowed my role as authority to change, too; I was no longer the "expert" who was there to direct and determine what went on. I became, in a sense, just another reader for them. Students came to me more often to talk—about writing, not grades—and we worked on their texts together, addressing concerns about writers' choices, not what was "right" or what I "wanted" the paper to be. I never got bored with this new role; I rather enjoyed being able to validate their group members' responses as I added my own. And I never found myself burdened with papers, something that was a pleasant surprise. I'd respond to drafts when they asked for response, and with everyone working at a different pace, I felt I had enough time and energy to respond to the few papers I got every class period. I never felt overworked. But most importantly for me, I was no longer the authority who decided when to start and when to stop a piece of writing; the students were in complete control of that.

When it came time to think about grades that first term, my students admitted in their self-evaluations and our final conferences that they were not afraid to hold their work up against the set of criteria for good writing we'd developed over the course of the term — because they now knew why those criteria were important. We agreed that writing in C portfolios reflected competent writing in the sense that the papers each had a point, had examples, and were free of error. But writing in B and A portfolios reflected more thinking, more elaboration and explanation, more crafting, more concern with the language. We agreed we wouldn't give each paper a grade then average them to determine the final grade; instead, we agreed to read the portfolio and get a general feel of the writer's ability. I was delighted to find that the students and I did agree about their grades when I read their self-evaluations; they reported they had learned about writing by focusing on texts, by being readers and responders, by being writers. They had thoughtful reasons for the grades they proposed: "I didn't work as much as I could have on P3 — the transitions between paragraphs are still rough so it just doesn't flow well. But P5 is the best one I've ever done; I did a good job of describing the way I felt. I think overall I do better than just making a point with examples, but I need to work on crafting. I think overall I'm a B writer." I was delighted to be able to agree, and to put a + on the B because that student had worked hard on multiple drafts, revisions, and responses for his group members.

## Portfolios — The Adjustments

For the first time, I felt that my students had actually learned some-thing about writing — and that grades were no longer an obstacle. Since then, I've structured the classes and portfolio evaluation in much the same basic way. I vary the number of papers depending on the length of the term, but I always include a self-evaluation as part of the portfolio. I keep a record of their homework assignments, drafts, conferences, attendance, and participation, but I've had to eliminate the end-of-the-term conference now that I have seventy— five or more students each term. And I've had to refine my response practices; I make it a point to respond to the first draft of the first two papers (long weekends, but I know they're coming), but after that I let them decide when they need my response and to what. And they can choose the kind of response they want—either a written one or a conference. From the ones who want written re- sponses, I get notes like this one: "Kathy, this is P3D2 [paper 3 of the 5 required, the second draft]—would you tell me what you think of my voice and if I've used enough examples. Can you see what I'm saying?" And I get longer, more reflective ones that help me when I try to decide how to respond: "Kathy, this is my writing from over the weekend. It's something that comes from the heart of a new college student struggling to adjust to a new way of life. I like some of the ideas I have in it but I'm kind of worried about the flow of the subject. It is kind of choppy. What do you think?" I find myself taking home a few papers after each class to read and respond to; I don't find this burdensome at all. I write back, answering their questions, adding comments about anything else I want to call to their attention, or I make notes about things I want to say in a conference.

I have made one other significant change: I don't give students a choice about portfolios anymore. I tell them the first day that I use the portfolio method only—but I tell them why. I explain that I feel writing to a grade (it's the one thing I don't "want" them to do) is not what I believe education or learning to write is all about. For the most part, the initial reactions I get are similar to this one: "It is such a relief knowing that this class is there to help me improve instead of evaluate and categorize me." But not all students like the idea of portfolios and this has created a new dilemma for me.

When I first encountered students who resisted the portfolio evaluation idea, I thought that they had not heard my message or didn't share my views; they felt that I was there to tell them what to do and how to do it—and the portfolio system didn't allow for that. Most often, these students show up in my office early in the term with one of two now-familiar complaints: "I don't know where I stand; I need you to grade my papers so I know how much harder I have to work to get an *A*." Or, "I still don't know what you want; tell me what I need to do to get an *A*." And while I've never really solved this dilemma, I have become comfortable dealing with these students.

I explain again that I'm not as concerned with their GPA as I am with teaching writing, that I want to allow them to learn to write, that I want them to do the best writing they can, that I want them to learn to make decisions. But some never do understand; they press me for exact answers, and I end up explaining that there isn't a magic formula for getting an *A* for me to give them. If they continue to worry about grades during the term, I give them "guesstimates" of a grade, but even that doesn't seem to satisfy some, so the most recent revision to the portfolio process I've made is to institute an optional mid-term evaluation. I'll review the contents of the portfolio and give it a grade (that has no bearing on their final one) if they'll do a mid-term self-evaluation, one that is extensive and asks them to discuss the status and revision plans for each piece and their estimate of the quality of their writing and their efforts. Those students who want mid-term evaluations — about twenty out of seventy-three last term — find comfort in having me put a grade on unfinished work; they tell me that helps them know how much harder they need to work to get the grade they want — especially if I give the portfolio a *C* when they think it's a *B+* or *A−*. They learn, too, that their evaluation of their work is a bit inflated, and some learn to refine their judgements. They seem more comfortable with the course after that, more willing to work and take risks. I admit to them (and to myself) that I feel very uncomfortable putting grades on unfinished work, but after I see how helpful this is to them, I bury my discomfort and try to see the situation from their point of view: Grades are a motivating factor for some students.

Those grade-conscious worriers are rare, though. Most of my students seem excited by the freedom portfolios gives them; in letters they tell me, "I much, much prefer this idea of having a chance to keep improving, keep working without having the pressure of having to do your best at a specific time" and "I think the portfolio idea is great because it takes the pressure out of writing each individual paper. It places more emphasis on writing and the process of writing, rather than placing unnecessary stress on 'getting a good grade.'" That student has said it best for me: because we can adopt this different perspective on evaluation, the students feel as if they are learning something — and they are. I continually get comments from them that tell me they are looking at education and writing: "The portfolio method seems to give a more comprehensive learning process" and "I think it's a good way to prepare for real life assignments. This gives us a chance to learn how to be responsible workers and produce our best work in a limited amount of time [I think he meant the term]." And students often tell me that they like the "chance to develop my papers beyond their usual extent." All these comments tell me that, for most students, attitudes, and perspectives are changing, and portfolio evaluation is largely responsible for it. But the portfolio seems to aggravate one particular problem for some of them — procrastination.

The students who can only get the work done if they have strict deadlines imposed by teachers often have a hard time dealing with the freedom and responsibility portfolios demand of them; I've found myself warning these students about procrastination (and the consequence in terms of their final grade) earlier and earlier each term. I've become strict about expecting and checking for drafts and revisions on group days; I circulate and check with the members of each group and record which draft of what paper each is working on. Some students never do anything about the procrastination, but I've discovered that they are also the ones who propose a C or D for their final grade because they know they haven't done the work they could have and have settled for papers that are "just okay," as they put it.

## Portfolios — Finally Being Comfortable with Grading

Using portfolio evaluation over the past seven years and in fifty-some classes, I've become more and more convinced that this is the only way I can teach and evaluate the writing my students do. Why? When I am asked that question by colleagues who don't use portfolio evaluation, I always cite the one aspect of the whole situation that seems most significant to me: Portfolio evaluation encourages us, even forces us, to focus on texts and not on grades. This focus changes the whole learning and writing situation in my classes from an artificial one that demands a work be begun, finished, and evaluated in a week or two, to a real one that allows texts to grow and mature as writers create, explore, risk, fail, and succeed over the course of the term. How? The key for me — and for my students — seems to be time.

Time allows the students to develop a sense of authority over their texts; one recently affirmed this for me in her weekly letter: "Instead of turning in a paper written the night before, we actually get time to work on them (that is when the time is available). The feedback is also very helpful. So the papers are definitely better quality; it [the process?] trains the writer to think a lot more about what is being written." As they respond to each other, they learn to make demands on writers: "But I want to know what happened so I can understand WHY this was so important." And they remember those demands when they become writers: "I tried to add detail to show the backyard so you could see why I was afraid. . . ."

I think time allows the students to see my role differently, too; I become the practiced reader who can show them how to read, to respond, who validates their group members' responses and has suggestions if they get stuck. The time portfolios afford us to work on drafts also gives me more opportunities to work with students in conferences. I require two, at least, and schedule one early in the term; after that, they are free to come whenever they wish (I've learned to carry a calendar with me so I can schedule appointments with the ones who don't get to see me during office hours). After they see me struggle to understand their texts and how I do it as I read, react, and question, after I suggest things for them to consider as they revise their papers, they know my responses are real, that I don't have an agenda for them to discover.

I notice a change as the term progresses: the grades that the portfolio will get seem to become secondary to each student's sense of how good she or he can make each paper. At least that's what it looks like to me as I read their letters and listen to them in conferences. They don't talk in terms of *A* papers or "getting it right" any more. The students usually make some joke about the amount of reading I have to do when they turn their portfolios in, but I surprise them (and myself) by confessing I'm actually looking forward to it. And I find myself admitting to colleagues who express the same kind of dread that I don't hate grading anymore; I'm anxious to read the final drafts, to see what choices the writers made, what responses they addressed and how.

When I get the portfolios, I read the papers first, and that's all I do—no marking, no comments. Then the self—evaluation. I usually find myself nodding in agreement with them as they discuss the strengths and weaknesses of each paper, and if by the end of this process my evaluation is different from the grade they propose for their work, it is usually very slight. That's when I turn to my record book and consider attendance, homework, participation, effort, etc. to help me arbitrate the difference.

But sometimes I do run into students who still have an over-inflated sense of their abilities; they are often the ones I've worried about all term for one reason or another. I agonize a bit over their grades, but I know other things about these students that help me evaluate their work and their efforts—that they rarely participated, that their responses to group members were weak, that they didn't really make an effort, that they didn't take advantage of the opportunities for responses and learning they were offered, that they refused to accept authority for their work. Their writing reflects all this; it's perfunctory and undeveloped. I don't see evidence that they tried to learn anything. So I don't agonize when I put a C− or a D on the grade sheet instead of the A they think they deserve because they were "always there and did everything." I know that I'm using the same criteria for them as I am for all the others, and I know my evaluation is fair.

But the writing of the students who did learn something and fairly evaluate their own work is always a joy to read. "I like the idea that I can use what I learn on all my papers before they are graded," one student recently told me; that suddenly made a lot of sense. He had learned something about using examples towards the end of the term; he had gone back and revised all his papers, incorporating examples in different ways, and his writing overall was better for it. Portfolio evaluation gave him the time and the opportunity to learn something; that's why grades seem — and are — fair now. One young man who struggled through several revisions of all his papers may have said it best: "I feel comfortable being judged on the total skills learned in the quarter. My first paper would have ruined my opportunity to get a good grade if I had to turn it in the beginning of the quarter." That's a very true statement in more ways than one, and I think it sums up best the reason I believe most students are comfortable with portfolio evaluation by the end of the term.

Thanks to portfolios, I can teach, and my students can learn to write. I can see their attitudes toward writing and grades change as they become confident writers and demanding readers. But most of all, I feel comfortable with grades and grading, and so do the students; I know portfolio evaluation has allowed me to achieve that.

# 15

# A Basic Writer's Portfolio

Sharon Hileman and Beverly Case
*Sul Ross State University*

Basic Writing classes at Sul Ross State University have undergone a number of changes since being implemented in the fall of 1982, but the problems in teaching Basic Writing have remained much the same: how to give students with weak academic backgrounds and low academic self-esteem maximum opportunities to develop their inadequate reading and writing skills for college-level work. A portfolio system eventually became our answer to the question of how we could best help students develop their writing skills.

Students in our English Department's earliest remedial courses, which were established before either of us began teaching at the university, had to pass exams in spelling, grammar, writing, and reading to pass the Basic English course. Grades were assessed only as pass or fail. Under this system, failure rates soared as high as 62 percent (fall, 1983).

In fall 1987, we implemented several changes in the course requirements. We complied with an administrative request to give letter grades instead of pass/fail designations; we dropped the spelling and grammar exam requirements; we kept the required 10.0 passing score on the standardized Nelson Denny Reading Test (offered four times a semester); and we instituted a holistically evaluated final exam (a writing sample), to be read by faculty members who taught Basic Writing.

Since this exit exam determines whether students pass the course, we wanted to be sure our students went into their final examination with adequate skills and self-confidence. The lab portfolio was our solution, and we have seen failure rates decline since we began

*Table 15—1*  **Pass and fail rates in Basic English classes.**

|  | No. of sections | No. of students | Pass | | Fail | | Withdraw | |
|---|---|---|---|---|---|---|---|---|
| *Fall 1986* | | | | | | | | |
| No portfolios | 3 | 111 | 50 | (45%) | 51 | (46%) | 10 | (9%) |
| *Fall 1987* | | | | | | | | |
| With portfolios | 3 | 90 | 52 | (58%) | 25 | (29%) | 12 | (13%) |
| *Fall 1988* | | | | | | | | |
| With portfolios | 2 | 72 | 54 | (75%) | 9 | (12.5%) | 9 | (12.5%) |

using it. (In fall 1986, our combined fail rate was 46 percent; in fall 1988, our second year of using portfolios, the fail rate dropped to 13 percent. See table 15—1.)

The major reasons for our initiating the lab portfolio system were (1) to increase lab tutor/student contact, (2) to build student self-confidence, (3) to provide a means to chart student progress and to individualize programs, and (4) to encourage students to develop self-discipline and become responsible for their own goal setting.

Our goals came partly from our evaluation of the Basic Writing students themselves. We find that our Basic Writing students are weak in grammatical skills, self-deprecating about their academic abilities, and unrealistic about their goals. Conditioned often by years of failure yet socially promoted, they know where they want to go (law school, medical school, Wall Street) but do not know the steps they must take to bring their inadequate skills up to college level. In assessing our students, we decided that individualized instruction, positive reinforcement, and self-discipline were vital.

Sul Ross is a small school, but our composition classes, especially Basic Writing, tend to be very large (about thirty-five per section). Unable to give individualized attention in classes this size, we knew students would have to obtain additional help from tutors (graduate students) in our Writing Lab. The portfolio requirement insures that students seek assistance at the lab on a weekly basis. Our students' papers and revisions must be placed in their portfolios in the lab by the dates specified on returned papers. This means students must make appointments with tutors to discuss and revise their work. No papers are filed unless lab tutors have gone over revisions with students; then the original and all drafts are placed in the portfolio.

We assign a course letter grade at the end of the semester, evaluating the lab portfolio after the student has passed the Nelson

Denny Reading Test and the final exam writing sample. The student's course grade may be based on the portfolio alone, or it may come from a combination of in-class grades (journals, homework, and so on) and the portfolio grade. Both of us evaluate portfolios for improvement as well as ending performance, and students know that an incomplete portfolio may jeopardize their grade for the course. Thus the portfolios become both the means by which students develop the writing skills necessary to pass the final exam and the end product by which they earn a letter grade for the course.

Our second goal, building student self-confidence, is much harder to assess. As Virginia Perdue has explained in a discussion of confidence versus authority, strategies are needed to "build personal confidence and social authority ... [to] help dilute the concentration of authority in the teacher and give students a stake in what goes on both in the classroom and in their own writing" (15). Our lab tutors, as well as the Writing Lab itself, help diffuse the authority of the teacher and create a more expanded sense of classroom. As students write in a different environment, scheduling their own times and work groups, they often begin to feel more comfortable and more confident about their writing abilities.

Students spend fifteen minutes to one hour per week at the lab, working with tutors to review and revise papers. One of our tutors believes that fifteen-minute sessions are ideal: "The brief time is not as big a threat to the student and there is plenty of time to concentrate on and explain one or two problems." Tutorial sessions may be one-on-one, or tutors may work with small groups of three or four students. In such an informal atmosphere, the students are more inclined to relax and express their fears and problems concerning writing. Conversely, tutors can more easily point out and praise accomplishments.

Another way we try to build self-confidence with our portfolio system is through positive evaluation of student papers. Many Basic Writing students' papers are very poor early in the semester, yet we do not want to discourage students by giving failing grades. Using a portfolio system, it is not necessary to grade an individual paper. Instead, we can evaluate a whole semester's collection of papers, a collection in which each paper is seen as part of the whole, not as a final accomplishment itself.

Thus, at the beginning of a semester we give no indication of the grade a paper might receive. About midterm, we begin to talk about evaluation procedures with our classes in terms of whether their papers would be passed or not passed by the committee evaluating the final exam. Students may do small-group evaluations of each other's papers as they practice holistic grading procedures themselves, and we will provide "guesses" if students want to know our opinions of specific papers. Near the end of the semester, instructors may exchange sets of papers or ask other department members to pass or fail a set of papers so students can have a "practice" assessment from a person who will be reading the actual final.

Some students have trouble adjusting to a "no-grade" class, but lab tutors agree that the no-grade method is less stifling for those Basic Writing students who have often been programmed for failure throughout public school and expect nothing different when they find themselves in remedial English in college.

Students do receive suggestions for revising each paper, however. Our procedure has been to have students do prewriting and writing in the classroom, but we have then tried different methods of returning papers, sometimes giving them to students in class and sometimes leaving them with lab tutors. Either way, students must go to the lab to revise and file papers.

Instructors may vary methods of evaluating papers, but error analysis and content comments are both included. We do not want students to be obsessed with error, yet we do want them to work consistently on the problems that interfere with the communication of their ideas. Early in the semester, students may need to have problem areas specifically located and identified; later they can "match" the errors checked on a checklist with underlined problem areas in their own papers.

Lab tutors have indicated that such a checklist makes their discussions with students productive because students can usually identify errors themselves and tutors can quickly see what grammatical areas instructors are emphasizing. By the end of a semester, checkmarks in the margin of a paper may be the only means used to identify the presence of errors and alert students to the need for corrections.

To encourage content revisions, primarily the development of ideas, both of us write marginal comments on the papers. At this point our tutors are especially useful because they can brainstorm with students during revision sessions. Since many of our students are from primarily oral cultures (inner-city Blacks; bilingual, border-dwelling Hispanics), being able to talk through ideas with tutors and receive immediate oral feedback undoubtedly helps them gain an understanding of "development." Instead of thinking a two-sentence paragraph is adequate to discuss a topic, students learn how to elaborate concepts fully for an audience.

One of our best experiences with content revisions occurred when a class had limited access to several computers near the end of a semester. A tutor worked with two students at a time as they wrote and revised their assignment using our two lab computers. Most students were so pleased with the "perfect product" that could be created by the computer printer that they spent extra hours working on revisions. Students seemed to be able really to read their own papers for the first time, and as a result expanded and reshaped ideas.

Recently, we surveyed students to see how they evaluate the portfolio system. Only one respondent said the portfolio had not been helpful but explained that the problem resulted from not attending lab. The portfolios were judged useful by 94 percent of the class, primarily because they liked getting immediate feedback from tutors and being able to concentrate on improvement from paper to paper. The students also believed that seeing all of their work at once was a definite advantage. One commented, "By looking back at my folder I can see where I'm going wrong."

Although the students' seeing where they are "going wrong" is one reason we require portfolios, we were pleased that the students found the portfolios helpful devices for correcting errors, learning to edit, and seeing where they were "going right." Half the students thought that they should evaluate their portfolios often themselves, at least an average of once a month. Their willingness to do self-evaluation this often makes us think that such evaluations also give them that sense of accomplishment that we want for them. The fact that 38 percent of them checked increased self-esteem as a benefit of their portfolio evaluations reinforces our belief that teaching writing goes beyond a mere imparting of skills.

The portfolio also enables us to achieve our third goal, that of charting student progress and individualizing programs for students. Throughout the semester, instructors can review students' portfolios to check lab attendance and to discover areas of persistent weakness. Instructors and tutors can discuss a particular student's difficulties and devise new teaching and tutorial strategies to help the student. The portfolio review procedure helps instructors determine what to reemphasize or perhaps present in a new way to the entire class.

As portfolios grow, instructors can require that students do self-assessments of their work, focusing both on areas needing improvement and on areas showing major improvement already. These exercises generate such comments as "I've conquered the comma splice!" or "I need to work on spelling from now on" or "My paragraphs are longer and better. It's not taking so long to write them." Lab tutors believe self-assessments are valuable exercises because students who have been working hard can list areas of improvement, and students who have not been working can see clearly their need for more effort.

Another advantage of our lab portfolio system, then, is that students become responsible for setting their own goals. Our own final goal was that students would take responsibility for their lab attendance and improvement in their writing. That they do so was evident in such statements as "I went and looked in my folder and there was ... not one single paper ... because they were all in my bookbag," after which the student usually begins going to lab and turning in papers. One student responded that those who want to improve "will make it a point to show up for lab and check on their own work."

Having complete portfolios available for review near the end of the semester can also help students make choices about finishing the course. Some students, especially if they are nonnative speakers who plan to repeat Basic English, may decide to withdraw from the course to avoid receiving a failing grade. Other students realize they are "borderline" and that the final exam is the best means we have of indicating whether they are ready to go on to standard freshman composition. We know that the extra time and extra help we provide for Basic Writing students will not be available in other classes. For this reason we consider the student's performance on the exit exam a fairly good predictor of performance in the standard composition course. By requiring both portfolio development and a demonstration of skills in the exit exam, we guard against producing students who can only produce passing papers after having errors pointed out to them.

With the portfolio system, we have had very few students who have been surprised at exam results. By reviewing their portfolios and conferring with tutors and instructors, students can usually determine their likelihood of passing the final writing exam.

Students, then, benefit from portfolios in a number of ways, and so do we as instructors. One major advantage is postponing the evaluation process until the end of the semester. It takes very little time to look through a student's portfolio and determine its completeness, the degree of improvement it documents, and the level at which the student is writing at the end of the semester. In the two years we have used this system, no portfolio has received a failing grade. Since we see the portfolio's most important function as being a record of development, a portfolio would fail only if it were missing many assignments or if it revealed no improvement in any writing skills.

We feel we can evaluate students' writing most fairly by looking at a complete, contextualized body of work and by remembering that we are readers, not just graders, of papers. We like the model for reading student papers that "views the writing always from the context in which it was created and brings to each reading a sense of other writings, assignments, and responses" (Jones 24). The most reliable judgments occur when many writings from a given student are read and analyzed together.

As readers of Basic English students' portfolios, we know that our responses to an isolated paper turned in during the semester may be very different from our responses to that paper read as part of the body of the student's work. Because we think the entire corpus is important in Basic English, we do not recommend any selecting of papers for the portfolio. Our students create developmental rather than professional collections of their work, and we want to see the entire process of that development.

In this respect our use of portfolios differs from that in standard and advanced composition courses in which the portfolio consists of selected "best work." Such courses usually rely on portfolios alone, with no final exam, to determine a student's grade, although the portfolios may be evaluated by a group of faculty members not teaching the course (Elbow and Belanoff, Burnham, Ford and Larkin).

Overall, we believe our portfolio system incorporates the best features of other successful portfolio users: deferred grading (Burnham), emphasis on writing skills instead of grades (Bernthal and Ludwig), transformation of a product-oriented course into a process-oriented course (Bishop), and provision of opportunities for student self-evaluation (Bishop). We agree with Elbow and Belanoff that since portfolios are criterion-referenced means of evaluation, "the ideal end product is a population of students who have all finally passed because they have all been given enough time and help to do want we ask of them" (this volume, 13).

Our interests in combining portfolios with Basic Writing led us to conduct a survey of the instructors who teach such courses in our state's two- and four-year public colleges and universities. Although the response to the survey was generally positive, we did confirm that few use portfolios in Basic English. Those that do, however, do so enthusiastically. The reasons our respondents gave for using portfolios are very similar to our own: primarily to encourage students to revise papers, but also to allow student self—evaluation, to allow faculty to evaluate students' progress, and to motivate students. One comment on motivation was that portfolios give students a "visual symbol of achievement."

The system used most often consists of students' keeping their own portfolios, which are made up of short essays written in class and revised out of class. The content of the portfolios varies more, with some instructors including both paragraphs and essays, both in-class and out-of-class revisions, and free writing or brainstorming materials. Forty percent of our respondents allow students to select only their best work for their portfolios. The majority agree with us that the portfolio for Basic Writers should be all inclusive. One instructor summed up our own feelings with the statement that portfolios provide "a comprehensive, systematic method for evaluation of students' progress."

All instructors replied that they alone evaluate the portfolios, and all assign a letter grade for a course. The number of times portfolios are reviewed may vary from several times during the semester to only at midterm and semester's end. Twenty percent of the respondents use the portfolio alone to determine the course grade; most rely on the portfolio and other requirements, usually a final writing sample.

Comments from our own students and lab tutors as well as from other instructors who use portfolios in Basic Writing indicate that the portfolio method is valuable and should be part of Basic Writing courses. Portfolios used in conjunction with tutorial assistance are well suited to address the special problems of Basic Writing students: low self-esteem, weak self-discipline, expectations of negative reinforcement, and the need for immediate, individual feedback as often as possible. Although we realize there are other factors besides using portfolios that may explain the steadily improving results in our program, we are so pleased with the ways portfolios have increased collaborative learning in the lab setting and enabled us to achieve our goals that we plan to continue using and improving them.

# 16

# A Portfolio Approach to Teaching a Biology-linked Basic Writing Course

Pamela Gay
*State University of New York at Binghamton*

In Reading, Writing, & Biology Watching, a basic writing course I created to link with an introductory biology course for students admitted to the university through the Educational Opportunity Program (EOP), I asked students to represent themselves as developing writers at the beginning, middle, and end of the course. Twice during the course, students submitted portfolios accompanied by cover letters in which they discussed their work, assessed their progress, and set goals for their ongoing development as writers. I wanted them to take charge of their writing lives rather than become victims of their writing biographies.

Introducing what I call a portfolio approach was not easy. In the middle of the summer, these non-Anglo students from New York City suddenly found themselves located 200 miles from city streets on a campus insulated by foothills. While they had hoped to be admitted to this selective institution, they were somewhat awed by the prospect. They were both proud and afraid — could they compete?

They wanted in. And they were ready to do whatever I told them. Obviously (in their view) something was wrong with their writing, as they had been placed in the lowest-level basic-writing class (they quickly ascertained) and they would most likely be placed in basic writing again the next semester. What did they need to do to get beyond the open door? They waited to find out.

One student expected we would write an essay a week as she had done in a high school college-preparatory English class. She had turned in her writing, received a grade, and then gone on to the next assignment. In the end, the teacher averaged her collection of grades to arrive at a final course grade. Her writing at the beginning of this summer program was undeveloped, ambiguous, and riddled with grammatical and mechanical errors. She resisted revision and didn't like writing because of all the errors she made. What she wanted was to get this college writing requirement out of her way: she didn't need to write — she was planning to become a head nurse in a hospital.

All students in this biology-linked course were science oriented. They had selected this link rather than an arts and humanities or social-science link. Most viewed science and writing as polar opposites. One student set me straight at the outset: "Look, I'm interested in science, not writing." I learned that writing to him meant English, a class in which you either read about literature or wrote about your feelings. "I don't like to write about my feelings," he informed me, "just facts." Another student, originally from Haiti, expressed concern that being placed in basic writing would hold her back from pursuing a degree in biochemistry. She was determined to get the education her aunt desperately had wanted but could not pursue. This course was holding her back. And what did writing have to do with science anyway?

While basic writers typically do not see themselves as writers, this science-oriented group was even more resistant to the notion. I knew they could not represent themselves as writers unless they first saw themselves as writers. But who takes them seriously? Basic writers are the invisible writers. Like Ralph Ellison's invisible man, they walk around with writing that does not represent them or that even misrepresents them. Most of them have not even thought about representing themselves; instead they have let others take charge of their writing and learning. Who are they to question?

From the start I treated them as writers. How did they see themselves as writers? I asked. They wrote and shared responses and exchanged their school writing histories. What kind of writing had they done in school? Book reports, papers. Had they written in courses other than English? Very little. What did they know about science writing? Lab reports. Who were their favorite science writers? Most had only read science textbooks. No one knew that the *New York Times* devoted a section each week to science news. What kind of responses had their writing received in the past? Most couldn't recall any comments; some recalled marks of error they couldn't understand. Rewriting, if practiced at all, was mostly limited to error correction. This was how we began, sharing our past lives as writers, our writing anxieties, and our goals.

I explained to them that I had been meeting regularly for several months with their biology classroom and laboratory instructors to coordinate the curriculum. They looked puzzled, as if wondering how these two subjects could be related. Were they going to do more writing in biology? We had actually decided to link or coordinate the two courses rather than have the writing course serve the biology course. For example, while we were discussing our writing histories in the writing class, in biology their instructor asked them to write about themselves as science learners, and she shared with them her story about how she came to make a career in biology and what her specific interests were.

Selected chapters from *Biological Science: An Ecological Approach* (1987) served as the basic text for the biology course. Topics included cell structure and reproduction, genes, Mendel's rules, DNA, biological classification of plants, and evolutionary change. In the writing course a packet of related readings I compiled served as a resource for writing and discussion. Readings included selections from *The Lives of a Cell* by biology watcher Lewis Thomas, whose work gave me the idea for this course; writings by Helen Keller and W. I. B. Beveridge on the power and importance of observation; a demonstration of careful observation by Loren Eiseley; selected writings by Stephen Jay Gould (on race and gender); a philosophical essay on nature by a graduate student teaching in the program; "Botany" from *The Notebooks of Leonardo DaVinci* (MacCurdy); sample field-notebook entries by a college senior majoring in biology; reading selections about women in science and cultural considerations in learning biology; selected articles from the *New York Times* and *Scientific American*; and a collection of viewpoints concerning animal rights, a social issue in biology. We decided to work collaboratively during the second half of the course on two writing projects, a lab report and a position paper.

I explained to the students that I would not grade each piece of their writing; however, it would be evaluated, as Berthoff (1978, 4–5) defines evaluation, that is, responded to by me and other writers in the class. (Their biology instructor would respond to a draft of their end-of-course position paper.) Through reading, writing, and talking about writing, they would slowly begin to develop evaluation criteria for particular writing situations. What makes a good field notebook entry? How is a biology watcher's notebook entry different? At the middle and end of the course, I would ask them to submit a portfolio of selected writings along with a letter assessing their work, progress, and goals. We would then arrive at a course progress grade and a final grade.

While they liked the idea of their writing not being graded in piecemeal fashion, they were also uneasy. How would they know how they were doing? What if they thought they were doing excellent work, and the teacher thought their work was mediocre and they didn't find out until it was too late? They wanted to know what the teacher wanted. They could select what to include in their portfolios? They were growing suspicious.

I went on to explain that we would not be doing extended writing the first half of the course (we would not be writing "papers"), except for one short research report. Instead, we would observe, read observations, and write numerous varied entries in a notebook. "Short writing assignments," says Ann Berthoff, "means that teachers can afford to encourage students to compose continually, habitually," leaving "more time for conferences; more time for considered responses; more energy to give to the ongoing review of writing careers" (4).

The first notebook entries ran several pages, demonstrating each writer's process of increasing powers of observation or looking and looking again, as Ann Berthoff would say. After reading a representative selection of notebook entries by Leonardo DaVinci (MacCurdy), students tried approximating his method. Later notebook entries were written, and perhaps rewritten, and edited for inclusion in their portfolios.

I used a quotation from the biology textbook to serve as the course theme: "The biosphere is a complex, living world. We look at the biosphere from many different viewpoints (*Biological Science*, 21). During the first half of the course, students practiced viewing nature from a biologist's viewpoint, from what we (borrowing from Lewis Thomas) came to call a biology watcher's viewpoint, from a critical reader's viewpoint, and from an artistic or creative viewpoint. I saw this course as an opportunity to introduce these students to various ways of viewing (or as Paulo Freire would say, of reading) the world and the role of language in changing points of view.

We began by observing the common American daisy. I asked students to write as accurate a description as they could. Initially, most students just wrote a few lines which included "white petals," "yellow center," and "green stem." Then they exchanged this writing with an observation partner. Were all these daisies alike? Some began to wonder, looking again at their own flowers. Everyone began to write more description. Someone announced her daisy (no

longer "the" daisy) had seventeen petals. Soon everyone was counting. Then someone else noticed that the yellow center of his flower
was flat in contrast to the bulging center of his partner's flower.
Some stems had leaves; others did not. Some stems curved. Since
this was an early classroom activity, it was also a good way for them
to begin to know each other. Students began writing rapidly, intent
on distinguishing one common daisy from another. Increased attention to the flowers, however, caused most students to move from
a more scientific viewpoint to a more personal, subjective viewpoint.
One student described her flower as "lonely," uprooted from the
family (rather than field) of flowers. These differences in language
and points of view became apparent during the first reading aloud.

I asked students to write two views of their daisy, a scientific
and a creative view. After trying these writings out in class (again
reading aloud and listening to each other's work), I showed them
two watercolors of daisies by Charles Demuth, one of the common
daisy (*Daisies*) and another called *African Daisies*, and O'Keeffe's
*Yellow Hickory Leaves with Daisy*. We also looked at O'Keeffe's, Van
Gogh's and Monet's different views of the sunflower, which is in
the same family as the daisy. And we looked at the closely viewed
flowers of Georgia O'Keeffe (*Jack-in-the-Pulpit* in six parts, for
example) and at her magnified jimson weed as well as her writing
about this plant. Her description is scientific, historical, and personal.
Why is this combination appropriate as a text accompanying her
painting of this plant? We talked about her purpose and the effectiveness of her writing. Why wouldn't her writing be appropriate in
a biology class? What's good writing anyway? We read a description
of the elm tree by DaVinci, who wrote for a different purpose than
O'Keeffe. Along with giving factual detail, he also writes about
seeds as having umbilical cords. Would a biologist be apt to see this
way? Would a biology watcher be more likely to take this approach?
I returned the students to their flowers, this time handing them
magnifying glasses to change their view again. They made more
notes.

Then I asked them to experiment with their flowers—to take
them apart and record their experiment. They smelled them, tried
painting with the yellow centers, deleafed them. Each began experimenting in different ways. Some immediately began to smell the
flowers; others began pulling off the petals. They jotted down the
order of their activities and talked about different ways of organizing
an experiment. In this case, the order was not important, just
interesting, but in many cases (in the biology lab, for example) the
order could be very important.

No one could remember what the scientific name for the flower's center was called. They tried to recall their botany lessons from school. We consulted their biology textbook to review the basic parts of a flower. (They were going to study gladiolas later in their biology course and do a lab report.) We also read about the naming of flowers and a scientific description of a daisy; we studied the place of the daisy in the classification of families of flowering plants and visited the campus nature area to observe daisies in their natural habitat and to take field notes. What were field notes? We read sample field notebook entries. Each student made notes on the daisies and one other plant. Many chose one of several kinds of ferns they were studying in biology. Some returned to the nature preserve on their own to make additional entries.

In their biology class, students were beginning to study classification and were preparing to give a brief oral report based on their written notes. Many were having difficulty remembering scientific names and understanding the classification scheme. The student who wanted to be a head nurse became hysterical trying to wade through a dense discussion of classification from her textbook. I helped her make a chart that resembled a family tree so she could visualize the relationships. After the oral presentations, many students rewrote their notes (on algae, for example) to include in their writing portfolios as representative of one kind of writing they were doing during this period of their writing lives.

At this time we also read "Observation" by W. I. B. Beveridge who describes observation as "much more than merely seeing something" and points out that different people viewing the same scene notice differences according to their interests: "In a country scene a botanist will notice the different species of plants, a zoologist the animals, a geologist the geological structures, a farmer the crops, farm animals, and so on. A city dweller with none of these interests may see only a pleasant scene" (100). Following Helen Keller's suggestion in "Three Days to See" (1933), I asked students to paint a scene with words so others could see what they saw. They could choose between a country or city scene. Many who were returning to the city for the weekend chose to describe faces, sounds, or sights from the city. One student who made an unexpected trip to Jamaica wrote an entry describing the sights and sounds upon her arrival there.

We made another observation entry, this time of an ant or anthill. Students went into the field, notebooks in hand, to observe and record. None had paid attention to an ant before, and what seemed like a silly assignment became fascinating for some. Some detailed accounts of ant behavior were read in class. Students who had not really looked, as Helen Keller (or Ann Berthoff) might say, wanted to look again. Some experimented. One student offered an ant a bread crumb and watched an army of ants carry it away. He was impressed with their organization and the speed with which they went to work — an hour later he was still watching and taking notes. Others wrote what we came to call biology-watching entries (like the philosophical writing of Lewis Thomas we were reading) or poetic-sounding entries. Some students surprised themselves with the analogies they made. A graduate student came to class to read a philosophical essay he had written based on his observation of nature and a particular ant. It was a wonderful piece of writing full of careful observations. The writer informed us he was reading his sixth draft and that he had written the piece from notes he kept while house-sitting in the country one week. The students were inspired. (I would now add to the packet Fabre's description of "The Red Ants," which William Zinsser brought to my attention while on a visit to our campus to talk about his book *Writing to Learn*. Another interesting addition would be the description of the battle of the red and black ants by Thoreau in "Brute Neighbors," *Walden*.)

We did not have time to go bird watching, but we did a careful reading of Loren Eiseley's "The Judgment of the Birds." (Zinsser in *Writing to Learn* includes another good selection called "Finally, Birds" from Glover Morrill Allen's *Birds and Their Attributes*.) I asked students to make a reader's dialogue notebook entry, what Ann Berthoff calls a dialectical or double-entry notebook. On the right side of their notebooks, they were to take notes and copy significant lines or passages from the article and on the left side to reflect on the notes they took — making notes on their notes. They found this reading difficult and did not at first understand what I meant by note taking and note making. How could you have a dialogue with yourself while you were reading? Wasn't reading a quiet activity?

We stopped to read "The Selves" from *The Medusa and the Snail* (1979) by Lewis Thomas. He writes about how we are made up of many selves and how it's perfectly normal to talk ideas over with yourself (your selves), one self to another. We talked about how we must switch from writer to reader in order to re-see our writing effectively and the difficulty of playing the role of critic. We also talked about active, as opposed to passive, reading and how writing can enhance understanding. I began reading Eiseley's "The Judgment of the Birds" aloud in class and having a dialogue with myself. I noted quotations and images and made notes on the board and discussed my reflections. They continued reading the essay and writing. Everyone decided to expand upon one observation and to share their writing (their reading) in class.

They laughed about how they hadn't known what Eiseley was writing about at first but now they did. Once they became engaged in the reading, they found it interesting that he observed nature from a hotel room on the twentieth floor in midtown Manhattan. Someone else might not have noticed pigeons floating outward to form a city of wings or associated those wings with the whirling depths of our minds. Suddenly they began to understand the powers of observation and how changing the angle of perspective or point of view (going into the wilderness, Eiseley would say) can bring insight.

In biology, their lab instructor took notes on a classroom lecture and shared his way of taking and making notes with the students. In order for their notes to be meaningful later for an exam, they began to realize they had to act on their notes. Slowly they began to understand the importance of dialogue in educating themselves as writers and learners. I encouraged them to include in their writing portfolios an example of note making in biology as a demonstration of one kind of writing and use of writing for learning (writing to learn biology).

We practiced writing summaries (from note taking) and critical responses (from note making), all of which went into their notebooks for possible inclusion in a portfolio. Students used various notebook writings to determine patterns of error and to make notes to guide editing of final drafts. Editing became a natural part of their process as writers preparing to publish or present their writing.

A reading of "Some Biomythology" (*The Lives of a Cell*) by Lewis Thomas led us to the library in search of mythical creatures. A reference librarian gave my students a tour based on this assignment to write about a mythical creature, using (and comparing) two sources. Students enjoyed looking for creatures, learning about different views, and reporting their findings in class. They began their reports by explaining their choices and describing their research process. Many were surprised to learn that stories of their creatures sometimes varied according to the culture or storyteller.

For the midcourse portfolio, students were encouraged to include a variety of notebook entries (field, biology watcher's, reader's dialogue, creative, and writing-to-learn biology) as well as their mythical creature study and a summary and critical reflection based on note taking and note making. But what writings would they select? How much should they include? What did a good portfolio look like?

The midcourse portfolio review served more like a preview or rehearsal for the end-of-course portfolio evaluation. Preparing for portfolio publication (that is, going public with their writing) forced students to develop some evaluation criteria. In a handout I prepared for a portfolio preview session, I wrote: "What is considered effective writing in a biology course may not be considered effective writing in a humanities course. A biologist, for example, wouldn't write about the 'lonely' flower. Scientific writing is more factual, unless you're biology watching like Lewis Thomas. Or unless you're writing about a social issue (genetic engineering, for example)." The idea that good writing is monolithic was soon dispelled, and students began talking about writing for different purposes and what constituted good writing for a particular writing situation.

We reviewed a list of possible kinds of writing that could be included in their portfolios and together determined a reasonable (and somewhat flexible) number. Students then met in groups to discuss which entries to select. As a whole class, we reviewed some selections and offered suggestions for revision. A comparison of several critical reflections based on reader's dialogue entries, for example, prompted us to list some criteria for excellence. An excellent entry would demonstrate critical thinking/observing. It would be thoughtful/reflective; detailed; and have little or no grammatical or mechanical interference. A poor entry, on the other hand, would appear dashed off, incomplete, undeveloped, and be hard for the reader to follow due to lack of development and/or grammatical/ mechanical problems. It would be more of a starting point for writing rather than writing ready for presentation. Standards began to get set within the class, based both on student writing and the published writing we read.

We also held whole-class editing workshops. Since all writing was done on the word processor (using WordPerfect on IBM-PCs), the physical act of making corrections was relatively easy. I taught students to edit "on screen," placing the blinking cursor at the bottom of the screen and working their way "up screen," sentence by sentence to check whether they had observed a particular convention. After editing their own writing, I then asked them to switch places with another writer to doublecheck the editing. If they found what they perceived to be an error, I asked them to place an asterisk at the end of the sentence in question and to consult with me or with other students who were confident in their application of this convention. Writers then returned to their own writing to recheck their editing. They later worked with individualized editing lists of five to seven items, which were revised as necessary throughout the course. We then practiced editing printed drafts (hard copy) after editing "on screen."

This kind of editing workshop activity can, of course, be encouraged without using a portfolio approach or computers as a writing and editing tool; however, preparing copy for portfolios (the final editing and literal printing) helps developing writers think of themselves as publishing writers and increases motivation. The classroom, especially the computer writing classroom, finally becomes a place for writing to go into production. Students select writing to be printed and prepare their selections for publication with the help of other writers at work and a teacher who serves as a writing consultant.

I asked students to preface their portfolios with a cover letter in which they discussed their selections, assessed their writing and editing progress, and set goals for themselves as writers. When assessing their progress, I encouraged them to use examples, such as a comparison of an original editing list with a revised one or a comparison of peer or teacher commentary at the beginning and middle of the course. Instead of just submitting their work for teacher review, I wanted them to scrutinize their own work and practices as much as they could on their own before we met in conference.

I chose not to have their portfolios reviewed by outside evaluators. I did not want these developing writers to enter a writing competition at this point in their writing lives; I did not want them waiting outside a jury-room door for an assessment of their writing performances divorced from the classroom as well as the writing context; nor did I want their writing to be judged as "proficient" or "competent" — or not. I wanted the emphasis placed on the developing writer rather than on the written products alone or a level of proficiency.

I met with writers individually to discuss their portfolios, using the letters they wrote to me about their work as a starting point for dialogue. I did not want to take the lead in the discussion; rather, I wanted to follow their lead. I thought of myself as testing what Lev Vygotsky calls the "zone of proximal development," that period in between what students can do today with help and tomorrow independently. To what extent and in what ways did they need my guidance to help represent themselves as writers? How could I be of assistance? Together we engaged in constructive dialogue about their collective work and their ongoing development as writers.

For their final portfolio, students could include some selections of their own choice from the first portfolio to be revised if they wished. The final portfolio would represent their work for the whole course, not just the second half, but would include a lab report and a position paper from the second half of the course as well as other writing samples which writers considered representative.

The biology classroom instructor and I collaborated on a peer review guide to be used for commenting on a draft of a lab report. When we told students about our collaboration, they groaned. Rewrite a lab report? It is writing, isn't it? Well, yes. We told them we expected them to write clearly and precisely and to edit for grammatical and mechanical errors. The report would be included in their writing portfolios.

Most of the second half of basic writing was devoted to reading and writing about animal rights, a current social issue in biology. In the biology classroom students read and discussed a policy statement on dissection and vivisection drafted by the National Association of Biology Teachers (NABT 7) along with a request by the Board of Directors for "thoughts on this issue." The board argued that too much time was being devoted to vivisection and dissection. Furthermore, such procedures could provide negative experiences for some students and perhaps even promote a disrespect for life. The NABT was recommending, where appropriate, the use of such alternatives as computer displays, films, videos, and other teaching strategies. Students talked about their own experiences and wrote a first draft of a letter to the executive director of the NABT.

In the writing class, students read various articles on animal rights (F. White), each time summarizing and responding and often changing their points of view. They reread their first drafts and wrote more informed responses. The biology classroom instructor then read their second drafts and commented. Even though this was an ethical issue, she wanted them to be less emotional and to support their arguments with facts or examples from their own experiences in biology classrooms.

We did not want our students to submit their first off-hand emotional responses nor did we want them to parrot back arguments they were reading or simply add information. Instead we wanted them to demonstrate what Kathleen Roth (22) calls "connected knowledge," conceptual knowledge integrated with the learners' own personal knowledge and experience.

They rewrote their position letters for peer review, again using a workshop guide we devised. We talked about supplying a context for the reader. Was it important for her to know they were beginning college students and not biology teachers? Should they make reference to the policy statement? Should they let the reader know that they had done some reading about this issue and perhaps even make some references? Finally the letters were rewritten and edited and submitted to the biology instructor who sent out the collection to the executive director of the NABT along with a cover letter asking for some response. Copies were also included in students' final portfolios.

What I'm calling a portfolio approach to teaching basic writing centers on the collective works of the developing writer, rather than on a series of unrelated writing assignments, and emphasizes progress or, to borrow again from Vygotsky, movement in the "zone of proximal development" (in this case, as writers and editors). This approach is similar to one frequently used in visual arts and creative writing courses (Gay, 1988; Schwartz), in which the work of developing artists is discussed regularly throughout the course and students submit a final portfolio of their best work for review.

A portfolio approach, based on the assumption that everyone in the course is a writer at work, a developing writer, seems especially appropriate for basic writers whose negative attitudes often interfere with their development as writers (Gay, 1983). Asking basic writers to build a portfolio of their work shifts the emphasis from a single writing performance to a collective and encourages them to take increasing responsibility for their development as writers and learners, thus enabling them to make a place for themselves in the academy and beyond. Through the process of selecting and preparing portfolio entries, participating in portfolio reviews and comparing later reviews of their work with earlier ones, basic writers learn to build an end-of-course portfolio that represents them as developing writers. From this base, they can continue their ongoing development as writers, writing themselves across the curriculum. Finally they have come to see themselves as writers—writers at work.

# 17

# Portfolios Evolving
## *Background and Variations in Sixth- Through Twelfth-Grade Classrooms*

Roberta Camp
*Educational Testing Service*

Denise Levine
*Fordham University; Community School District 2,
New York City Board of Education*

It is clear that a transformation is afoot in the assessment of writing and that portfolios are part of the transformation. There is evidence in this book as elsewhere of a diversity of writing-portfolio projects, each creating a model for portfolio assessment that serves a particular purpose and arises out of particular needs.

The first part of the present discussion is intended to help place these exploratory efforts, including our own, within a shared historical and theoretical background. The later part focuses on the experience of students and teachers with portfolio projects in Pittsburgh and New York, and in particular on a characteristic of portfolios that makes them especially valuable for instruction and learning: reflection by student writers on the pieces of writing they include in their portfolios.

## Background for Portfolio Approaches to Writing Assessment

Over the last fifteen to twenty years, an enormous shift has occurred in the way teachers and researchers look at writing and writing instruction. We no longer believe, if we ever did, that "writing is writing." We are aware that the skills and strategies needed for writing vary with the purpose for writing, the situation, and the intended audience. We are much more inclined to think of writing as an extended process that occurs over time and that draws upon different approaches to thinking and expression at different points in that process. We have become more interested, too, in helping students become aware of what it is they do when they write — what they think about, what strategies they use, what alternatives they consider (see Hairston; Mayher; Britton et al. 11–18; and Applebee and Langer).

The result of these changes is a lack of fit between current models for teaching and learning, on the one hand, and traditional models for writing assessment, on the other. In the traditional models for assessment, tests were designed separately from curriculum and, in large-scale assessments especially, were expected to be independent of curriculum. Writing tests were given under controlled conditions, with established time limits and standardized tasks. For tests of writing, the prototypical test was made up of a series of multiple-choice questions and a single impromptu essay (see R. Camp, *Changing the Model*).

Fortunately, the models for assessment are now changing. The designers of forward-looking assessments are now aware that tests can influence and even distort curriculum. In the case of writing, we have seen that multiple-choice tests of grammar and sentence structure are likely to encourage instruction in sentence-level skills and that the single impromptu essay is likely to promote an overly simplified view of the multiple and varied processes involved in writing.

In the models for assessment that are now emerging, curriculum and assessment are based on a common, articulated concept of learning. Instruction and assessment are complementary, two faces of a unified classroom experience. Assessment is conceived broadly, so that it includes much more than stand-alone tests; it may be immersed in instruction; its primary purpose may be to inform teachers' decisions about instruction and to enhance students' awareness of their own abilities (see Archbald and Newman; Anrig; Frederiksen and Collins; and Wiggins). In this brave new world, assessment may in fact be based on work that engages students over a period of time inside and outside the classroom, and on teachers' evaluations of the work. Clearly, the new view of assessment is more congenial to portfolio assessment than were its predecessors.

The changes evident in new paradigms for writing and in the models for writing instruction and assessment are reinforced by the views of teachers' and students' roles that have come out of the educational reform movement of the last ten years. The emphasis on teacher professionalism leads to greater awareness of the importance of involving teachers in the design and implementation of curriculum and assessment. The view of students as active rather than passive learners suggests that students should learn to assume increased responsibility for their own learning. As a result, we have begun to look for assessment approaches that are adaptable to a variety of curricula and teaching and learning styles and are directly informative to teachers and students (Wiggins).

### Emerging Models for Writing Portfolios

The idea of portfolios is certainly not new. Artists and student artists have long used portfolios to demonstrate the range and quality of their work. To the extent that the writing portfolio idea borrows from the artist's portfolio, it is likely to be a demonstration of the range and quality of the writer's work—most typically drawing on examples of only the best of a writer's work. However, in the present pedagogical climate, a portfolio of writing will probably show as well some evidence of processes and strategies used to generate writing, of the writer's awareness of those processes and strategies, and of the writer's development over a period of time. In these cases, a portfolio will include a variety of finished pieces of writing and at least one piece accompanied by the brainstorming, notes, sketches of ideas, and early drafts that preceded the final product. In addition, it will probably include some record of the student's experience in looking back at his or her work, both for processes and strategies used in writing and for development over time.

How the expected variety among pieces and how the evidence of process is defined will vary with the assessment purpose for the portfolio and with the instructional and institutional context in which it is developed. The need to make portfolios manageable and interpretable requires difficult decisions about what to include and what to leave behind, about how much to standardize and how much to leave flexible. In the many portfolio projects now underway in this country and others, these decisions have been made in a variety of ways in order to meet the range of needs and purposes that are addressed by the portfolios.

As a result, we now see multiple models for portfolios, with different requirements for the pieces to be included in the portfolios and different procedures for selecting them. Certain commonalities appear across a number of projects, however, suggesting an emerging definition of portfolio approaches in terms of the characteristics that make them worthwhile:

1. Multiple samples of writing gathered over a number of occasions.
2. Variety in the kinds of writing or purposes for writing that are represented.
3. Evidence of process in the creation of one or more pieces of writing.
4. Reflection on individual pieces of writing and/or on changes observable over time.

Each of these four features contributes information to the overall picture of student writing ability that is not available in traditional, nonportfolio approaches to writing assessment. However, the experience of teachers and students in portfolio projects in Pittsburgh and in New York as we have observed it suggests that the last feature, reflection, appears in some respects to be the one that brings greatest rewards to student and teacher. Students' reflections on their writing, in these projects at least, represent the portfolios' greatest opportunities for student learning and for information that teachers can use to guide instruction.

Reflection makes visible much in learning that is otherwise hidden, even from the student writers themselves. Through reflection accompanied by the pertinent pieces of writing, teachers and students alike can discover how students find their way through the process of creating text, what they see as their own purpose or agenda in a piece of writing, and how they look at their work and at themselves as writers.

As part of the discourse surrounding our collective portfolio efforts, it might be helpful to look more closely at the explanatory projects in Pittsburgh and New York, each of which arises from a different set of circumstances. Together, the two projects suggest some of the strengths of portfolio approaches to writing assessment in middle and high schools and especially of portfolios that are built around reflection, the practice of students' looking back at their work.

## Arts PROPEL: A Report from Roberta Camp

*Imaginative Writing and the Environment for Portfolios*

Arts PROPEL is a Rockefeller-funded collaborative project involving teachers and supervisors from the Pittsburgh Public Schools and researchers from Educational Testing Service and from Project Zero of the Harvard Graduate School of Education. Its primary purpose is to create assessment closely integrated with instruction in the arts, particularly in three areas of the middle-school and high-school curriculum: visual arts, music, and imaginative writing.

In the first three years of the project, researchers, supervisors, and teachers in Arts PROPEL have devoted much of their attention to creating sequences of classroom activities that emphasize three aspects of learning in the arts: perception of the techniques and effects evident in other artists' work or performances, production of one's own work or performance, and reflection on the work or performance created. The emphasis on reflection in these classroom activities has helped students learn to look back on their own work. With time, it has also created a climate in classrooms that is conducive to portfolios.

Arts PROPEL imaginative writing takes place in Pittsburgh in language arts and English classrooms, where the collection of writing folders has been long established. In the past, because the folders had been used primarily as a basis for conversations about student writing between teachers and supervisors, there was little need to create a consistent approach to the collection of student writing across classrooms or schools. The task for Arts PROPEL has been to help teachers create an approach for portfolios of imaginative as well as academic writing and to ensure that the portfolios will be consistent enough to facilitate conversations and, as appropriate, comparisons across classrooms. What has been far more important, however, is that the experience of creating writing folders (collections of all writing) and then portfolios (selected pieces accompanied by reflective comments) be made useful to students' learning, and that the portfolios that students create be made informative to teachers' instruction.

### Portfolio Explorations in Arts PROPEL

The project in Pittsburgh has pursued two avenues of exploration. The first involves researcher interviews with individual students in a limited number of classrooms in order to discover how students look at their own work, what they value in it, and what options they see for revision or for alternatives to be explored in future pieces of writing. In some of these classrooms, teachers have tried out a series of guided reflections that helps students toward the creation of portfolios. The second course of exploration has involved groups of teachers, supervisors, and researchers in discussions in which teachers identify and describe what they find most informative in samples of student folders and portfolios and what further information they would like to see provided.

By comparing and synthesizing students' and teachers' perceptions, the researchers in Arts PROPEL have developed tentative sets of procedures and guidelines that teachers use to help students create portfolios. These procedures, or variations on them developed by teachers, help students engage in reflection about their writing, select pieces of writing from their folders to create portfolios, and reflect on changes in their writing and in themselves as writers over the course of the school year. The procedures and guidelines are being tried out in a half-dozen classrooms to evaluate the feasibility of the approach, the benefits for student learning, and the assessment value of the information obtained.[1] Then they will be refined and explored further in a larger number of classrooms.

## The Value of Students' Reflections on their Writing

The practice of looking back at their writing is relatively new to most middle- and high-school students, even those in Pittsburgh schools who have had experience with reflection in Arts PROPEL classroom projects. If students are to profit from such complex reflective experiences as making comparisons among multiple pieces of their writing or selecting from their writing the pieces they will put into their portfolios, they need considerable support from their teachers and the classroom environment.

To prepare students for more elaborate forms of reflection, the Arts PROPEL classroom teachers first model the use of reflective questions and set up occasions for students' oral reflection on one another's writing. After about four months of teacher modeling, oral reflection, and small-scale written reflection on individual pieces, students are ready to look at the body of work they have created. At this point, usually in mid-January, they take their first formal step toward creating portfolios: they each select a single piece of writing for their portfolios and focus closely on that piece, using a series of questions to guide their reflection. Well grounded in the reflective experiences of the first months, the students are then able to move fairly steadily toward more complex aspects of portfolio creation: looking at multiple pieces of writing and at processes and strategies for writing, selecting pieces of writing to illustrate what they can do as writers, and writing about changes they see in their writing.

Even in the first few months of the school year, however, students' reflections are quite informative. As can be seen from the work of even a very few students, portfolio reflections make visible for students and their teachers much that is useful to teaching and learning:

1.  What the student believes she has done well in a piece of writing:

    "I feel that I did pretty well on how much facts I wrote on the topic, but I could do better on sentence structure." (eighth grader)

2.  What the student values in writing:

    "My favorite type of writing is something like a book report where I have to do much more than just write about something I already know." (tenth grader)

3.  The student's own goals and interests as a learner and developing writer:

    "I decided to create a fictional person and be slightly funny." (eighth grader)

4.  The student's strategies and processes for writing and his awareness of them:

    "I'll sometimes get a wide variety of ideas at once and take forever to choose one. Once I get an idea I tend to stick with it." (tenth grader)

5.  What the student understands she is learning about writing:

    "I've finally figured out what I want to do. The most difficult thing for me was taking all my ideas and organizing them." (twelfth grader)

When students look back on their work and their strategies for creating it, when they describe what they see and what they value in their work, they provide a strong basis for their own learning, for richer responses to their peers' writing, and for comparisons with their peers that lead to expanded awareness of strategies for writing and criteria for evaluating writing. Students who learn to reflect on their writing not only provide their teachers with information that can directly guide instruction, they engage in a form of assessment that has greatest potential effect on their learning because it addresses directly their own awareness of what they have done and what they can do.

## The New York City Writing Project: A Report from Denise Levine

*Writing and Learning as a Context for Portfolios*

The New York City Writing Project has been at the forefront of the shift in the way teachers have come to view writing and writing instruction over the last decade. Like others in the composition field, members of the project perceived a lack of fit between the project's model of teaching and learning and traditional models of assessment. We were especially concerned about this lack of fit as we approached the evaluation of the Junior High School Writing and Learning Project, a professional development program in writing across the curriculum. We were looking for a model of assessment that would provide us with a window on the classrooms of the participating middle school teachers and students—a window through which we and others would be able to perceive and understand the learning taking place in schools and subject areas very different from one another.

### Creating "Authentic, Legitimate" Assessment

Working with researchers from Educational Testing Service, we sought a model of assessment that would build on students' strengths rather than highlight their deficits. We wanted a model that would allow students and teachers to demonstrate what they could do, one that was based on a common, articulated concept of learning. We were looking for what Wiggins has described as an "authentic test," one that would "ferret out and identify strengths." The aim, we believed, would be "to enable students to show off what they can do" (711). Portfolio assessment seemed a most appropriate form of evaluation for our purposes—a test that would be contextualized.

Yet, in the earliest stages, each of us working on the portfolio development (researchers from Educational Testing Service and members of the Institute for Literacy Studies, which houses the New York City Writing Project at Lehman College) had a different vision of what a portfolio should look like. Portfolios had looked different in each of the different contexts and settings that we had previously explored. However, near the end of the first year of our explorations, using the art portfolio as our inspiration, we reached a consensus. The portfolio would be a demonstration of a student's use of writing to learn during the course of the school year. Actual student drafts and final products as well as works in progress would provide what Wiggins has called a "legitimate assessment, responsive to individual students and school contexts" (704). Through the use of portfolios, we hoped students would become aware of, and demonstrate, the ways in which they used writing as a tool for learning, as well as the ways in which the writing strategies they used had changed over the year. Reaching that consensus turned out to be the easy part. Next, we needed a common, articulated view of learning.

## Identifying the Common Underlying Principles of Our Work

At the midpoint of our Summer Seminar in the Teaching of Writing (an intensive, experiential four-week graduate course for middle school teachers of all subject areas), we asked the participants to think about the "common underlying principles of our work." Teachers brainstormed, wrote, and discussed theories of writing and learning in small groups. They produced a set of fifteen principles, which fell into four categories: using writing to find meaning, using writing to communicate, being aware of the processes one uses to write, and creating a context for learning through writing. These principles became the heart of our portfolio project.

Our next step was to turn the principles into a set of questions to guide students' portfolio selections. The teachers piloted the "guidelines" during the first of three selection periods. Each student portfolio included a letter to the reader of the portfolio about the selection process, in addition to a letter to the teacher describing changes the student noticed in reading, writing, and learning attitudes and strategies. Each class set of portfolios contained a cover letter by the teacher providing his or her impressions of the portfolio selection process, in addition to any contextual information necessary for making sense of the work in the portfolio.

There was no limit on the number of entries students could place in portfolios, and from student to student, from class to class, from subject area to subject area, portfolios differed. Some teachers instructed students in the portfolio selection process; others preferred not to interfere with students' decisions about what to include. Some students made use of the guidelines; others did not and opted instead to include only "best" works or "favorite" pieces. In this sense, the portfolios were organic. Each reflected the classroom context from which it had grown. The selection process and the portfolios that resulted from it were as rich and as varied as the classrooms in which they took shape.

## What We Learned

While we saw evidence of students' use of the writing process (through drafting and revising) and evidence of students' use of writing for a variety of purposes and audiences in the portfolios, we were left with many more questions than answers. We began asking, for example, how we could develop a language to talk about student work and what it represents. "What is 'writing to learn,'" we again asked ourselves, "and what does it look like? What is the social context for students' writing and learning and how can we get at this and other aspects of the classroom ecology through the portfolios? When students are responsible for portfolio selections, what gets left behind and of what significance is it?'" Finally, we questioned whether any process as idiosyncratic as portfolio assessment could ever be standardized.

In spite of the persistent questions and the unresolved issues around portfolio assessment, however, the students, teachers, researchers, and evaluators involved in our project agreed on one point: the reflective student letters were the most significant entries in many of the portfolios. Not surprisingly, we found in our experience with our "authentic test" that "self-assessment becomes more central," as Wiggins has suggested (711). Kerry Weinbaum, one of the teachers participating in the project, explained why:

> The reflective self-assessment letters were the most important aspect of the portfolio process. They were meaningful to me because they provided me with a "window on [students'] thinking" (Sowers) enabling me to see beyond the printed pages of my students' work. They were significant for my students because they allowed them to reflect on their own growth and learning over the course of the school year ... [enabling] my students, too, to see beyond the printed page. (213, this volume)

Gabriel, an eighth grader, spoke even more forcefully about reflection and "seeing beyond the printed page" in his letters to his teacher, Anne (see figure 17–1, a & b). Gabriel saw his mind "maturing" as he reflected on the change in his primary focus over a two-month period. In looking beyond the printed page, he realized that the content of his recent writing seemed to "concentrate on real life more than the fantasy world," and he concluded that this shift was part and parcel of his desire to "explore and expand" his horizons. In the process of reflecting, his understanding of himself began to evolve and he was reminded of the importance of keeping an open mind. His letters are testimony to the power of portfolio reflection for exposing the edge of students' thought.

While reflection is an important and powerful tool at any stage in life, we would argue that it is particularly critical for young adolescents, who are attempting to make sense of the world and their place in it, to understand themselves and the nature of their relationships with others, and to clarify values and establish habits of mind.[2] To this end, we believe that portfolios, with their built-in opportunities for reflection, offer young writers a leg up on establishing their identities and their goals while, in the language of the Carnegie Commission, "rejoicing in the knowledge of [their] personal strengths" (17).

C

JHS                      Gabriel
                         11/17/88

          Dear Ms. _____,

              My writing has changed drastically,
      for the better, since last year. I have
      learned new words to express myself and my
      falings. I have found it easier to write
      more and have sense in my writing. I also
      can pick very intresting topics to write
      about.
              I also have the ability to edit my
      mistakes and someone else's. The topics that
      I write about is mostly about fantasy. I
      use my imagination alot in my writing. I
      don't like toning in to the real world,
      I pretty much like my worlds.
              I like to write about things that
      my imagination can conger up because in
      that imagination world I can be whatever I
      want to be, I can do what I want to d

Fig. 17-1a   Gabriel's Letters

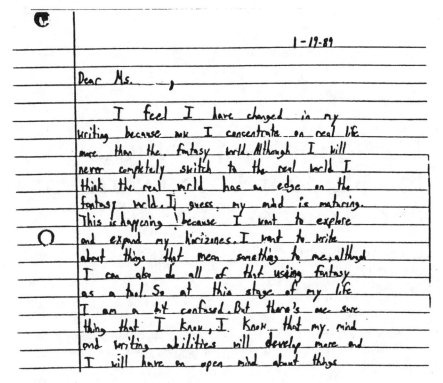

**Fig. 17–1b  Gabriel's Letters**

## Notes

1. For a description of the experience of one teacher with the Arts PROPEL approach to portfolios, see Kathryn Howard; for a detailed description of the Arts PROPEL project and the PROPEL approach to portfolios, see Roberta Camp, "Thinking Together About Portfolios."

2. For a more detailed discussion of the education of young adolescents, see *Turning Points: The Report of the Task Force on Education of Young Adolescents*, Carnegie Corporation of America, 1989.

# 18

# Portfolios as a Vehicle for Student Empowerment and Teacher Change

Kerry Weinbaum
*Community School District 10*
*New York City Board of Education*

> Now as a learner I'm still the same, except that now I know a lot more about responsibility since now it's really left up to me. But I like it better this way and I know you do too.
>
> —Elissa, grade 8

I smiled as I began to reflect on Elissa's growth over the course of the school year. What accounted for her insight into her own learning?

Last September I had agreed to participate in a portfolio evaluation project conducted by the New York City Writing Project at Lehman College and the Educational Testing Service. I was one of a group of fifteen middle school English and content-area teachers, from various districts in New York City, who were using and assessing writing in their classrooms as a tool for learning. What follows is the world in which I work and the story of my year.

As I approach my school each morning, I am continually struck by its imposing nature. It is an old building, erected in 1914, and it has housed various other schools throughout its history. It always seems to me that this building deserves a more refined location, a place more worthy of its past. And yet it is not so. Located in the Bronx, it is severely overcrowded, as are all of the schools in the district. There are not enough classrooms for all the teachers and many "travel" or share rooms. Such had been my lot for the past six years as I fell into both categories. I was a squatter. I only had the use of my room when another teacher was not scheduled to teach in it and, due to programming errors, I traveled to other rooms several times a week as well. My main classroom was long and narrow with little room for walking around. Due to the age of the school and the years of neglect, plaster falls from the walls, lights blink in disco fashion, and rooms are either frigid or stifling for no particular reason. From time to time we are visited by families of mice and various other creatures. Although technically not in the South Bronx, the surroundings are run-down and on the low end of the socio-economic scale. Drugs and crime are an everyday part of the students' lives. With it all, there are those who come from caring, cohesive families. It is in this atmosphere and under these conditions that my eighth graders and I embarked on a journey into the world of portfolios.

Class 8E consisted of thirty students, most of whom were Hispanic. The rest were Black or Asian. This ethnic breakdown correlates with the area in general. I chose 8E to participate in the portfolio project because, with the exception of about six students, I had taught them the year before. I felt they would respond positively to the continuation of a whole-language approach toward English/language arts since they had done so well with it as seventh graders. Furthermore, I believed I knew these kids and what they were capable of. It seemed right to involve them in the project. I was worried, though. As I talked to the class about the project and described what had to be done, my own initial reactions were of not knowing what to expect and not feeling sure of *my* capability to carry it all out. I questioned whether my writing assignments would be useful. Would an impartial reader learn anything from reading pieces self-selected by students and placed in a folder and, more to the point, if not, how would this reflect on me as a teacher? I had not yet come to the realization that this project was to be as much about me and what I was willing to risk as a teacher as it was about my students.

Three times during the course of the school year, students chose the pieces to include in their portfolios, following specific guidelines. At the end of each selection round students wrote cover letters to the portfolio-reading committee, as well as to their teachers, addressing specific points regarding their growth and learning and their reasons for selecting the pieces they had. For most participating teachers, the portfolio project ended at the conclusion of each selection round. For me, and five other teachers, that was just the beginning.

The purpose of the portfolio project was to research whether students' growth and learning could be assessed by studying their writing over one school year. As part of this smaller group of six, our task was to study portfolios as an alternative to standardized testing. We met twice monthly to discuss and examine assessment, our students, their writing, and portfolios in general. Each of us kept a teaching journal in which we reflected on our teaching and recorded everything that occurred in our portfolio classes. In addition, we responded to various articles and readings. Finally, we selected two students from the portfolio class who served as case studies in order to provide a more in-depth look at the process. Over the year we interviewed these students, examined their writing, and discussed their selections in general and their portfolios in particular. It was hoped that, through them, we would begin to uncover what effect or impact, if any, portfolios had on the students' own assessments of growth and learning. It was at this point that a sense of uneasiness settled into the pit of my stomach and remained there until this project was nearly over.

From the start I wondered if I had bitten off more than I could chew. I knew that research was to play a major role in all of this. The very idea of research and especially research on assessment intimidated me and I had written about it in my teaching journal:

> Assessment? Tests. Exams. What have I learned? What have you learned? Did we do it right? Judgment. Stress. Having to prove something to someone. Was it worth it? Should we do it over? Grading. I'd rather be the person doing the assessing than the one being assessed. I do not like research. Tedious. Boring. Playing with data. I like answers but I don't like the hunt.

Well, here I was at the beginning of the hunt and I did not like it at all. My first problem was choosing the two students who would serve as my case studies and, in effect, represent the other twenty eight in the portfolio class. I was obsessed with selecting the "right" students, those who would provide me with the information I needed, whatever that was. I selected Elissa and Sam, sensing that I could learn from them both and, with not a little reluctance, I proceeded as planned.

Elissa was a very self-possessed, outwardly mature thirteen-year-old Hispanic girl. I considered her to be one of the best students in my class as she was very disciplined and always attended to the task at hand. In class, she appeared to set herself apart from the others, yet I knew from observation that she had many friends. This description remained constant, yet as the year wore on, I felt subtly disappointed in Elissa. I had higher expectations for her than she appeared to have achieved. Although she always got her work done and, usually, it was more than acceptable, there was something missing. The sparkle was just not there. It was flat. As time went on I learned that Elissa's mother was divorcing her alcoholic father. Needless to say, this situation affected her greatly, as it did her work, attitude, and attendance at school. I kept this information in mind each time Elissa and I spoke or reviewed her work. There was always much to discuss, however brief the time in which to do it, but afterward, I always felt I had come up empty. I did not learn much from what she said or from her writing beyond what was obvious. I felt I had no data at all upon which to base the conclusions I knew would be expected of me. At one point I began to study the self-assessment cover letters that she included with her portfolio selections. In her letter of November 17, addressed to the ETS reader, she went on about why she selected certain pieces for the portfolio and ended with the revelation that "although I chose them, I feel they are boring and that I am not a creative writer." This struck me because I, too, felt many of her pieces were boring. However, that she and I agreed on this point did not indicate that there had been no growth or learning. I later questioned her about this and she said, "When I select a topic it's interesting to me but once I finish the actual writing of the piece, I like to forget about it and go on to the next one." Once written, the pieces became meaningless and boring to her. The fact that writing presented no problem for her and that she thought about what she read and learned indicated, at least to me, that she had grown. Still, I felt a great sense of incompleteness. I had not gotten what I needed from studying Elissa or her writing and, in desperation, I began to think that I was not likely to.

Sam presented even more of a problem. A funny, outgoing thirteen-year-old black boy, he was what I call a "reluctant writer." He did his work, but it seemed to take him forever. Many of his original pieces were about the same thing: action or adventure stories in which he and other class members were the characters. He also liked to write about sports. Sam was easily distracted and liked to talk to others during class; yet once engaged in his work, he proceeded with little difficulty. He considered himself to be an average student, as did I. Sam was aware that his writing was often not mechanically correct but had indicated in an interview that he disliked revision and editing simply because it was a lot of work. He said, "It takes too much effort to revise and edit." When he took the time to do it he was pleased with the result and felt more satisfied with his work, but at other times he just did not care. This pretty much says it all. Despite our discussions, interviews, and reviews of his portfolio I continued to have the nagging feeling that, as with Elissa, I was not learning much. I wrote about this copiously in my teaching journal. I continually brought it up at our seminar classes. I felt that I was getting nowhere very quickly and I couldn't understand it. The class was writing. They were reading, and they were learning, weren't they? Why couldn't I uncover concrete evidence of this in Sam and Elissa's portfolios? What was I doing wrong?

In the midst of this dilemma, I was dealing with a huge time problem, ever present for a teacher in an urban, inner-city school. Between snow storms, class trips, days off for standardized testing, holidays, assembly programs, and so on, I felt that I had no time to teach, let alone to figure out how, why, or if my students were learning. I was becoming more deflated, frustrated, and demoralized. More than once I wrote in my journal that I hated the portfolio project and that I wanted to walk away from it. The problems were, it seemed, insurmountable and the questions and concerns about portfolios were endless. Added to all of this, the class itself seemed to be, upon reflection, regressing. After nearly two years of offering my students freedom of choice, or so I thought, there was a definite breakdown. It was now the end of February and the class was involved in reading short stories and plays. I had taught and discussed the value of literature logs, which the class began to keep at this time. At first it went well. Students wrote comments, questions and reactions to what they read. They made connections to their lives and to the world in general. Often students would trade logs and respond to each other's comments. The logs would then be shared with the whole class. It was new, it was different, and everyone seemed to like it. More importantly, they appeared to be learning from the experience. After a time, however, I noticed what were, at first, imperceptible changes. The literature logs were often forgotten at home or remained undone. Work that was completed was shoddy or perfunctory at best.

By now, it was mid-March and the class began to read *To Kill a Mockingbird*. We had moved from short stories to the novel and the students seemed genuinely intrigued by this one. A few had heard of the book but no one had read it and, best of all, no one had seen the movie. I was delighted because the book had always been one of my favorites and, frankly, it was the only novel of which I had enough copies to go around. This is another reality of life in a big city school. In almost no time, however, I noticed a definite lack of productivity. Again, the work was either forgotten, poorly done, or not done at all. I could not understand what was happening or why and the portfolios provided few answers. I first chalked it up to spring fever and the fact that the class was looking ahead to graduation. I talked to the class about it in an attempt to ascertain what had gone wrong. They responded with what they thought I wanted to hear, but there was no improvement in their output or caliber of work. After nearly two years with this class, what I had done and tried to instill in the students seemed lost.

I was in a panic. I hated the portfolio project and the seminar more than ever. I wanted to forget I had ever heard of alternate methods of assessment. I blamed the portfolio project for what was going wrong in class and I felt that whatever meager data I had accumulated would be worthless, as I was learning little or nothing from my two case studies. Endless discussions with the class were an exercise in futility and I did not know what to do next. Then I recalled an article my seminar was asked to read. It was a case study report entitled "I, Sam and Science: An Exploration in Teaching" by Thomas Latus. I was struck by Latus's assertion that "only by taking the risk of sharing control can the teachers and students start to do their work." (4). Since I agreed with this premise, I began to question whether I was really sharing control with my students. My teaching methods were certainly different and nontraditional, but I wondered whether I was assuming all of the control and direction in the class.

Not long before, I had read another article entitled "The Unteachables" by Jane Juska. This article really spoke to me. Juska, an urban teacher, talked about the never-ending frustration she felt as she tried to get her low achieving students to make "a consistent effort to learn" (1). No matter what she did, it never seemed to happen. She bemoaned the fact that despite all her attempts, the responsibility for learning always fell on her shoulders, and that for a long time she had been aware that it was she who worked the hardest in her classes. In trying to find a way to change this situation she came to the realization that "while school offers them [her students] survival and belonging, at the same time, it refuses them power and freedom" (2). She wondered, "What would happen if I turned over my power to them?" (2). The rest of the article described how Juska pulled back, relinquished control of her class without abdicating authority, and, in the end, how her students assumed responsibility for their own learning. It had worked. In her words:

> Here's the real difference: the kids are reading, they are writing, they are talking about the book. Maybe none of this is getting done as

quickly or as intensively or as efficiently as if I were center stage. But no. I remember what Dave told me way back in October: "Face it, Ms. Juska, nobody read 'Fall of the House of Whatever'!" Now they're proceeding, and in fact, not just in my wishful imagination. Whatever is happening in this classroom is really happening; it's not pretend. (26).

Could this be the key I was looking for? Perhaps Juska and Latus were on to something. I was determined to find out. For a long time I had looked to my students for the answers and they were not forthcoming. It was now time to look within myself. Perhaps I had not given them as much freedom as I thought. My techniques might have been different but the focus of the class was largely directed by me. I did, indeed, work harder than any of my students. The words of Dave, Juska's student, echoed in my brain. It might as well have been any of my students shouting, "Face it, Ms. Weinbaum, nobody's reading 'To Kill a Whatever'!" It was time for me to take a risk and I came to the conclusion that to give my students true freedom meant I had to relinquish control of my class.

I decided to have the students contract with me, in writing, what they would do from the end of March until just before graduation on June 22. They were permitted to work on any projects they wished as long as they related to English language arts. Each student presented me with a written contract indicating the work to be accomplished. Considering the time period left, and that I had never done this before, I conferenced with each student after which I deemed the contract acceptable by signing it, subject to renegotiation. This left my students and me free to deal with any unforeseen problems that might arise. This contract system wound up being the piece that provided meaning for the portfolios.

Surprisingly, the majority of the class chose to continue reading *To Kill a Mockingbird* and to keep a literature log. Some opted to read books from the library, and/or stories, plays, and poems from their anthology. In addition, all the students contracted to write self-generated pieces. Some wrote a number of narratives, poems, and essays, while others concentrated on one longer project, producing entire magazines devoted to sports or fashion. Most of the class also continued to work on an oral history project that began earlier in the term. Tuesdays were set aside for reading groups where the students discussed any and all aspects of their reading and reviewed their logs. They worked in writing groups on Fridays at which time they listened, responded to, and edited each other's work. The rest of the class time was spent with each student working on his individual contract.

I did not assign homework. Each student was responsible for figuring out how much work had to be done at home based upon what was accomplished in class. All I required for a passing grade was that the contracts be fulfilled. The higher the caliber of work, the higher the grade would be. I was no longer center stage. I facilitated, answered questions, and joined reading and writing groups. I conferenced with students and, in some cases, renegotiated contracts but, at long last, the class had grabbed hold of the reins. They were now responsible for their own learning. It did not always work like a charm. There were days when there was a lot of unproductive talk but, for the most part, the students were truly engaged in their work.

It was now mid-May and time for the third and final round of portfolio selections. As before, the students chose their pieces according to the specific guidelines previously set forth. They also had to write the two requisite cover letters: one to the portfolio reading committee and one to me. This time these letters had to be more detailed. In addition to explaining why they made the selections they did, students reflected on and addressed such points as (1) what they learned about themselves by looking at the entire year's portfolio, (2) how they had changed as writers and learners, (3) what they valued about their work, (4) how they now felt about English/language arts as a result of the writing and learning they had done throughout the year, and (5) how the writing had helped them to learn. Again, time closed in on us but finally, on May 19, I arrived home with a complete set of portfolios in tow.

After reading them, I was totally overwhelmed. I could not deny that progress had been made. The quality of the writing and the sophistication evidenced in the cover letters alone told me what I needed to know, so much so that the pieces themselves became almost secondary. Nearly every student, some more eloquently than others, spoke about the changes and growth they had noticed in themselves over the course of the year. Many included their contracts and talked about the impact they had made on their work. Jayson and José, for example, had produced little during the first half of the year. However, on the third round, both had filled their portfolios with work primarily generated by their contracts, and their letters to the portfolio readers gave them the opportunity to reflect on the change. Andrea was never interested in reading. Now, things were different. In her words: "As a reader, I was never interested in that subject. Now, that is all I want to do . . . This year I know I learned a lot . . . The thing that made my big change toward reading was when I started doing the literature log. Before, I used to read without thinking. Now, when I read, I write down anything that comes to my mind. That's when I improved a great deal." Natisha said, "I feel English class has helped me develop into a better writer. ... The contract we made with Ms. Weinbaum has given me responsibility and helped me to time myself ... Writing and keeping track of a lit log helps me understand what I am reading." Is this progress? I would say so. All of the students, in one way or another, expressed what and how they learned and the progress they made. But I think Rochelle said it best when she wrote, "Writing has helped me learn to simply write." I could not have said it better myself. The contracts and reflective portfolio cover letters seemed a perfect fit for these students to explore their own development as writers and learners.

And what about me? What have I learned? The first thing is that in concentrating on finding the answers from my two case studies, I neglected the forest for the trees, as all of my students had something to teach me. I also discovered that the actual pieces contained in a portfolio are not always as important as why they were written, how, and under what conditions. There are just too many variables for which to account. These, as well as what is going on in a student's life, and the need to have some control over it all are factors that must be considered. The reflective self-assessment letters were the most important aspect of the portfolio process. They were meaningful for me because they provided me with "a window on [students'] thinking" (Sowers) enabling me to see beyond the printed pages of my students' work. They were significant for my students because they allowed them to reflect on their own growth and learning over the course of the school year. Simply filling portfolios with completed work was not enough. It was the process of reflection that enabled my students, too, to see beyond the printed page.

Finally, I realized that I had to be willing to take risks, too, if any learning was going to happen. I could not sit back and wait for my students to produce wonderful portfolios based upon my assignments and expectations alone. Will contracts and portfolios work every year with all classes? Who knows? The point is that all writing and learning has to have a reason for being, an intrinsic value to the learner. In this case, the contract system personalized the portfolios for my students; that is, it helped them to make the portfolios their own. If one method does not elicit this end, another one must be attempted. Portfolios work when classrooms and students work, when the value of what is being done comes from, and is seen by, the students themselves. This, I believe, is a most valuable lesson for any teacher.

# 19

# Going up the Creek Without a Canoe
## Using Portfolios to Train New Teachers of College Writing

Wendy Bishop
*Florida State University*

The portfolio system is not designed to check up on the TA's, it is designed to promote the concept of the TA as coach, not evaluator. The place where this concept falls apart is that I grade all my papers, as do, I think, all or most of the other TA's. So the concept of TA as coach and peer can only go so far. And in any case, the TA has to give the final class grade.

I cannot see any alternative to grading each particular paper. My students would go ape-s--- without grades. I will also admit that I would have trouble keeping track of how each student was doing in terms of final grade[s] without some sort of paper to paper grading system.

—Steve

I am so pleased. Everyone of my students got in his or her portfolio and arrived to class on time. What a wonderful feeling; I was so proud of them. . . .

I read the midterm self-evaluations that they wrote in class yesterday. I'm impressed by the fact that they really do know what grade each of them probably deserves and will probably get. They all seemed very close. Some were a little harder on themselves than I would be. I think they're impressed with the work they've done.

Some feel that their portfolio draft is the best paper they've ever
written. Many of them were also actually surprised by the
difference between the first rough draft and the portfolio draft. . . .
Monday was a very good day.

—Peg

In their teaching journals, Steve and Peg register distinctly different
reactions to a new teaching practice. To a great extent, their reactions
prompted this narrative review of issues that developed when I
used portfolio evaluation as a cornerstone of a pedagogy class for
new teachers of college writing. There is limited information available on portfolio evaluation (see "Portfolio Assessment"), yet there
is growing interest among process-paradigm teachers and teacher
trainers for using portfolios because they promise an evaluation
method consistent with process-teaching practices.

To prepare for portfolio evaluation, I found it necessary to review
available literature, tailor the plan to the program, design training
materials, try materials with my freshman class, and explore and
then evaluate these materials in the graduate pedagogy seminar.
Simultaneously, and often problematically, any changes I was making
in training practices might affect not only the new writing teachers
but also the composition director, department chair, TA mentors,
and department professors. Although these may seem like simple,
linear steps and unsurprising issues, as I was developing and
exploring portfolios as a teacher-training strategy, I encountered
complicated problems: confusion among some new teachers and
resistance and alarm from some TA mentors and department
colleagues.

## Getting Ready

When higher-level administrators at this northwestern university
started discussing writing proficiency, word sifted down to the
English department that the university or even the state legislature
might impose some type of exit or proficiency testing for required
writing courses. Until that time, the department had experienced
remarkable freedom for designing and evaluating the freshman
writing program. Students were placed in writing classes by entrance
test scores, which were confirmed or questioned only by first-day,
in-class diagnostic writing. There was no exit testing.

Clearly, mandated proficiency testing would strongly affect an

English department that had, up to that time, involved itself very little with composition issues. The composition director began to investigate alternative testing possibilities with the support of the current chair, hoping to develop a contingency plan to forestall any nondepartmental proposal.

While talking to the composition director about alternative possibilities, including a holistically scored exit test or a junior or senior year writing-in-the-discipline course, I suggested portfolio evaluation along the lines proposed by Ford and Larkin, Burnham, and Elbow and Belanoff, since I had been using writing portfolios for several years in composition, creative writing, and technical writing classes (Bishop "Revising").

Actively pursuing the idea, the composition director requested and received university funds for a guest "specialist." Four months later, in the fall of 1987, Peter Elbow visited the campus for a week to discuss proficiency-testing options and to talk in general to the department about composition. It was certainly a pleasant visit for me, for the composition director, and I hope for Peter Elbow, but after his visit, I had the distinct feeling that few in the English department and/or administration knew why Elbow had visited. Equally, no concrete plan for instituting a portfolio system was developed in response to that visit. For the administration and non−composition faculty members, Elbow was perceived as a guest lecturer rather than the consultant for curricular change that he could have been.

By early spring 1988, however, several interested teachers planned an informal, grass-roots, practice reading session. We agreed to gather midsemester papers from our EN111 (freshman English) classes, evaluate each others' class essays, and discuss our findings. When we met, in March of 1988, we spent the first thirty minutes of our available sixty minutes explaining how each of us (eight individuals) had all misunderstood our own good intentions. Some of us had not brought essays, some had already graded and marked our essays, and so on. We finally managed to read an available ungraded set, listing our evaluations on a separate sheet of paper. Each participant evaluated each essay in that set as being pass (set at C or above) or no pass (set at D or below). Then, we shared our results.

Evaluation specialists who have followed me this far may well blanch−we had no anchor papers, no rubric, no control on paper type, no reader training, and no common understanding of a portfolio-evaluation system other than what each of us had gleaned from a mimeographed copy of the Elbow and Belanoff article. We left our meeting with no plan for continuing that was any better than the plan we had followed that day.

That's where our grass roots efforts stood by the end of spring 1988. At that time, the threat of imposed proficiency testing was (by rumor) diminishing, Peter Elbow's visit was less than a memory for all but three or four of us, and I was offered the opportunity to train the new teaching assistants in the department's composition pedagogy course for the upcoming fall semester. I would have the summer to prepare. I was also teaching a freshman composition class that summer, so I could develop training materials if I wished, a sample syllabus and class handouts, for instance. Most important, I could decide, as I did with the support of the composition director, to institute a full-fledged portfolio system within the pedagogy seminar.

Reflecting on the problems we had encountered in even beginning to develop an informal portfolio evaluation system, I became more convinced that the best place to explore such testing and evaluation issues was with the new teachers. I felt that new teachers of college writing would benefit from an immersion, not only in process pedagogy but also in a process evaluation method: writing portfolios. If researchers like Arthur Applebee are correct—that process teaching is not going on in the classroom at the rate our journal articles concerned with the topic would seem to indicate (instead, research and theory usually outpace practice)—then new teachers of writing might benefit from the opportunity truly to experience new methods before their own teaching and learning histories or departmental constraints asserted primacy. My own research with writing teachers led me to believe I would best be able to effect change in evaluation procedures with teachers who were, relatively, ideologically uncommitted (Bishop *Something Old*).

Equally, my experiences during the preceding year with our informal program for change had taught me that even a grass-roots try at portfolio evaluation would have to be instituted and overseen by at least *one* individual, especially in a department with little commitment to or expertise in composition studies and with minimal experience with testing and evaluation in general. Although idea sharing and collegiality *could* be spin-offs of such an investigation, unorganized collegiality would not coordinate a rather complicated undertaking.

During summer 1988, then, I began reading more widely about evaluation issues and collected the reading materials that I would present in the pedagogy seminar in the fall: work by Larson and Knoblauch and Brannon on teachers' commenting practices and grading, work by Beavan on evaluation alternatives, work by

Burnham and Elbow and Belanoff on portfolio evaluation, and so on. I adapted a generic grading rubric used for individual papers to include portfolio categories, and I wrote handouts to explain the method to my class and shared them with the composition director. When I couldn't explain myself clearly to him, I often saw the necessity to revise materials again.

Also that summer, the composition director and I read one set of each other's class papers at midterm and at the end of the semester. We assessed papers using the rubric I had adapted as a preliminary run-through for the system. Although our evaluations were highly subjective, since they were verified by no other readers, our discussions at this time proved invaluable in clarifying the project and in assuring I had the support of the director.

For the fall 1988 semester, I assumed that new teaching assistants would participate in the portfolio system fully, by following my sample syllabus, or partially, by agreeing to ask students to prepare a mid- and end-of-semester "best" paper for evaluation by an outside reader. These "outside readers" would consist of members of our pedagogy seminar.

Beyond inculcating a drafting cycle in TAs' classes and introducing them to evaluation issues they might not consider on their own, sharing papers would allow me to explore proficiency testing issues with a limited number of teachers. For each TA's class, should a student's paper receive a C or above (pass) reading, the teacher would set the student's class grade according to whatever class criteria she or he used normally. Should the student's paper receive a D or below (no pass) reading, *it was suggested* that the student receive no higher than a D class grade (D is a passing grade at this university; students receiving a D may still go on to the required sophomore-level writing class). We raised our "outside reading" pass level from D to C because we felt, due to the revision opportunities offered in our writing classes and the help available through the writing center, it was reasonable to expect "average" writing from a student at the end of a semester of writing instruction.

By the time I completed my preparation for the pedagogy seminar, I had already learned valuable lessons. First, departments may resist instituting a portfolio evaluation system unless mandated to test existing students. Equally, departmental support for such a project will fluctuate with upper administration's pressure: more pressure, more support; less pressure, less support.

Second, hiring an outside writing specialist *is* useful for those involved in designing a project and as a public relations event. However, the specialist's expertise may be wasted if this individual is brought in before enough groundwork has been laid in terms of

gaining department commitment, developing teachers' understanding of goals and methods, and assessing teachers' degree of
interest.

Third, a project to "change" department evaluation methods on
this scale should be headed by one or, preferably, two or more
interested and knowledgeable individuals or the project will (a) take
a very long time; (b) send confusing messages, undercutting the
effect of any work done; or (c) fall apart. Ideally, released time
for research and pilot testing is necessary to perform this work
professionally.

And fourth, those department members who are coordinating
such a project should realize that until the professional materials
regarding portfolio evaluation develop sufficiently (or unless they
have access to CCCC workshops or have strong backgrounds in
rhetoric and composition *and* testing and evaluation), they will have
to prepare a great amount of site-specific training materials for new
teachers, as well as clear explanations and rationales for possibly
more resistant continuing teachers.

## The Pedagogy Seminar Semester

One week before the fall 1988 semester began, the composition
director and I conducted a two-hour-a-day, five-day workshop in
which we reviewed department policies and immersed the thirteen
new and returning teaching assistants in writing-process activities
along Bay Area Writing Program/National Writing Program lines
(see Daniels and Zemelman). That week, all TAs designed their
course syllabi and reviewed them with department-assigned mentors.
The composition director was one mentor and two faculty members
trained primarily in literature were also mentors. I refer to them as
literature mentors since they held positions in relation to the TAs
and to me distinct from that of the composition director (who also
was a mentor). The literature mentors did not attend the writing
workshop section of the orientation.

Throughout the semester, these three mentors met regularly
with department TAs and visited each TA's class twice. Additionally,
they reviewed three sets of TA evaluated papers. Unlike the composition director, neither literature mentor had been involved in the
Peter Elbow visit — one was on leave, one chose not to attend — or
the informal portfolio-evaluation session, conducted the previous
spring semester.

As the project began, I gave the literature mentors copies of my training materials—the sample freshman English syllabus with its accompanying letter to incoming TAs and a description of portfolio evaluation. Since, normally, mentors examined three sets of *graded* papers with TAs, I explained to TAs in this letter that they might choose to evaluate papers with written comments or critique sheets but might also feel obliged to show mentors separate grade estimates or to mark papers according to some type of scale—check, check plus or check minus, numbers (1−5) or grades (A−F).

The pedagogy seminar enrolled eight new teaching assistants and five local teachers and graduate students; our weekly meetings progressed fairly uneventfully up until midterm. There were all the usual problems experienced by new teachers; they were learning too much and needing to put new practices to work immediately in the writing classroom. And there was a growing but always inexplicit ideological split between, on the one hand, the teacher trainer, me, and the composition director mentor (both of us process pedagogy advocates) and, on the other hand, the literature mentors, who were clearly less committed to composition studies.

During the course of the pedagogy seminar, the TAs and I discussed evaluation articles. Participants responded to readings and the class through teaching-process journals and responded to each other's journals in groups that met once a week outside of class. Just before midsemester, as a class, we conducted an evaluation session using sample papers gathered from my summer English 111 class; in this session we agreed upon anchor papers at the pass (P) and no pass (NP) levels, clarified and modified our rubric, and shared reading concerns.

At midsemester, during a pedagogy seminar class meeting, we evaluated student papers from the freshman composition classes of participating seminar members. Readers included TAs, other enrolled M.A. students, the composition director, and me. Each paper received two or three readings, until at least two readers agreed on a pass (P) or no pass (NP) rating. This midsemester evaluation session with "outside readers" clarified the system for several teaching assistants who had questions about portfolio logistics and holistic reading. The session also shook the faith of several others who were faced with returning nonpassing papers to students for the first time.

Between midsemester and the end-of-semester evaluation session, mentors and new teachers and I, all in our own ways, expressed dissatisfaction with certain elements of a portfolio-based training seminar. Particularly, I was concerned that the teaching assistants were being put under unnatural stress in trying to meet the expectations of their mentors and of the pedagogy seminar. For instance, seemingly aware for the first time that a new evaluation system was in place, one mentor phoned the composition director and expressed chagrin that TAs, evaluating a single piece of writing, might disagree on their readings and that I was encouraging such a process. This mentor in particular seemed never to have shared his own readings of papers nor participated in holistic evaluation sessions. For him, the portfolio evaluation method seriously questioned what he felt was natural and needed teacher authority in the classroom.

Since we had no department forum for airing these worries, they surfaced unexpectedly at a department colloquium intended to share scholarly works-in-progress. The composition director presented a critical paper on reading response. Without notice, the discussion afterward veered to a critique and defense of the pedagogy seminar and the portfolio system. The talk was sharp; the department chair mediated briefly and then dismissed the colloquium.

A week later, the chair called a special meeting to discuss issues that simply had not gone away. Primarily, the literature mentors were concerned that students were learning multiple revision practices and evaluation procedures that they would encounter nowhere else in the university. They pointed out that students in biology and math and psychology would be taking essay tests and be graded on single drafts of research papers, not on their writing process. Additionally, they expressed concern that I was encouraging teaching assistants *not* to assign final grades for individual papers.

Increasingly, it became obvious that, despite department approved guidelines which encouraged process classrooms by recommending conferencing, journal writing, ungraded writing opportunities, and so on, these mentors had found some of the classrooms they visited unusual and disturbing; students were working in groups and teachers did not appear to be teaching. Finally, one mentor felt I had not "proved" that portfolio-based classrooms (and, implicitly, the entire process methodology) produced better student essays. These critiques made me understand more clearly that my focus had truly shifted from products ("better essays") to people and their processes. Through portfolio evaluation of the workshop classroom, I intended to affect people as much as I intended to affect papers; I hoped to produce better writers and better teacher evaluators. I realized that I would need to make these goals more clear.

We completed the semester and the pedagogy seminar with a final portfolio-evaluation session. In addition to the pedagogy seminar members and composition director, one of the literature mentors attended and participated as did two interested faculty members and several second-year TAs. The following semester, four of the eight new TAs from the pedagogy seminar decided to continue using portfolios, including the two who most worried about their ability to return nonpassing papers to students after their first portfolio-evaluation session experience.

## Seminar Lessons

For all of us, learning compounded exponentially as the pedagogy seminar progressed. New teachers of writing received immediate experience evaluating student writing as they taught their first composition courses. However, they still needed infinite support from mentors, trainers, and peers as they worked to understand the fallibility and strength of their own judgments. This became clear in the following cases.

1. Some teachers who assigned grades or points on papers before the portfolio found their grades in conflict with the outside readings of a paper and didn't know how to go back to their students with such results.

   What a night. I felt all sorts of things but none of them are particularly uplifting. First, I can't believe the students who didn't pass and I can't believe the students who did pass. I'm really off-balance because of this. I think I need to think about this over the weekend. One thing is certain, I can't give these papers back tomorrow morning. I need some time to figure out how to break the news to some of these students. (Scott)

   Some teachers were sure students couldn't survive without a grade until midsemester; several other teachers found their students adjusting to the new evaluation quite smoothly. I learned to suspect that our own evaluation fears are easily transmitted to students: those teachers who worried that students would be worried about not receiving grades tended to find that students *were* worried, and vice versa.

2. Teachers did not know how to explain a split reading to students (two teachers not passing and one teacher passing a paper equals a not pass). They had never brought up the issue of subjectivity in evaluation in class. New teachers of writing strive to appear less fallible than they always feel. Admitting subjectivity can shake teachers' belief in themselves.

   For those students who had to go to 3rd readers I feel there is strong potential for them to wonder what on earth is going on, and they may feel like they passed by luck of the draw. Those papers didn't show consistency of policy. (Sara)

[note added later by Sara: "This worked itself out in class — as I talked with those students individually."]

3. Some teachers did not *believe* in holistic evaluation either because they had never experienced this type of evaluation themselves or because they distrusted the readings given to their papers by other inexperienced teachers or by class members who were not currently teachers (although trained in the same practice session and reading the same seminar materials):

At one point I felt some papers were being judged solely on choice of subject.... I was feeling very protective towards all of the writers being evaluated in that class. (Sara)

One observation: of my four students who did not pass, all but one of the NP readers were non-TAs. I'm not sure if this means anything but I wonder. (Scott)

4. Conflicting attitudes on the part of mentors, composition director, and teacher trainer toward the system were quickly communicated to the teaching assistants and sometimes confused them. For instance, literature mentors did not, themselves, understand how a paper that did not receive a letter grade and copious on-text markings could have been properly evaluated.

[My mentor] expressed reservations about the fact that I was not actually marking the [student's] paper itself. He was not sure that a student could find mechanical/LOCs [lower order concerns] if I did not specifically point them out. I agreed that this was a problem.

[He] said that he did not want to push me in a specific direction as far as grading was concerned. He understands that we are all pushed towards a grading system that is more like what I am doing than what he would do if he was in charge of the ranch. I sense a certain disdain on [mentor's] part for the highly process-oriented approach that Wendy and [composition director] advocate. I told him that I felt lucky to have instructors/mentors that *do not* have the same views. I figure a good balance can be struck. (Steve)

In this instance, the teaching assistant resolved conflicts. In other cases, resolution may not have been so simple.

5. Teachers' syllabi or grading practices could contradict the evaluation system. Teachers might simply add on the external reading but not integrate it into their grading system, so the Pass/No Pass reading functioned as a test more than a teaching device. Some teachers also decided that readers' evaluations contradicted the evaluations they wished to give. It appeared that, to use the system effectively, teachers may need *actively* to adapt materials

and methods to their classroom, which not all new teachers are knowledgeable enough or willing to do.

I don't know. I don't think that the Portfolio thing is a total disaster. It just didn't do anything for me this time around. If I wanted it to work for me I guess I would have to restructure my entire class plan. (Steve)

6. New teachers of writing, using any system, have to face the issue of "failing" students they have become close to. The portfolio system, which encourages withholding grades on individual papers, and the process classroom may exacerbate this problem.

I really had no idea this portfolio stuff would be so intense. I really like the idea, I like using other readers and I like getting an idea of how (and what) other classes are doing. I need to find a way to be less emotionally involved with my students. I have been completely consumed by this, even dreaming about it. (Scott)

7. A belief in portfolio evaluation may be closely tied into beliefs about process instruction. Those less committed to or successful with process instruction may remain equally uncommitted to or unsuccessful with portfolio evaluation.

So if the Portfolio system does not really promote the coach/peer mystique, and it does not check up on the TA's, then what practical purpose does it serve? At this point I think that all it does is get in the way of my own class plan. (Steve)

8. The portfolio system is not simple, particularly since it frustrates traditional grading expectations. Portfolio methods will have to be discussed again and again; they may not make sense until they are experienced.

For the last ten minutes [of freshman composition] I talked again about the complete portfolio and answered still more questions. In all I've covered the portfolio system at least five times recently, but there are still questions, still fears, and I suspect there will be until they've got it handed in. It's just so different from anything they've had to do before. . . .

All of this seems pretty crazy to them. I see the anxiety and questioning. It's almost like they somehow expect everything will blow up in their faces. This is why I'm trying to do most of the preparation in class time, so I'm there to answer questions. . . . They just seem to need to hear it over and over again. (Peg)

[Entry from the beginning of the semester] Until [the portfolio method] is proven to me, I am not going to commit myself to it. . . . What if a large portion of the 111 students flunk the portfolio evaluation? Especially if these students are not "bad" students? Wouldn't we then be, as instructors, up the creek without a canoe, much less a paddle? (Steve)

9. New teachers are highly sensitive to departmental divisiveness and will appreciate support and solidarity for their undertakings, including portfolio evaluation.

> I think the final portfolio evaluation was a great success. I was very pleased that [mentor] and [interested professor] showed up. As a student it is a wonderful show of support for us. Their presence and seeing what they passed and did not pass was also insightful — gave us better perceptions of our perspectives on what passes and doesn't pass. I'm not sure if they'll ever know just how nice it was for us to have them there. (Peg)

10. Teachers have emotional reactions to this process (learning any method in general but learning portfolio evaluation in particular) that should not be underestimated:

> At any rate, I had another dream (not about rats this time!). I dreamed Wendy had evaluated every single line written in our journals and marked them each with a red pen ... and gave me a D at the end.... I woke up laughing wondering at the same time if I should cry ... and think it was me wondering if I've been too harsh on some of my students. (Sara)

## Going up the Creek Without a Canoe

Reviewing teachers' journals taught me much of what I have tried to share here. The pedagogy seminar experience did not greatly change those new teachers who entered it with strongly expressed reservations about using portfolios. It appeared that changing, fully, to portfolio evaluation would have required substantial time commitments from them at a moment when they were already undergoing a great deal of stress. However, even TAs who were resistant to portfolios, like Steve quoted above, still enjoyed the camaraderie of the evaluation sessions; Steve participated as a reader at our next evaluation meeting even though he was not using portfolios during that semester.

Conversely, those teachers who expressed strong interest in and commitment to this type of evaluation still experienced many ups and downs, particularly Scott and Sara, quoted extensively above, but those TAs continue to use portfolios. What appeared to them as panic over portfolios, or what Steve aptly called going up the creek without a canoe, was as much panic over predictable teaching issues, panic *any* new teacher of writing may experience. As a teacher trainer, I learned it was tricky if not downright dangerous to subvert a department's accepted practices; I instituted portfolios at the cost of some hard feelings and unexpected confrontations with less involved faculty members. At times, I was on the defensive. However, by meeting with mentors and the department chair, I was forced to confront my avoidance of confrontation. I became more adept at explaining and defending my theory-based beliefs concerning writing evaluation to mentors and teachers, and I modified my training documents to be clearer and more explicit. I do expect to continue to use portfolios to train TAs, because working with new teachers and current faculty in this manner taught me a great deal and constantly challenged my thinking.

Some time after the pedagogy seminar, I asked former members to fill out a questionnaire concerning their current feelings about and practices with portfolios. Four teachers—Ellen, Jill, Carolyn, and Sara—responded. All saw some value in the system and all mentioned problems. Two TAs felt the problems that they listed diminished as their own experience increased; these two teachers continue to use portfolio evaluation. Two other TAs felt that their worries over reader reliability for the outside reading had not diminished. These teachers no longer use portfolios, preferring to rely on their own judgments for paper grading.

In general, the four teachers felt the concepts of portfolio evaluation were well presented in the pedagogy seminar, although one teacher strongly desired more written guidance. Teachers also suggested they would benefit from more practice evaluation sessions, occurring earlier in the seminar, and from regular, informal sharing with peers about portfolio practices.

As a teacher trainer, I will take these suggestions to heart, remembering that new teachers of writing value *every* opportunity to share grading and evaluation practices. I'm also pleased that these TAs proved so willing to go up the creek without a canoe, to explore alternative and perhaps even "radical" evaluation methods; through exploration, we all became more professional. Together, we found that using portfolio evaluation in a pedagogy seminar is a productive practice, one that results in meaningful dialogues, one from which participants continue to learn, and one that teacher trainers will want to consider.

# IV

# Political Issues

# 20

# Introducing a Portfolio-based Writing Assessment
## *Progress Through Problems*

William Condon and Liz Hamp-Lyons
*University of Michigan*

Everything, Nancy Sommers suggests, begins in narrative ("Understanding Student Narratives"), and certainly our assessment of the problems we encountered and the progress our program has made in converting from a timed impromptu exit assessment to a portfolio exit assessment does. We tell the story of our journey because as we look back upon it, as we view it as story rather than living it as drama, we find that we are able to "make sense, retroactively, of the past and project a meaning onto the future, knit past and future together, and create, suspended between the two, the present" (Rose 6). From our current vantage point, we can perceive a narrative strain, a plot of a sort, which reveals aspects and influences of the change to a portfolio-based system that were not recognized as such when they occurred. In other words, a number of important discoveries have occurred along the way — discoveries that have affected every aspect of our program, that have involved us in considering new problems and new kinds of progress, and that have kept us moving forward as we respond to each new facet of portfolio assessment. While many might view what follows as a drama, a play in four acts, we like to perceive our story as action research. But perhaps it is just a story, still incomplete: the story of how a seemingly simple change from one form of exit assessment to another has opened up a wealth of issues, which in the beginning we did not even realize were there, and of how the examination of those issues has allowed our program to move forward and has brought us as a faculty closer together professionally.[1]

## Understanding the Problem

Before the fall of 1987, the exit assessment from the English Composition Board's Writing Practicum consisted of a fifty-minute impromptu essay that was read and scored by two (or three) readers in the well-established process of holistic scoring. The readers were also the ECB's professional writing faculty. The procedure used at Michigan was adopted in 1978 (see Fader) and existed, more or less intact, until about 1986. Indeed, the entry assessment remains essentially the same: all entering students (except from the School of Business Administration) write a fifty-minute impromptu essay during orientation, and their performance on that essay places them at one of three levels within the university's writing program: into Writing Practicum, Introductory Composition, or exempt from the first-year writing requirement. The English Composition Board, reporting directly to the dean, is responsible for all aspects of the writing program and also teaches the Writing Practicum courses from within its own faculty. Approximately eight hundred students, freshpersons and transfers, take these courses each year, in classes of no more than sixteen students taught by highly qualified and experienced writing faculty (most with Ph.D.s). The practicum is a half-semester, credit/no-credit course for students who need more practice writing before they are able to compete successfully with their peers in Introductory Composition and in their other university classes. The practicum provides an intensive experience — two two-hour class meetings and a thirty-minute individual conference per student per week — geared to allow students to progress quickly through the course and on into the main track of the university's writing program. From the beginning, in 1978, until the fall of 1987, students concluded the practicum by sitting for another fifty-minute impromptu essay, identical in format and with the same possibilities for placement: Writing Practicum, Introductory Composition, or exempt. This system was designed to render valid placement decisions for students coming out of the practicum, since the instrument that placed them into the course was the same as the instrument that governed their passage out of that course.

Several sources of dissatisfaction arose, however, some of which concerned the assessment instrument itself, but most of which were endemic to the whole concept of using a fifty-minute impromptu essay as an exit assessment. One fifty-minute impromptu argumentative essay could not, many felt, adequately assess either the students' writing skills or the progress those students had made as a result of their work in the practicum. While the university's schedule for orientation left us shackled with the fifty-minute impromptu as an entry assessment, our experience in the classroom, as well as current theory in writing, made us question the definition of writing competence this procedure assumed. We questioned whether the results obtained by this method did justice to what the students had learned, and the questions we raised then have become central issues in the still scant literature surrounding portfolio assessment. Roberta Camp, of the Educational Testing Service, reports that the movement toward portfolio-based assessment grows from a definition of writing that recognizes the value of varieties of writing and stresses the writing process. Assessment must fit into the larger context of a writing process (Camp, "Portfolios Evolving"). Assessment must also fit into the larger context of a writing program, certainly, as well as within the even larger context of the university (Anson and Brown; Bridwell-Bowles 6), or it can hardly be viewed as fair to the students passing through it. Perhaps most telling, though, are the doubts cast by those such as Elbow and Belanoff on the conclusions drawn from one-shot proficiency tests: "The research movement that gives high marks to holistic scoring for validity . . . also shows that no matter how accurately we may evaluate any sample of a student's writing, we lose all that accuracy if we go on to infer the student's actual proficiency in writing from just that single sample" (this volume 4–5). In our dissatisfaction with our own status quo, we had arrived at many of these same conclusions, based on essentially the same theoretical misgivings regarding our method for assessing the writing proficiency of students exiting the Writing Practicum.

Our immediate problem, however, seemed less theoretical than practical: requests for "overrides" from class instructors, for students who the instructors asserted had been wrongly placed by the exit impromptu assessment, had become frequent enough to cause us concern. Moreover, several faculty believed that using the fifty-minute impromptu actually undermined instruction by letting the students in this credit/no-credit course concentrate on only a small portion of the course, on impromptu writing. Students often resisted revision (not possible on an impromptu), and they ignored much of what was presented with regard to invention (no time for much of that on an impromptu either). Such resistances made teaching writing as a process difficult, almost hypocritical. Since the impromptu exit assessment clearly emphasized writing as a product, students felt entitled — perhaps even empowered — to ignore the importance of process. As long as exit assessment was in the form of impromptu writing only, there was a mismatch between what instructors propounded and what they were seen to practice, a mismatch that became increasingly unacceptable to more and more of the faculty.

Another problem that became apparent when we began to re-examine our exit assessment was that faculty differed in their view of its function. Some felt that it should check that students leaving this level and moving into introductory composition were at the same level as students placed directly into introductory composition; these faculty tried hard to read exit impromptu essays in the same way as they read entry impromptu assessment essays. Other faculty felt that students who were completing a writing course at the University of Michigan should be better writers than entering students, and they seemed to apply stricter standards. Still others felt that no one should have to take the lowest-level course twice, and seemed to be generous to the very weakest writers. All of the faculty were using their contextual knowledge, reading rhetorically, as described by Haas and Flower, and contextually, as the work of Bruffee, John Harris, and others shows we always do. Yet our impromptu entry assessment was built in the traditional manner, in which all identifying markers about the writers are removed and decisions are as decontextualized and "fair" as possible. Such measures make sense, of course, in the context of an entry assessment, but we found such procedures to be unacceptable on the exit assessment. Faculty knew these students, knew their writing, felt strongly that this student should be exempt or that this other student needed another practicum, no matter what the result had been on the impromptu. The student had a bad (or a good) day, faculty would say, and the result does not reflect how well (or poorly) this student can really write. These faculty, with increasing conviction, argued that rather than continuing a decontextualized exit assessment, we should find ways of taking advantage of what we could not eliminate: the context of the practicum, where we could take the time to allow students to show what they could do in and through writing, and where we might find ways to take advantage of our knowledge about the writers instead of deliberately eliminating it.

## Working Toward a Solution

But we tell our story as though it were a simple chronological narrative: it wasn't. Strange though it may seem, looking back on that time from our present moment, we realize that we did not then fully realize the nature of our problem, and so we could not immediately or simply know how to proceed toward a solution. Portfolios did not just emerge as the instant solution to this difficulty; instead, we faced what seemed to be a leap in the dark. Poised on the edge of the abyss, we knew only that we did not like where we were standing. We had little idea of where we would end up should we decide to jump off.

We began by discussing ways we could develop a richer, more extensive instrument. Working groups within the ECB began to explore proposals to, for example, augment the prompts we were using by incorporating a text or several texts into the test, stressing the reading/writing connection. That was eventually rejected because in effect we would lengthen the class time spent dealing with impromptu writing, which was not what we wanted. We also explored substituting an evaluation instrument that would give more specific feedback on the student's writing, thus allowing the outcomes to be more accessible to the students being tested and to their counselors within the university. Although such a system was implemented for entry assessment with some success (Hamp-Lyons and Reed), it was rejected for the exit assessment because, while it addressed some critical inadequacies in our entry assessment, it could not solve the problems, well known to us all, at the heart of impromptu writing assessment. Further, it addressed none of the theoretical and practical objections we had raised to using an impromptu essay as the sole means of performing an exit assessment. Gradually more of us, and gradually more confidently, began to talk of a richer form of exit assessment, one that would employ portfolios. We were then aware of several contexts in which writing portfolios were used to assess writing ability, and in the years since that beginning, we have become aware of even more.[2] Yet since none of these models seemed precisely to fit our context — exit proficiency assessment from a nongraded, multiple-section, pre-composition writing course — we decided to proceed with caution.

We began a flirtation with portfolios during the 1986–87 academic year, when they were introduced as a backup to the regular impromptu exit assessment. Though these portfolios were compiled from writings done in the practicum, there were no uniform guidelines regarding the length of the essays included or the kinds of essays (except that there had to be at least three pieces of writing and that at least one piece had to be an impromptu other than the one written in the formal exit test). These early portfolios were only consulted in the case of a student's or an instructor's appeal of a placement result, and so they did not alleviate the problems the exit impromptu presented. They did, however, give our faculty enough experience reading and evaluating portfolios to make us certain that (1) portfolios could provide a means of evaluating student writing that would be more fully consistent with a process-based writing pedagogy and (2) even though the introduction of portfolios would present many difficult problems, both logistical and philosophical, the benefits to be derived from using portfolios made introducing them worth the trouble. And so our faculty began to require every student in their practicums to prepare a portfolio "in case" their instructor wanted to appeal their exit placement.

From here, the observer at our play can predict the new problem that our makeshift created. Appeals grew more frequent and more successful, convincing even more of us of the inadequacy of our impromptu exit assessment, to the point that we could no longer deny a need to read portfolios as a normal procedure for exit assessment. As time passed, we faced an ever stronger, ever more pervasive desire for a richer form of assessment, as if the portfolio had become a self-promoting artifact. Nevertheless, we knew that we faced a difficult time of transition, for introducing portfolios would, in a real sense, transform our established program and alter our own roles within it.

## Searching for Consensus

Our difficulties began before we had even started, in deciding what the precise makeup of a portfolio would be. Obviously (in retrospect: it was not then so immediately apparent to us), nested within that question lay the need to formulate a new definition of writing competence, a definition that would in turn ensure that the specified contents of these portfolios would allow students to display their full potential for competent writing. Perhaps most obviously, this new context for judgment presented the need to define competence in such a way that it could include revision. But competence also had to be defined in a way that allowed students to present a variety of writing within their own portfolios and that allowed instructors to teach with various approaches, methods, and materials, with the result that a variety of writing would appear from portfolio to portfolio within any single class. We faced the difficult task of serving apparently contradictory needs: to ensure uniformity, we had to dictate the contents of a portfolio, while acknowledging diversity among students and classes meant leaving the essential form open. We had to learn what we felt we needed to know about the students' writing while leaving room for them to show us the full range of writing that they are capable of producing. Thus, even the decision that a portfolio would contain a revised argumentative paper, an in-class timed essay, and a second revised paper, preceded by a cover letter, required a good deal of discussion and negotiation among our faculty.

Ultimately, the decision of what to include grew out of what we felt we were teaching in the practicum, which in turn required us to reach some firmer consensuses about course content than we had previously established. This was not as easy as it may sound, especially for a faculty that has resisted, and continues to resist, a detailed written curriculum, standard syllabi, or prescribed texts, priding itself instead on its professionalism and emphasizing the benefits of utilizing each faculty member's individual skills and knowledge. There were, though, some things that as a faculty we already agreed upon. We were agreed that our courses needed to focus on academic writing and on argumentation in particular, since two successive surveys of Michigan faculty had told us that these were the two categories of writing that professors most often assigned (Keller-Cohen and Wolfe). We were also agreed on a process-oriented approach that necessitated a less teacher-centered class than is perhaps usual in college composition. Faced with the need to work collaboratively, which the portfolio method of assessment presented, however, these points of agreement were clearly insufficient. Our definitions of academic writing differed greatly, as was clear to us even before we began the intense self-examination the move to portfolios required. We also differed as to how much we emphasized writing processes and which processes we stressed, and on the importance we attached to written products.

Since portfolios are read not only by the class instructor but also by at least one colleague, we needed more formal and open consensuses that would allow one teacher to read and respond reliably and justly to the writing of a student in a colleague's class, but that would not define what we would teach so narrowly that the consensus began to infringe upon an individual faculty member's freedom to design and conduct a practicum as he or she thought best. So we defined the contents loosely, including an argumentative essay because we could agree to make argument the heart of the course. We refused to specify the form of the second essay further than the understanding that it would be some sort of academic writing or writing that was intended to act as a bridge to academic writing. Both these essays, we decided, could be revised as often and as extensively as time allowed, and the faculty's expectation was that these pieces would represent the best that the student could produce.

The third piece was to be an impromptu, timed, in-class essay similar to the existing exit assessment. Thus, students would receive a certain amount of practice for the impromptu they would write at the end of the course. Some faculty felt this opportunity was important because timed writing is common within the university, while others believed that including an impromptu would also serve as a check on authorship. Finally, the last piece of writing was a cover letter, written in class on the last day before the post-test. The cover letter was to serve both as an introduction and table of contents, giving students a chance to establish a direct relationship with their readers, as well as a chance to display their ability to write effectively about their own writing. This combination of in-class and revised writing allows students to demonstrate competence within a richer context than either a timed writing or revised essays alone could allow, and even more important, the portfolio grew out of the work the students were doing in the practicum. Where once the exit assessment was essentially unconnected with many of the most important elements of the course, now it is an integral part of the instruction.

## Extending Consensus

As we shape our experience into a narrative for our readers, inevitably the tale is told as though we knew, when we began, where we would go and how we would travel. That is not the reality. In reality each piece of the portfolio represents a compromise between differing views of what was important, as well as with our inability to know what the right decisions would be. As two years have progressed, we have come to understand our own definition of writing competence very clearly, by looking at ourselves and our practices through the portfolios we have collected and evaluated. We have learned rather precisely where our differences lie, and we have done much to articulate why those differences exist. We have also moved closer together in important ways. For example, when the faculty first discussed the "argumentative" essay in the portfolio in order to decide what, for our purposes, we meant by argument, we were unable to reach any shared sense of the term. Now, however, we have agreed on multiple but closely related definitions, and have achieved considerable clarity and richness in those definitions.

Within the context of an assessment based on a fifty-minute impromptu argumentative essay, we had felt no real need to find out what our colleagues were teaching in the name of argumentation.

The brevity of the essays the students wrote, together with the kind of argument the essay prompts dictated, essentially shielded that whole pedagogical process from the evaluators' eyes. Thus, although we stressed the importance of argumentation in everything we said about our program, if we were assessing for it at exit we were doing so only trivially. In reading a portfolio, though, faculty faced more writing; longer individual essays; revised and, theoretically, perfected essays, one of which had to be an argument. And the quality and structure of that argument revealed much more fully the kind of approach the student had learned in practicum. Thus, we found that some of us taught classical argument; some taught the argument-objection-response pattern as it appears, for example, in Meiland's *College Thinking*; some of us taught argument based on thick description or personal writing; and others taught from the broad perspective that any piece of writing that attempts to make a point — to persuade — is an argument. For some instructors argument meant critical thinking, multidimensionality; for others it meant a formal textual pattern and specific formulaic strategies. Once the portfolio system brought this variety into the open, we had to learn to deal with the discrepancy between what the reader thought of as argument and what the student had been taught about argumentation; otherwise, our evaluation certainly would not be fair. We had also, and perhaps most importantly, to find a way to incorporate that diversity, once recognized, into our collective definition so that we could preserve the richness, which we recognized as a strength of our program, while continuing to serve our students' needs. Working with portfolios helped us move toward agreement, and the agreement, as we refined and refined it, helped us read and interpret portfolios.

We were able, after several valuable discussions and exchanges of written text — discussions that continued for over a year and were particularly facilitated by our colleague Barbra Morris, who brought together all our rich complexity of definitions of argument and helped us all to see the patterns of agreement among the complexity — to agree on certain elements that we all expected of an argument, but which could be realized in different ways. Thus, our faculty grew closer together, our curriculum became much more clearly defined, and we gained a document that we could share with students and other colleagues so that practicum itself became less of a mystery.

There were many such discussions and much need to move closer toward consensus along the way as we moved from discussing what students would put into the portfolios to resolving the issues surrounding our responses to them. For example, we discovered that we needed to know how faculty were reading, interpreting, and responding to the content of the portfolios. We had constructed our version of a portfolio based upon what we believed we were teaching and valuing—and in some cases on what we would like to teach more effectively—and now we were having not merely to read the portfolios prepared by our own and our colleagues' students, but also to understand them as "texts" (Fish). The important role of content, of the weight of ideas and evidence built into a credible schema by the student writer, is increasingly clear to us as we read and talk about more and more portfolios, but we are not yet at the stage of being able to specify how important it is or how to judge that importance. This is just one part of the story that remains unfinished.

In addition, our decision to read portfolios in "teams" of three faculty members forced us to examine our notions about the course we were all teaching. For each portfolio, one reader is the class instructor and the other is a team member, with the third team member reading portfolios about which the instructor and second reader disagree on placement. To make sense of other instructors' portfolios, we had to use our understanding of the common aims and goals of our program (so far as they exist/existed then), together with our understanding of how our teaching preferences and our expectations matched with those goals, and place those in turn against the perhaps quite different preferences and expectations of the other instructors in the same portfolio team. Ultimately, we had to create an interpretive community in a context where the stakes were rather high—the success/failure of our own group of students, looked at in equal terms with the success/failure of students we did not know, but who were in their turn dear to the heart of a colleague. In the wholly criterion-referenced system we had decided on for portfolio reading, we (represented by two or three instructors from among us) had to decide directly whether each student's writing was strong enough to move the student forward, and if so, how far. This step in the process moved us onto ground which, to the best of our knowledge, was untrodden.

Responding holistically to what amounts to a short first draft according to long-established criteria is, whatever else one thinks of it, a relatively easy thing to do. The portfolios, however, presented a reader with more writing to judge, with more of the writer's abilities to contemplate, and with a wider range of writing, both within a portfolio and across a class set, than is possible given the limitations of a timed essay. Suddenly we were dealing with more than one piece of writing, some of which had been revised extensively. Suddenly we needed to know a great deal, not just about what a teacher teaches, but how he or she teaches. We had to work out how to approach the reading and how to solve the problem of forming a judgment about the writer's competence in a way that was at once context-rich and impartial. Just seeing the writing before us was not enough to ensure a fair and reliable judgment. We needed more context: what the assignment had been; the methods and objectives of the particular section that student was in; how convinced the instructor was of the virtues of timed impromptus as an assignment type; how keen the instructor was for students to take risks in their writing, as opposed to emphasizing a safe approach that might generate pedestrian texts. In short, we found that we needed a much higher degree of shared knowledge than we had needed before, when every student simply wrote an exit assessment essay, and that need for shared knowledge led to still-emerging consensuses about the nature and the objectives of our course, about the range of pedagogical methods that might best achieve those goals, and about the kinds of writing we would expect in a portfolio.

Thus, just as the portfolio incorporated the writing process into the product the students produced for evaluation, so the portfolio-based exit assessment incorporated the processes involved in program development into the product that our faculty produces: an assessment of student writing. We discovered a powerful forum for faculty development, for the best kinds of learning and sharing of methods, assignments, approaches, and attitudes—a sharing that led to the kind of consistency among sections of practicum that is often attempted but seldom achieved through the sorts of external controls often found in composition programs. None of those external controls exists in the English Composition Board, yet the portfolio system has allowed us to learn so much about and share so much of each other's work in the classroom that the effect is, more and more, precisely the kind of shared knowledge that external controls seek to impose—but without the resentment and sense of threat that we often hear of in externally controlled contexts. And this kind of consistency is extremely flexible, since the learning process continues with each new testing period, with each set of portfolios we read. As students' needs change, portfolios furnish a mechanism that allows our program to change with them.

As we learned more and more about reading portfolios and about each other's approaches to teaching writing, our new knowledge, wavelike, affected both curriculum and community and, wavelike, those effects further eroded fundamental assumptions and revealed new questions. We have already touched upon one example of this kind of development, our emergent definition of *argument*, but finding a consensus about argumentation was not the only adjustment that portfolios required us to make. We had also to determine, collectively, how we would respond to writing that had been subjected to extensive work in conferences with the instructor, as well as in peer review groups. We affirm our belief in the value of revision, both as a tool that skilled adult writers ordinarily use (and which, therefore, a writing course should teach) and as a technique that teaches students how to produce better writing by leading them to work on a piece of their own writing until it is better than they could have written it before they started. In order to achieve either of these goals, revision must have a place in the classroom. However, reading these sometimes heavily revised essays in order to judge a writer's competence raises difficult questions — primarily, of course, of authorship. If the students produce their essays in class and hand them in on the spot, then taking precautions against plagiarism is a simple matter. Once an essay can be revised out of class, however, the problem is more complex, though not by any means unsolvable. In fact, guarding against outright plagiarism — ghost-written essays in the portfolio — simply meant prohibiting students from placing in their portfolios any essay that had not actually been written and revised as part of the practicum, a context that always includes weekly half-hour conferences with the instructor and often extensive peer review sessions as well. In such a context, plagiarism would be extremely difficult to accomplish, and it is further guarded against by the inclusion of two pieces of in-class writing.

The second problem is a more subtle form of the first; that is, this problem still involves authorship, but without the implication or the accusation of plagiarism. If an essay has been through several drafts and has been critiqued along the way by the instructor in conferences and by classmates in peer review groups, then who is the author of the essay? How well can the student really write? We had to find ways of discerning when a piece of writing stopped showing what the student could do and started showing the value of the coaching the student had received. Again, this was a problem that had not arisen when students wrote post-test essays, but it had existed beneath the surface of our former method of assessment. The portfolio let it out.

These problems of authorship, like the other tensions and conflicts in our story, yielded to the narrative force, to the irresistible (as it was beginning to seem to us) movement forward of our plot, which by now had as its central theme the simple fact that at some point the building of a community ceases, and the community begins to build itself. The consensus in favor of a process-based approach was sufficiently strong to dictate that revision would remain a central part of the practicum, so we designed the portfolio so that it enables us to check whether the writer in the revised pieces is the same writer, literally and figuratively, as the writer in the "finished" essays. While the bulk of the writing, in number of pages, (two of the four texts, and the two longest) is still writing that has been revised, two of the four pieces are not (the in-class impromptu and the cover sheet). In addition, the cover sheet is quite a complex piece of writing in itself. It demands a degree of metacognition, for the student must write about writing. Thus, the student can show the extent to which the strengths in his or her writing are conscious strengths, and it stands to reason that writers who have made lasting improvement are more likely to be conscious of the reasons for the improvement and more likely to point out those reasons, while writers who have merely been helped to the appearance of competence will not only betray that impression in their in-class writing, where they could not receive the same level of support, but they will also be less able to write about the strengths of their own writing, thus betraying their lack of accomplishment yet again.

## Reaping the Benefits

In the case of our lack of consensus about argument, as well as in our struggle to deal with the question of just how much support is too much, using a portfolio-based system of exit assessment did not so much create as uncover problems that were present in the system, but that the former method of assessment could not reveal. Far from being a weakness of portfolio assessment, then, we see the problems the use of portfolios raises as one of its most critical positive elements, one of the strongest indicators that it is meaningful assessment, one of its greatest promises of progress to follow. And perhaps the most fruitful source of that promise lies in the fact that portfolios link assessment with instruction, with the result that a portfolio-based assessment aids in strengthening even an already strong writing program by motivating faculty to reach consensus on important aspects of the courses a program offers. In addition, and perhaps just as important, the fact that instructors are reading portfolios from each others' classes produces, of necessity, a high level of interaction among faculty, which in turn results in a high level of shared knowledge of the kind that need not lead toward any consensus. That is, our teacher/readers exchange information about assignments and pedagogical approaches to such a degree that each of us has, in effect, a kind of smorgasbord of teaching practice to draw upon. We know who is using what kind of theoretical base, and who is using what kind of pedagogy, so that if one instructor wishes to adopt a certain approach or specific technique, she or he has not only a ready resource for beginning, but also an effective model close at hand.

This high level of shared information and shared commitment affects students as well as teachers. Students find that the common experience of preparing a portfolio knits peer review groups together more securely than when the goal is to produce just one essay or to write, eventually, an acceptable exit assessment essay. Faculty regularly report that students bring their awareness of the portfolio to bear, both individually and in peer groups, from the very beginning of the term, and that it serves as an individual and a group motivator. On the individual level, students are more committed to writing that counts, so they are more willing to put a heavy investment into a piece of writing because they know that, ultimately, this piece of writing may go into a portfolio and determine their further placement within the University's writing program. Thus, a student will work harder to begin with and be more open to multiple revisions than students were before, when the revisions did not, as far as the students could see, affect how they would do in the exit assessment. In addition, the portfolios give more impetus to collaborative learning situations such as peer review or other group work. Again, when students know that their writing counts, they are more forthcoming with advice and more willing to take advice than is usual in peer-review situations, where the end of the process is a single essay that will be graded and become just one minor component in determining a course grade or, as in our case, formerly, an impromptu post-test essay that had absolutely no connection the students could see with the current writing task. Peer review ceases to be a cute trick composition instructors impose on long-suffering students, valued, as Freedman tells us, more by writing teachers than their students. It becomes a real compact between learners who can have a stake in helping someone else succeed and get the same kind of help themselves, without an element of competition interfering in the cooperative effort.

Perhaps more important than the shared knowledge among students or teachers, however, is the knowledge that portfolio readers share during the process of assessment. And while it is important to remember that the classroom teachers are also the portfolio readers, it is equally important to remember that these are two different roles — roles that may and often do reflect on each other, but that remain separate, both because assessment comes at the end, when there is no more class to teach, and because, for the teacher of an ungraded course, assuming the role of evaluator marks an abrupt change from the persona adopted in class. In class, the teacher is supportive, coaches, coaxes, facilitates. In the portfolio reading, the teacher must read the same texts she or he has seen before, in class, in conference, in the dark of night, but in a new, harsher light. Now these texts are public texts, and they must withstand the full light of day, or the light shone upon them by another teacher in the same program, one who has not been in class, or in the student's journal, or in the conferences; who does not know how far the student has come, or by what path, but only where he is on the journey. Now the teacher must become evaluator, must apply shared criteria, to the extent that we in our interpretive community have moved toward establishing criteria; and she or he must apply the criteria agreed on by the portfolio team.

The difference in these roles produces a different point of view for the instructor/reader, one that enables that reader to look at pedagogy in a different light. For example, participating in a portfolio-reading group allows teachers to explore the role of the portfolio in setting assignments for their students. Since each member of a reading group supplies the others with copies of that class's assignments, readers can see what sorts of assignments produce essays that are assets to a portfolio. They can evaluate the difference between the essay assignment with a rigid structure — geared, for example, to teach students specific lessons about organization or structure or to help them get started on the conceptual level — and the portfolio with more open assignments that give students less structure and less of a conceptual head start. How much guidance one gives students initially is governed by how one feels about the outcome of that guidance: one gives a level of guidance or support that seems to work best for one's students, trying neither to go too far beyond nor to fall short of the support most students need. Portfolio-reading groups offer a place where the teacher, now a reader, can compare different levels of support, both in discussion with the other members of the group and in examining the products, both those from his or her own students, as well as those from students in other classes. Thus, readers themselves receive a great deal of information about solving the problem of how to construct assignments, and they carry that information back with them into their roles as teachers.

We can think of the unfolding of story as teachers and students and readers move into a portfolio system as a spiral, in which shared information works its way into others' teaching, and into one's own, producing changes in students' texts, which produce more shared information, which works back into teaching, turning and turning in a widening sphere of influence, so that, at least for this community, it is not possible to see or foresee where it will turn in the end.

## Conclusion

From our current vantage point, however, two years into a portfolio-based assessment, we can at least see that portfolio assessment is far more than just another method of assessing student writing. It is a tool for change, perhaps subversive to the establishment, occasionally threatening to the insecure, always challenging. We can also share several of the conclusions our experience has led us to draw. First, portfolio assessment is not a method to be imposed from the outside, to be conducted by somebody else's rules and by somebody else's standards. Since portfolio assessment directly links assessment with instruction, the method must be different for each site, since each program that installs it will begin by taking advantage of different strengths as well as by finding that it needs to reach consensus in different areas. Second, portfolio assessment provides an important source for program development: it is a powerful form of faculty development ("faculty" as group noun, not singular noun); a program-evaluation tool; and a means of curricular development. Third, portfolio assessment is a process, not a panacea; it is not to be undertaken lightly, and it is probably not a wise model in situations where power roles are sharply defined, where a few can dictate interpretations to the many. At its best, portfolio assessment establishes a genuine community of writing teachers, held together by mutual interest, cooperation, and respect, rather than the detailed rules and procedures many programs use to ensure "uniformity." At its worst, it could become a bigger stick to students and teachers than any impromptu, timed, essay exam ever was. But a good system of portfolio assessment embodies a multiplicity of processes that leads faculty to look at products that open still more processes to scrutiny. Finally, while we have spoken of some major implications and consequences of adopting a portfolio system of evaluation, we have only scratched the surface of what has happened, and what will happen. After more than two years of intensive study of and involvement in portfolio assessment, we are still not all that far from the beginning. However, we remain enthusiastic about continuing to make discoveries about ourselves and our program, about continuing a process that has already gone beyond all our expectations in leading to a reformation of our program and our visions of ourselves as writing teachers.

## Notes

1. The authors wish to acknowledge the Post-Test Committee of 1987–88 (Jan Armon, Barbra Morris, and Ellen Westbrook) for its work on new models for exit assessment writing tasks; the Stimulus Committee of 1987–88 (Jan Armon, Helen Isaacson, Barbra Morris) for its work on new models for impromptu assessment prompts; the Portfolio Committee of 1987–88 (Emily Jessup, Mike Lyons, and Barbra Morris) for feasibility studies and data collection; and all our other colleagues at the English Composition Board (1987–89) who have worked with us to develop, implement, and continue questioning a portfolio exit-assessment system: Heather Buda, Cheryl Cassidy, Francelia Clark, George Cooper, Kathy Dixon, Louise Freyman, Janise Honeyman, Martina Kohl, Phyllis Lassner, Ele McKenna, Mark McPhail, Toni Morales, Kenn Pierson, Sharon Quiroz, Martin Rosenberg, Bill Shea, Kim Silfven, Maureen Taylor, and Carol Winkelmann.

2. Although portfolios are not widely used in writing assessment within the United States, several programs do use them, and for a variety of purposes. The most intriguing of these purposes represents an adaptation of England's use of writing folders in proficiency testing at several grade levels, a possibility currently under study at ETS (Camp) and at the American Council on Education (GED). And essays in this volume attest to the many ways portfolios are being used at present. Individual instructors have long used portfolios as a way around simply averaging students' grades on essays in order to arrive at a semester grade. In this way, portfolios allow students to continue to revise their earlier essays so that all the writing for the course reflects the level of skill the student has achieved by the end of the term (McClelland). Writing programs, as well, have adopted the portfolio as a way to ensure uniform competence in students passing out of an otherwise standard freshman composition course (Elbow and Belanoff) or as a way of testing the writing proficiency of students identified as being at risk, no matter where they are in their undergraduate curriculum (Holt and Baker). In still other cases, portfolios are used to evaluate, not a student's proficiency, but the adequacy of a university's curriculum (Larson). Though such uses are still scattered, portfolios are proving to be a powerful and versatile tool for assessing students' writing, writing programs, and even school and university curricula.

# 21

# Large-Scale Portfolio Assessment
## *Ideological Sensitivity and Institutional Change*

Chris M. Anson and Robert L. Brown, Jr.
*University of Minnesota*

> What would recognizing the idealogical freight of our tests cost us?
> ... We would have to give up a naive faith in objective, externally
> verifiable and knowable and measurable and replicable reality. We
> would have to produce tests that allow for social construction of
> knowledge, that place student writers in interactive, collaborative
> settings. And we would have to find systems of measurement that
> allow for pluralistic and multiple ways of knowing and being.
>
> — Andrea Lunsford, "Assessing Assessment:
>   Challenges to the Tradition of Testing"

When most people think of strategies for writing assessment, what
usually comes to mind are questions about the design of writing
tasks, the nature of scoring criteria, the training of essay readers, or
issues of validity and reliability. Much less obvious but equally
important to the design and implementation of any writing assessment program are issues relating to the institutional or educational
culture surrounding the assessment itself. Where has the motivation
for assessment originated? What purpose is it thought to serve?
How will the institution react to the prospect of assessing students'
writing? As experts in writing assessment are increasingly pointing
out, large-scale testing is a political act. Before we can respond to a

conviction, mandate, or real need to test students' writing abilities, we must understand the educational and political context in which we will build an assessment program.

In comparison to more established methods such as the holistic rating of single-sitting test essays, portfolio assessment seems innovative and theoretically rich (see Belanoff & Elbow, this volume; Elbow & Belanoff, "Portfolios as a Substitute for Proficiency Examinations"). Over a decade ago, the little-used portfolio method was already being described as a powerful alternative to traditional grading, a way to "unify the department while putting the emphasis where it belongs in a writing class—on the student's writing" (Ford & Larkin 955). But like any method designed to enhance a curriculum, portfolios can take many forms and be variously implemented. What they will look like and how they will work are questions that must begin with a careful analysis of the institutional context in which they will be used.

To foreground the relationship between context and implementation, in this chapter we will describe and critique our efforts to create a large-scale, cross-curricular portfolio program at the University of Minnesota. In steering university administrators away from regressive writing tests and toward an instructionally valuable portfolio assessment, we have seen ourselves as agents of change, aspiring to turn a potentially damaging process into a means of educational enrichment. In this role, we have found it necessary to analyze the politics and ideology of our institution and develop specific strategies for enhancing literacy at a site where writing plays a limited role in undergraduate education.

## Conflict and Debate

The University of Minnesota is an enormous, state-supported institution. Over the years, it has developed an increasing focus on research while struggling to uphold its original mission to provide a decent post-secondary education to residents of Minnesota. In 1985, Kenneth Keller, its new president, outlined a bold plan, "Commitment to Focus," which promised to place Minnesota among the top five state-supported research universities in the country. The plan called for decreasing undergraduate enrollments at the Twin Cities campus (from a high of more than 30,000), eliminating or consolidating the least effective units, upgrading graduate degree programs, recruiting top scholars, and motivating faculty to spend even more time on research.

Reaction to the plan was mixed. Some agreed wholeheartedly with its principles, while others saw in it a campaign for elitism and exclusionary practices. Individual departments responded with sometimes embarrassed or defensive self-scrutiny, measuring themselves up against national norms and questioning their success at encouraging scholarship. Among faculty, this had two effects: those who already put most of their time to their own scholarly work were pleased to imagine even more support for their endeavors, while those devoted to teaching and community service felt anything from apprehension to panic. Some department chairs, perhaps as a way to shock the rank and file into scholarly activity, even broached the idea of counselling unproductive faculty out of the profession.

At a university where one is more likely to see large classes taught by teaching assistants than small groups of undergraduates led by distinguished faculty, writing was already a rather scarce commodity. The unveiling of "Commitment to Focus" only made more grim the prospect of increasing attention to writing. "Unproductive" faculty searching for ways to free up their time for research will, when pushed hard enough, slash away at the most time-consuming and seemingly least essential processes in their instruction. Because writing is so often used as a way to test instead of teach, to many faculty it is plausible to substitute objective exams for essays, term papers, or short writing assignments.

In the midst of this change in the University's climate, a historical undercurrent of paranoia about the quality of students' writing began to surface in the early weeks of the 1985 school year. Motivated by several high-ranking colleagues who were passing rumors about the abhorrent writing that they had collected from juniors and seniors in their classes, the dean of the College of Liberal Arts began assembling a committee of faculty from various departments to examine the issue of writing standards at the University. The resulting task force would study the issue and then make recommendations for assessing students' writing as a way to impose more stringent standards for written literacy among undergraduates.

When we and our colleagues in the Composition Program caught wind of these plans, we felt insulted and mistrusted. At our institution we are the most likely group to be consulted about writing assessment, yet the dean had not bothered to call us before taking action. Instead, a faculty member from the Department of History who had been appointed temporarily as an associate dean invited us to participate on the dean's Task Force on Writing Standards, which, he said, would recommend minimal standards for writing measurable by a test. Coming at a time when the president had seriously proposed reducing the number of freshman admittees, this unexpected drive for a major writing assessment was all the more disconcerting.

These political circumstances made the first two or three meetings of the task force rather tense. The composition faculty were asked why we had never used an entrance test before, to which we replied that we had never needed one. We described ways that such tests can deteriorate instruction and further marginalize students in need of help (Lloyd-Jones & Lunsford). We explained that Minnesota has a very homogeneous student population and that we had never had problems with placement because only a very small percentage of entering freshmen take "remedial" writing or are exempted from the regular course. We described the formula used by Admissions for this placement—a combination of high-school class rank, grades, and College Entrance Examination scores—and, given its reliability for our purposes, defended it next to a placement test. We explained our philosophy of instructional empowerment, our conviction that teachers, not mandated tests, should make recommendations about students' writing abilities. And we expressed our concerns about relying on the "quantification" of skills to judge something as complex, with so many interpretive and textual levels, as writing (see Wiener).

In spite of our rationale for not testing students' writing, the committee was at that point embracing misguided suggestions from some members who had used very little writing in their own instruction and knew almost nothing about its large-scale assessment. Meanwhile, our own remarks about the dangers of ill-wrought or hastily constructed assessment programs fell on deaf ears. As we grew more defensive, the members of the task force only became more adamant. Put simply, we faced a conflict of vision and ideology: faculty at the university were troubled by the poor skills of their students (from whom they asked very little writing) and were pointing their fingers at the secondary schools and the Composition Program for not adequately preparing those students to write. A mandated assessment—"toughening up" the entrance and exit gates of the University—was the only way they knew, at the time, to improve the situation. We soon realized that to create an environment for change, we had to think more carefully about our institutional culture and its attitudes.

In as supportive and questioning a way as we could, we began turning the issue back on the committee by discussing and documenting the impoverishment of writing at the university. We had evidence, for example, that beyond their composition courses many undergraduates write only one or two papers over four years. We cited examples of departments in which 90 percent of the faculty use lectures as the exclusive teaching mode and where the main learning activities for students are note taking and filling in dots on machine-scorable objective tests. We described a situation in some departments in which professors encourage their students to buy lecture notes from sanctioned note-taking services, which further disengages them from the learning process and makes it unnecessary to own a pen.

In sharp contrast to these circumstances were the personal histories of most of the task-force members. As our discussions of undergraduate education inevitably called up memories of college days, the group shared anecdotes of their own development as writers — how important a role writing had played in their education, how at their alma maters every course had involved or required some writing, even how individual writing projects had helped to etch their academic careers.

After many months of heated but eventually wide-ranging and productive discussions, a noticeable change came across the task force. Instead of a group of strangers from diverse departments arguing about the best way to test students' grammar, we had become a community focused on integrating writing into the entire Minnesota curriculum. In spite of our politically charged context, we experienced what many experts in writing across the curriculum have described as the "magic" of faculty workshops and other consulting efforts (for a range of descriptions, see Connelly & Irving; Freisinger, Fulwiler, "Showing, Not Telling" and "How Well Does Writing Across the Curriculum Work?"; Herrington; Maimon; Nochimson; Raimes). Our focus on writing — how to describe it, how to judge it, and how to teach it — had moved us away from "mindless quantification" and toward an alternative vision in which, as Wiener has put it, a "concerned, interactive professoriate can establish commonalities for judgment and can anchor them in rational thought and liberal learning" (15). Later, during one of our final meetings, the chair of the committee would admit that even after producing scholarly books and articles for thirty years, he had never understood writing as such a complex process until he had discussed it so intensely with his peers.

In the first phase of our work, the task force slowly developed what can only be called a changed "ideology" of writing — a system of shared values about the goal of an educational enterprise (see Bernier & Williams; Mosenthal). The process of that change was so professionally and personally meaningful to the task-force members that our focus had shifted from the quality of students' writing to the role our faculty could play in its enhancement.

## Toward Rich Assessment

Still faced with its original charge, the task force now had to devise a way to bring about large-scale reform (and build a WAC program along the way) as a *consequence* of an assessment program. We had managed to bring to the surface what the members of the task force knew tacitly all along: that literacy grows through constant practice and that a ten-week course, no matter how successful, no matter how well "tracked" by an assessment program, would simply not fix the problem. Focusing instead on the university as a context for the development of literacy, we began rethinking the role that assessment could play in restoring our faculty's attention to writing.

As the task force reconsidered its mission, we reached consensus about three principles of writing. First was the view that individual departments should be involved in developing writing standards for their own majors. To accept this view, members of the task force had to understand that the characteristics of good writing (and the relationship between writing and the development of disciplinary knowledge) vary from field to field and across University departments (see Jolliffe). They also had to be convinced that people in other disciplines do, in fact, know a great deal about writing and can, with a little guidance, talk productively about instructional uses for writing in their own curricula.

Second, the task force began to see that assessment is neither inherently desirable nor necessarily evil. Depending on how and why it is used, it has the potential to create positive change that benefits the entire institution (Edward White) but just as easily can lead to discrimination, political crisis, and law suits (Lutz, 1988). This principle helped the committee to question its original charge — to develop a writing assessment program — by focusing discussion on whether such a program was needed, what forms it could take, and what it might accomplish if implemented.

Finally, we agreed that multiple samples of writing, gathered over time from various contexts, would more fully represent a student's level of achievement than a test essay (see Gordon 36). The idea of using a portfolio of writing samples as the means for our assessment not only supported this conviction but also furthered the cause of reintegrating writing into all departments at the university, empowering faculty to teach and assess writing (see Belanoff

& Elbow, this volume). Students would have to write to create a portfolio; departments would have to build writing-intensive courses in which students could work on their writing; and teachers would have to rethink the role of writing in their own instruction.

The process of drafting what would become the "Report of the College of Liberal Arts Task Force on Writing Standards" was equally illuminating for the committee members. For several weeks, two subcommittees worked independently, each drafting half the document (one focusing on entrance standards and one on exit requirements), and then circulated their work among the entire committee for discussion. After several rounds of revisions and discussion, the document represented the collaborative efforts of an extremely diverse group of faculty.

A draft of the report was then circulated among all units in the University and was sent to nearly 150 principals, English department chairs, and faculty in Minnesota secondary schools for comment. Working from its fundamental conviction that the quality of writing improves only through increased attention to writing across the curriculum, the report made five essential recommendations:

1. *Require the submission of an entrance portfolio for admission to the University.* As a minimal requirement, this portfolio would contain a piece of narrative or descriptive writing; a piece of deliberative writing such as an academic essay or media review; a piece of persuasive writing such as an editorial or issue-oriented research paper; documentary evidence of the student's writing process, such as notes, outlines, drafts, and revisions for at least one text; and a one- to two-page letter by the student introducing the portfolio, reviewing its contents and the circumstances of production, and describing the student's writing process. The portfolio would contain ten to twenty-five cleanly typed pages and include a document certifying that they were produced by the student in the contexts described.

   It was felt that simply requiring a high-school portfolio would encourage the secondary schools to build their own writing-across-the-curriculum programs. The portfolio would be used as the primary means of determining placement into the first-year composition course (on the basis of a two-point general impressions reading of "adequate/inadequate"). Although the task force did not go so far as to recommend which unit would conduct the placement reading, it was generally understood that this would fall into the hands of the Composition Program. In support of this first requirement, the College of Liberal Arts would set up a communication system with the secondary schools and provide consulting whenever possible.

2. *Require the creation of a portfolio to be assessed for exit from the junior year.* At a minimum, this portfolio would contain writing produced at four stages:

   a. At least four pieces of writing produced in the freshman year.
   b. A single longer piece of writing produced in the sophomore year.
   c. An extensive research paper produced in the junior year.
   d. The written component of a senior project produced in the fourth year, and only after a "pass" assessment of the portfolio at the end of the junior year.

   The responsibility for assessing the students' exit portfolio would fall into the hands of the departments, in tracking and advising their own majors. Consultations with faculty in composition would help departments prepare for this assessment as the requirements would be phased in.

3. *Restructure the course requirements in composition.* Students are currently required to take one quarter (ten weeks) of introductory composition as freshmen and then, as juniors, one of twelve advanced composition courses in generalized disciplinary areas (Writing for the Social Sciences, Technical Writing for Engineers, Writing About the Arts Other Than Literature, Writing for the Health Sciences, etc.). The new plan would add another freshman-level course, which would be "linked" with a content course in the disciplines.

4. *Build and require writing-intensive courses.* To support the junior-level component of the portfolio, departments would create writing-intensive courses. Students could enroll in more than one such "W-course," but at least one substantial, certified paper would be entered into the portfolio at this stage.

5. *Enhance existing senior-project courses.* Although all students are technically required to produce a senior project before graduating, the original requirements have decayed so badly over the years that some departments no longer require the project or, in some cases, accept presentations, performances, art work, or other material in place of a written document. Under the new plan, students in all departments would be required to prepare a substantial written senior-project report as the final item for their exit portfolio. Existing curricula would be revised to accommodate the new requirement.

As the responses to the plan trickled in, they were copied to various deans and associate deans as well as the members of the task force. After another round of discussions and a few minor modifications to the proposal, a final draft was prepared for examination by the Faculty Assembly of the College of Liberal Arts.

In the winter of 1987, the assembly voted hesitantly to accept the plan but to wait for full implementation until 1990, after pilot projects could be conducted to determine its feasibility. The committee was generally happy with this response, in spite of some strong criticisms of the proposal. While the real business of designing and carrying out the pilot program was now in the hands of the Composition Program, faculty on the committee felt that their proposal would play an important part in improving literacy at the University.

Over the next year, we began several small projects focusing on writing across the curriculum (Anson, "Piloting Linked Courses Across the Curriculum"; Anson & Bridwell-Bowles; Bridwell-Bowles) and publicized the plan to receptive audiences (Anson & Brown; Anson, Bridwell-Bowles, & Brown; Brown). During this time, we made repeated pleas to the deans of our college to provide the needed support—even by way of a single additional faculty member or several administrative assistants—yet nothing came our way. Temporary retrenchments and financial setbacks were apparently to blame. Finally, after almost two years of struggling to carry out our pilot projects with no release time, financial help, or funded assistants, we received notice in the spring of 1989 that the dean—again without consulting us—had decided to cancel the portfolio project indefinitely.

## Starting Over: Learning to Read the University

In a recent article, Blair has argued that writing instruction *can* become fully interdisciplinary—that a true writing-across-the-curriculum program will be based on consensus achieved through dialogue. Our experience on the dean's task force gave us faith in that assumption and encouraged us to proceed with our plans. In light of this initial success, we had mixed feelings about the project's suspension—dismay that new support for writing turned out to be so much lip service; renewed concern about the quality of literacy at the university; and a kind of nihilistic relief that we had forestalled an otherwise dangerous testing program by convincing our colleagues to recommend in its place something richer and more powerful. We

also faced some challenging questions: Is the portfolio method possible on a large scale, across the curriculum? If so, how can it be
implemented in a culture that devalues undergraduate education in
favor of professional research?

No story of assessment design is benign. Historically, the development of assessment programs around the country reads like a
long epic of struggle, accommodation, fear, and, very occasionally,
triumph. In this context, our own difficulties are not rarified or even
unpredictable. Even so, it is clear that large research universities
present a particularly difficult set of hurdles for reform.

At base, the portfolio method and the literate culture it seeks to
produce probably confront the institutional foundations of many
research universities. From this perspective, it became useful for us
to rethink the context of our proposal as a method for potential
educational reform. The most powerful data we had were the dozens
of responses from faculty, department chairs, and high school
teachers to our original proposal—responses that are fundamentally
political texts amenable to analysis, mirroring the major roles within
the academy. As Tompkins has pointed out, discourse is never
merely a way of ordering and presenting information; it is, rather, a
way of making meaning—social as well as linguistic. It reflects
ways of knowing, ways of structuring our cultural relations, ways of
being.

Working from these principles, we began to reread and critique
the many letters of response to the task-force proposal. Our critique
led us to construct a complex and interrelated series of influences,
arranged from the most overarching to the most local and specific,
which not only *explain reactions to* (as in our own case) but also
*provide a heuristic for* the creation of principled, cross-curricular
assessment programs.

### Cultural Ideology

At the highest level, how the members of an academic community
think about writing originates in the ideology of the surrounding
culture. As Piché has pointed out, educational institutions are by
nature "socially constituted relevance systems, reflecting and ampli-
fying larger sets of social and cultural values in the emphases they
give to kinds or ways of knowing" (17). In spite of great efforts by
theorists and educators to reform our culture's educational ideology,
we still cling to uninformed notions of what it means to "learn" or
"know," and nowhere is this more apparent than in the area of
writing. Many of the comments we heard from experienced pro-

fessors during the early task-force meetings sounded no different from what we hear again and again in public discourse about education. Kids can't write any more. Their punctuation is terrible. Why don't the schools teach them how to spell? Oh, you teach English? Better watch my grammar. Although university faculty obviously have a more sophisticated understanding of educational practice than what might be found among the general public, many responses to the task-force proposal betrayed "current-traditional" attitudes toward writing that have been systematically overturned in composition theory for over two decades (for similar accounts, see Young & Fulwiler). In spite of some strongly stated language in the report favoring a complex, process-oriented, and intellectually meaningful view of writing, the phrase "traditional writing skills" occurred frequently. Typical is the following response from a faculty member in East Asian Studies: "The most valuable *skill* that most of our graduates can hope to *take away* with them is the *ability* to *get their thoughts in order* and *to communicate them clearly and intelligently*" (italics added). While most would agree on some level with the principles of this statement, we found it remarkable that a proposal so concerned with using writing to enhance learning would be read in such a product-centered way, with such a focus on skills and abilities as the "outcome" of imposed standards.

Another respondent agreed wholeheartedly with the report's argument that writing across the curriculum would help students to write continually, but again understood the chief benefit to be "a substantial improvement in writing skills" rather than general intellectual development or improved learning of subject matter. Interestingly, this faculty member went so far as to offer his own method of using writing in large lecture courses (he was the only University respondent to do so).

> In my courses I assign an expository writing Homework nearly every week. The student has to explain in clear logical steps the causal relationships (the causal mechanism) underlying some particular part of the economic system. The homework paper (typically one or two typed pages) is read and graded by an undergraduate T.A. (a senior with a good GPA record in Economics). The T.A. simply assigns a letter grade. He or she does not annotate or rewrite. But the student gets his graded paper together with a mimeographed Model Answer provided by me. If the student compares his answer with the Model Answer, he can figure out what he did wrong. Homeworks that are not clear and which display careless logic and organization receive D or F grades.

While this faculty member's practice is laudable in a department where undergraduates do very little writing, it is instructive to note how an otherwise learning-oriented assignment is cast in the dualistic language of correctness and adherence to organizational and stylistic formulas, all of which are "economically" assessed.

In contrast to the responses of University faculty, letters from the secondary schools showed a far deeper understanding of contemporary educational theory, a fact we found ironic next to the usual blame directed at the public schools for their various inadequacies. The following excerpts are representative:

> I feel that your emphasis on the writing *process* itself is laudable and is grossly neglected by most teachers and students alike. Secondly, I also agree with the point made by the committee that writing samples should not be restrictive and narrow. High school teachers often construe such strict guidelines as the *only* writing skills needed to be taught whereas this is not so.

> We applaud the attempt of the Task Force to emphasize the composition concepts of process as well as product, and the attempt to make use of current research in the field of composition. The idea of writing in an area of content, rather than simply treating writing as though it were a subject in itself, has strong appeal to secondary school teachers.

Although most of the secondary school responses came from teachers of composition or English (whereas all of the University letters came from faculty in other disciplines), we were surprised to find a greater rejection of the "current-traditional" or public ideology of writing among the former than the latter. One candid response from a local high school even offered a plausible reason why the secondary schools often emphasize surface mechanics — to prepare students for college composition!

> The University's recognition of writing as a process will begin to dispel the popular notion among secondary teachers of the typical freshman composition course where the instructor sits, red pen in hand, ready to evaluate a paper solely by the number of comma splices, fragments, and run-ons. This notion has often been the rationale for converting writing classes into grammar and usage classes.

In place of terms such as "skills," "measures," "competency," and the like, the secondary school responses seemed dominated by the words "process," "ongoing," "development," and "learning." Four letters from high schools many miles apart all praised the report using the nearly identical language: its recognition of/emphasis on/ attention to "writing as a process" and to the "ongoing collection" of writing in the creation of a portfolio or the "ongoing function" of writing in WAC programs.

Of course, the routing of the University's request for reactions by the high schools might have landed our proposal in the hands of the most eager or competent teachers and administrators. We believe, however, that the culture of Minnesota high schools (some of which are regarded as the best in the country) is steeped enough in pedagogy to push many teachers beyond current-traditional beliefs and methods. Public schools run on a reward system that has admittedly poor resources but is clearly oriented toward excellence in teaching. Wisdom and expertise in the practice of teaching may be considerably more important there than at the research university.

Finally, it is worth noting that while many of the university respondents objected to *their department's* role in our proposal, most were nevertheless encouraged by the idea of imposing tougher "standards" (many used this or similar terms in an opening line of diplomatic praise). Receptiveness to the process of tracking, chaneling, sorting, or excluding students on the basis of test scores is so much a part of our cultural ideology of education that such a response is not surprising. As Andrea Lunsford has described the situation:

> In general, patterns of assessment (like our schools) reflect a *factory* or *industrial* model, one that goes along with a view of knowledge as a packageable commodity. This industrial model in testing is everywhere prevalent—little worker bees go through the steps of the system producing little pieces of machinery. ... Conditions are rigorously controlled. The student worker has one shot at effective productivity— one missing cog and the product is failure. (8)

In this context it is interesting to consider the objections of the chair and the director of undergraduate studies in the English Department to our plan. After expressing "gratitude" for the "heartening" attention to "writing standards," these colleagues criticized the complexity of the portfolio method and recommended a test essay in its place:

> Within a formal setting, ask for an essay on one of several topics announced at the time of the examination, and give forty-five minutes to draft an essay; after a break of, say, fifteen minutes, have applicants revise, edit, and rewrite the essay within the space of an hour.

What stands out in this response is the way the *purpose* of the program has been interpreted—in terms of Lunsford's "factory" model of education. The more highly mechanized the method, the more "reliable" and "feasible" its implementation. Portfolios invite, as another respondent observed, an "element of subjectivity":

> Modes of thought are as various as human personality. As scholars, we

often disagree sharply in our evaluation of the published work of others in our fields. What constitutes a valid argument? When has a claim to have proven something been fully satisfied? How good is the evidence that is used? Where does a technical vocabulary become an insufferable put-on?

Such questions were precisely those we hoped all our colleagues would see as the rationale for decentralizing assessment through a cross-curricular, departmentally controlled portfolio program. As Belanoff (1986) discovered in the very early stages of SUNY-Stony Brook's freshman writing-portfolio program, it was the inescapable element of subjectivity that rapidly led to the idea of "clusters" of instructors who would collaboratively decide on their own assignments and read each other's portfolios. Thus, what had started as an assessment soon turned into a powerful means of instructional enrichment.

### Institutional Ideology

A second source of response to proposals for reforming writing instruction has its origins in what we call *institutional ideology*, a more specific set of beliefs related to the mission(s) and culture(s) of an educational context. Many of the responses to our proposal suggested a view in which writing is an unnecessary burden, an "add-on" to existing responsibilities, a threat to protected time for research and (ironically) writing for publication. Typically, department chairs and faculty members with this view seemed to stand their ground against the imposition of yet another curricular mandate that would lead to more work. Resisting writing on the basis of its "unfamiliarity" to the discipline or the inability to teach it was one defensive strategy. More appropriate to the recent political climate at the university were some criticisms that the proposal opposed the University's new agenda for becoming a premier research institution. The following excerpt is typical:

> My final concern about the report is whether or not [the proposal] is in accordance with the shift of emphasis from undergraduate to graduate education. When I read the report, I thought of situations in several small colleges where the faculty is so occupied with carrying out the details of undergraduate programs that they have no time for scholarly work ... [S]hould we rather be looking at schools that give comparatively little attention to their Bachelors and concentrate primarily on research and teaching of graduate students?

Another faculty member from psychology asked whether a "labor-intensive program of this kind at the undergraduate level [is] an appropriate expenditure of resources at a graduate-training, research-oriented university." Another urged the task force to "expand significantly on the realities [of resources], particularly in terms of what the proposal will ask of the faculty."

Here the issue is, ostensibly, distribution of effort in a scarcity economy: can we afford time to teach and monitor literacy? But the rhetoric bifurcates and asks readers to align themselves with one of two positions. The terms of this *bifurcatio* are two varieties of "work": scholarly, which is individualized and inherently private; and "details of undergraduate programs," which are intersubjective, time consuming, and incompatible with research. At the ideological center of the issue is the culture's definition of work and its value, represented in a system through which the academic culture rewards and reinforces the behaviors of its members. Intuitively wise and self-protective, faculty in institutions circumscribed by a research mission are reluctant to work against their own interests.

Even a cursory reading of the various University responses to our proposal clearly shows that resistance to reform in the area of written literacy has its strongest roots in the prevalent institutional ideology at Minnesota. Building a rich, interdisciplinary context for integrating writing and learning takes time, money, and commitment. If the dominant mission of the institution is to create intelligent, literate citizens — readers, writers, and learners — then the institution will allocate its resources accordingly. Administrative problems associated with a program to improve literacy will be seen as challenges to be met eagerly and diligently by a committed professoriate. Yet even minor logistical problems in our plan were puffed up into an "ordeal" to be "endured," an "administrative nightmare," a "horror," a "scheduling monster," a "quasi-tutorial process engaging great amounts of instructional and intellectual time," "drudge work [eventually] assigned to graduate students [so that] the standards will become nothing more than a hurdle." Some chairs of departments even used the occasion to ask for a 50-percent increase in the size of their faculty, or a specific (impossible) budget increase to begin implementation:

> In total, I estimate that in order to undertake the proposed change our department would require between $131,865 and $206,730 per year in additional resources. ... Without [these] resources, our teaching of writing would be at the expense of teaching and research about politics. The teaching of composition would become an onerous burden for all of us.

Even more calculating was the response of a dean in the wealthy and powerful Institute of Technology, which controls programs in such areas as engineering and computer science:

> I think the idea of more stringent evaluation of writing ability for admission and for graduation is excellent. My only concern is with the magnitude of the task. To store 16,000 portfolios, each ¼ inch thick, requires 330 feet of shelf. Reading 4,000 a year at one-half hour each requires the equivalent of a full-time person.

Here, the section before the understood *but*-clause ("my only concern") voices the institution's received wisdom: tougher is better under the myth of meritocracy. After the *but* comes the real force of the message, expressed in logistical terms. Institutional ideology is at work in the reluctance to dedicate resources—space (measured in shelf-feet) and time (measured in person-hours)—to the labor-intensive business of intersubjective teaching. Early in our work we frequently mentioned and disparaged this response. After all, it came from a part of the institution that had just built a multimillion-dollar, eight-story computer science and electrical engineering complex with four of the stories in an underground, atmospherically controlled, natural-disaster-proof environment. Surely these future-looking technocrats were not intimidated by shelf space or a few full-time graduate assistant appointments? We missed the point.

Though it may not always be apparent, discourse configures academic culture. And writing programs address the politics of discourse directly; they intervene in the most sensitive cultural issues. We might have expected an interesting lack of consensus, since the culture of the large research university is multifaceted, organized by disciplines, and highly competitive. But the issues, reflected and amplified in the discourse of the responses, run even deeper. At base, they suggest how radically disruptive contemporary writing theory is to some key ideological premises of the research university. In suggesting changes in the place of writing at Minnesota, we were suggesting changes in the culture of the University, in its very lifeblood.

## Disciplinary and Departmental Ideology

The university itself is, of course, made up of many units and departments whose faculty are so specialized that they often have little desire even to talk with members in their own fields who may be working in different subdisciplinary areas. It is at this level that we can begin to see traces of what we call "disciplinary" ideology (Anson, "Toward a Multidimensional Model"); and, at a more specific level, "departmental ideology" (Anson, "Resistance to Writing"), a system of shared values held by individual departments which, over the years, have taken on a clear orientation within their subject area. (Classic examples include the "Skinnerian" psychology department, the "traditionally empirical" or "ethnographic" department of education, or the "new critical," "Marxist/feminist," or "poststructuralist" department of English.) Departments can also be seriously fragmented by competing disciplinary ideologies, as when faculty who run writing programs in departments of English must struggle to implement new methods against the will of their "traditional" colleagues.

While most responses focused on the more global, Universitywide implications of our proposal, it was hard to miss the undercurrent of disciplinary ideology in a few letters. Faculty in the humanities urged more attention to the sort of "consummate forms of writing which we banish from practical forms of discourse," including "the epistolary style; some work in literature; dissertative discourse, to be sure." Faculty in the Department of Art History expressed concern "about the effect of the plan on students whose area of emphasis is some form of non-verbal communication, such as music or studio arts." Faculty in the Department of English felt that traditional rhetoric got "short shrift" in the proposal and disliked the emphasis on multiple audiences for writing, arguing that most writing at the University "should be addressed to one's scholarly peers and instructors." Faculty in the Department of Spanish and Portuguese argued quite convincingly that the plan for a portfolio had excluded any provisions for writing in a second language and asked whether it were a "viable alternative to allow foreign-language writing samples as part of the portfolio." The Department of Psychology challenged the entire charge of the task force by asking a series of questions which, if answered in a way that would justify the proposal, would take a form not unlike a typical research proposal in the social sciences (background, statement of the problem, subjects, data, etc.): "Question 1: What, exactly, is the problem? ... Question 2: Is the recommended course of action the best solution to the problem (whatever 'the problem' is, cf. Question #1 above)?" And so on.

Finally, we were interested to note differences in comments about the writing of the proposal itself. Some faculty praised it highly as a "masterpiece of clarity, thoroughness, and academic idealism," with "so much attention and intelligence expended on subjects so important to us." Others, however, were quick to criticize the proposal for a few stylistic infelicities that the task force did not catch in the draft sent out for review. The Department of English, upholding its public stereotype, called attention to an unidiomatic use of "writing" in the terms "a deliberative writing" and "a narrative writing," as well as a few typos. Another respondent from the Department of French and Italian offered this advice:

> I praise the style of the document in general but note that, as in so much administrative writing, it betrays some erosion of English. There are far too many run-on substantives ("evaluation process," "writing experience," "performance goals," "performance criteria," "a several year period," "writing assessment"), catch-all pieces of jargon ("students will be routed . . .," "phased in" . . . for "program purposes" on a "principled basis," etc.). The document should pay closer heed to its own principles. It might also appeal gently to the very trope it appears to repress: irony, the mode that allows criticism, pleasure, and perspective to animate writing.

Ostensibly stylistic advice and relatively harmless, this response actually carries out some political action. The features singled out— nominalizations and reduced relative clauses — are markers of distinct discourse communities, including those of the social sciences and education (Brown & Herndl). By calling into question these stylistic features, the writer defines his own affiliation: he is *not* a member of groups who write this way. Significantly, this writer represents a moderately radical modern-language department in which he is a recognized deconstructive theorist. Derrida receives his nod through the comments on the trope of irony.

Clearly, specific noetic characteristics of the fields within which our faculty were responding partly explain their reactions to the proposal. The research university is organized by discipline and department, and thrives on defining and maintaining difference. The selective undergraduate institutions, organized in coherent communities, are often able to suppress disciplinary difference in favor of unity. Yet even at these sites — oriented as they are toward excellence in teaching — considerable lack of consensus among the disciplines presents barriers to centralized, cross-curricular assessment programs and suggests something other than a top-down approach.

### Personal Ideology

Struggling amidst these various layers of cultural, institutional, disciplinary, and departmental influence stands the individual faculty member, coming to terms with his or her own beliefs and pedagogical practices. In critiquing the general response to our proposal, we are

acutely aware of the good will, enthusiasm, and humane beliefs
of many faculty members across our institution. Faculty heavily
committed to teaching may have chosen to reflect the dominant
institutional ideology at Minnesota for fear of too strongly opposing
its research agenda at a moment when it was being systematically
reinforced. Yet some found it difficult to hide their own frustrations
as concerned educators in departments preoccupied with scholarly
reputation and productivity:

> The report is quick to say that T[eaching] A[ssistant]s might be hired
> (which is what professors will hooray) or, if professors are used, that
> they must be paid. I would suggest that professors should do the tasks,
> at least in significant part, and that each and every person should take
> his or her turn without exception and without pay. I'd vote YES with
> such an understanding. But I am perverse. Undoubtedly that proviso
> would be a formula for failure.

Here there is an unmistakable energy in the fantasy that the entire
Minnesota faculty could, through an institutional mandate, be compelled to engage in teaching and monitoring literacy; but all too
quickly the fantasy vanishes as the reality of the institutional context
washes over this faculty member's personal convictions. In speaking
of "professors" as the other (in spite of the fact that he is one), this
writer clearly positions himself in an ambivalent relation to his
community's attitudes toward writing instruction. His position is
inevitably conflicted. Aware of the prevailing reward process, he
focuses his attention on the questions of who will do the work and
how they will be paid. He can thereby speak sincerely *for* commitment
to education, while ironically inscribing himself as "perverse" for
doing so.

Others offered their own beliefs about writing in the form of
suggestions for setting up the portfolio requirements:

> A fairly standard bibliography might be established and sent to high
> schools across the state. ... It could include Strunk and White, the
> *Chicago Manual of Style*, or other major works. ... I think, too, that the
> Task Force should implement a list of writers and writing which define
> outstanding prosody. Models from our perspective would be Melville
> and Henry James, who do more to extend the affective and perspectival
> range than any in the modern canon; Frame's translation of Montaigne,
> which reflects great suppleness of style; or Cervantes in good English,
> which betrays a syntax that we can strive to emulate through our
> relation with the Hispanic traditions. And so forth.

Reflections of personal ideology were generally more rare than
we heard during our task force meetings, perhaps because the
writing situation constrained the respondents and forced them to

write as representatives of their departments. The influence of personal ideology is also subtle and is best studied through a much closer analysis of teachers' beliefs and practices than what is afforded in two-page responses to a bureaucratic document. Nevertheless, in our consulting efforts with faculty members from various departments (especially when these take place away from the university), we find personal ideology one of the most meaningful places to begin talking about writing.

## Hope and Renewal

It might seem, we have realized in telling our story, that we present a hopeless case for cultural change in the research university, and bleaker still for using something as complex as a writing portfolio to enrich literacy there. As our history presents them, the institutional forces informing departmental and personal attitudes seem absolutely to determine policy.

But the case is really far less daunting. We learned not that change is hopeless but that it must always begin with cultural understandings—a hard thing to achieve when we are implicated in the patterns we seek to understand. What our short history brought to the surface were the underlying structures of one research university: disciplinary, organized as a loose confederation of departments, privileging individuality over collectivity, primarily rewarding research and publication, and always paradoxical—a place where individuals' beliefs may not fit their conditions of employment.

Our mandate for assessment came from college-level administration whose motivation, in turn, came from difficult political and economic conditions in the University itself. Significantly, the mandate fit *no* departmental, disciplinary, or personal configuration very well. Thus, we learned that complex educational policy is not happily set by mandate, from the top down.

Well after the task force proposals had found their way to the shelf of financial exigency, we received a call from a colleague in the University's School of Dentistry. Would we be interested in working with them on ways to build writing into their new, revised curriculum? Interested but perplexed, we agreed to meet.

We soon discovered that the School of Dentistry knew nothing about the task force proposal (apparently many medical and health-science departments had not been consulted, perhaps because they function fairly autonomously within the University). Nevertheless, they were in the early stages of major curricular reform and had become interested in the idea of "saturating" their curriculum with writing. To that point, dental students produced almost no writing in four years of post-baccaulaureate instruction. Classes took the form of large lectures with objective tests and small clinical practicums spent mainly in observation.

Our perplexity arose from our being able to think of few ways in which writing figured in the lives of practicing dentists. We approached our meeting with an informal proposal for a mixture of preprofessional writing and writing in the health sciences, a mix of practical and research-based writing.

"Dentists don't write," we were quickly told by one of the more outspoken members of the curriculum revision committee; "there's really no such thing as 'dental writing.'" What the School of Dentistry had in mind were ways to enrich teaching by incorporating writing experiences into the whole curriculum. They spoke — without using the terminology — of active learning experiences; of open-ended, discursive evaluation; of using informal writing to encourage learning; and of teaching based on problem solving. They reported some resistance to these ideas on the usual practical grounds (for example, professors who would not want to revise their courses or spend lots of time grading papers). But they also reported solid support for a richer teaching and learning experience, again, on very practical grounds: faculty in the School of Dentistry were concerned that their graduates were not learning "disciplinary thinking abilities," which they considered central to good dental practice. They feared that rote learning dominated the central curriculum. Although they were uninterested in assessing writing ability as such, they had also broached the idea of collecting students' writing in a sort of folder or file in order to measure whether the new, writing-intensive curriculum was having an effect on students' *learning* of dentistry. These folders, which they soon began calling "portfolios" after we introduced the term, would serve as a catalyst for faculty to think of new ways to build writing into their courses.

We were amazed. Clearly these one hundred or so health-care professionals had not been reading our literature on teaching and learning; they were not in the business of writing across the curriculum. Yet their workplace experience had led them to as clear an understanding of active learning as we had heard anywhere. They presented us with exactly the arguments our colleagues in the Liberal Arts had so strongly resisted.

In the months that followed, we established a remarkably satisfying relationship with the School of Dentistry, a relationship that has led to a new undergraduate course for pre—health science students, a rich revision of the dental curriculum, faculty workshops, a booklet of innovative assignments by the faculty, and over $15,000 of grant money to begin a longitudinal study of the effects of the new writing-intensive curriculum on students' abilities in scientific inquiry.

Against our experience with a large-scale portfolio system, our collaboration with the School of Dentistry contained two clear and central lessons. First, *we* had misconstrued dentistry. Dentistry, as we conceived it, was a matter of facts, data, and technique. It now seems obvious to us that we were inscribed, trapped by part of our discipline's ideology. We had unwittingly subscribed to the terms of an old opposition of arts and technology, the opposition that separates many state university systems into the "university" and the "agricultural-technical campus." In constructing dentistry as technology and technology as simplex, we fell into the same invidious disciplinary comparisons that led our colleague from the Department of French and Italian to fault our report for too many nominalizations and too little irony.

Second, we ignored our own good advice for writing specialists as change agents. Working from our own disciplinary perspective, we saw dentistry through its *content*, its body of knowledge — as if the making of knowledge were the unquestioned goal of all education (certainly an assumption that had been reinforced in our earlier experience on the task force). We should have remembered our own advice: read schools and departments as complex institutions engaged in *varieties of production*. While we may produce research as our primary product, the School of Dentistry produces dentists. As a dominantly educational enterprise, the School of Dentistry was primarily focused on its students. Aware of the problem-solving nature of good dental practice, the faculty wanted to teach scientific inquiry. Aware that metacognition consolidates and clarifies all types of problem solving, they turned to writing as the best means to ensure some of this necessary, higher-level thinking.

Teaching and assessing writing, when they work in consort with the cultural operations of the institution, have a good chance of success. When they counter the cultural operations, they will always fail. We learned the lesson of all good ethnography and, finally, of all good teaching. We could not assume that we knew our culture simply because we lived and worked in it. The research university is an immensely complex institution, and much of the complexity is hidden and mystified by the very structures we were seeking to change. We needed, first, to know the world in which we worked.

That done, we could begin.

# 22

# The WPA,
# The Portfolio System,
# and Academic Freedom
## *A Cautionary Tale with an Optimistic Ending*

Marcia Dickson
*Ohio State University at Marion*

There once was a new Ph.D. whose first job was as a writing programs administrator (WPA) at a midsize four-year liberal arts college. In the fall of her first semester—when the WPA (flushed with the success of completing her Ph.D. and solid in her belief that academia was ripe for her ideas) took her place among the tempered, mostly tenured, literary faculty—she introduced a plan for a portfolio assessment system. The plan had its flaws, but it had been basically sound at the university where she'd studied and seemed, as far as she could see, a fair and reasonable program for assessing the students' level of competence and creating a community of cooperative and collaborative faculty readers.

One day, shortly after she placed the proposal in the mailboxes of her colleagues, she left her office to make her way to the English Department office to perform some mundane task of administering. As she started down the hall, she found the way blocked by the rather imposing figure of the department's most senior (and most vocal) professor.

He was a tall and rather grandiose man—one who obviously had spent most of his life torn between being a gentleman of letters and a regular guy. He smoked a cigar, which he used like a weapon while he talked, and his plaid lumberjack shirt stood out proudly against the corduroy of his manly jacket. He did rather look like the legendary Mark Twain, but what in Clemens was caustic wit became, in his demeanor, merely caustic.

"Excuse me, young lady," he rumbled. "But I feel it is my duty to discuss this portfolio nonsense with you."

Now the WPA (who though she was new to faculty status was hardly a naive spring chicken) knew a threatening situation when she encountered it. So in her best "May I help you?" manner, she cocked her head, looked attentive, and said "Yes?" with a smile that could charm a rock.

If he had been a rock, it might have worked, but he was more in the nature of a railroad train, and her small effort at congeniality disappeared under the thunder of his next comment.

"I have never, in my entire career as a professional educator seen such a flagrant violation of ACADEMIC FREEDOM! (And he did, although I don't know how, manage to say "academic freedom" in all capital letters.)

"Are you aware," he continued, "of the catastrophic consequences which your proposal will unleash?"

She wasn't.

But she wanted to know.

So she asked him.

"According to your memo, other teachers would be able to come into *my* class and tell *me* what grade I should give *my* students! They could call into question what *I* want to teach and how *I* want to present it! According to THE LAW (he did it again), that classroom is my kingdom; I rule there. You're trying to undercut my authority with this shared grading nonsense. It's UNAMERICAN, and the faculty here won't have it."

Now I wish I could tell you that she argued brilliantly, slew the giant, and brought portfolios to the masses within the first year of a golden age—but she didn't. The best she could manage was a direct attempt to explain the philosophy behind the program, which (as the Californians say) he couldn't hear. The departmental proposal was rejected by the tenured faculty, who did agree, however, that it was an excellent means of keeping tabs on the part-timers (whose academic freedom no one seemed concerned about).

Thus ends the tale—but not the saga.

Although my cautionary tale is exaggerated, it is far from inaccurate. The WPA is not always a junior female, the professor not always the senior male, and the exchange is not always heated, but one of the recurring objections to the portfolio system does involve the question of academic freedom. You will find allusions to this critical area of academic concern in nearly every article in this collection because, even when a department designs and implements a portfolio system with the consent of the majority of its faculty, a rather vocal minority tends to remain fearful that somehow portfolio assessment will limit the autonomy that has been guaranteed instructors under academic freedom rulings.

The right to academic freedom is a serious and legitimate concern for all members of the academy: tenure-track professors, part-time instructors, and graduate students, as well as for the undergraduates they teach. But few members of our profession have ever read the AAUP's "Statement on Academic Freedom and Tenure," and fewer still have any sense of the obligations that this statement outlines. Academic freedom is a rallying cry based on myth as well as fact. Although its authors saw the statement as a means of guaranteeing free speech, the academic freedom statement has sometimes been used to suggest a control of the classroom that borders more on license than freedom.

What exactly is academic freedom and who is entitled to it? Although the concept of academic freedom dates back to fifteenth-century Germany, American documents on academic freedom date back only to the beginning of this century and the formation of associations that, like their counterparts in industry, were formed to protect those who studied and taught in universities from those who set policy and administered it. According to the American Association of University Professors' (AAUP) handbook, *Academic Freedom and Tenure*, this is the way it all began. The first statement of the organization's concerns appeared in 1915, shortly after the founding of the association. In 1925, at a conference called by the American Council of Education, the "Conference Statement of Academic Freedom and Tenure" was drawn up and endorsed by the Association of American Colleges. In 1926 the American Association of University Professors also endorsed this new conference statement. The statement was once more examined and interpreted in a series of conferences held between 1934 and 1940. The resulting text, "Statement of Principles on Academic Freedom and Tenure," along with three "Interpretations," was adopted by the two associations in 1941. This 1940 statement has served as the model for numerous organizations and as part of negotiation contracts between universities and their faculties (Joughin 33–34) and has remained unchanged (sexist language and all) to this day.

At present, the statement appears in a collection of union documents called "The Red Book."[1] The 1984 version reprints the basic statement with an addendum entitled "1970 Interpretive Comments."

The basis statement has become, as my AAUP officer explained with a sense of humor, rather like a sacred document upon which someone comments occasionally. The collected comments attempt to clarify the teacher's responsibility to *his* subject, profession, and institution (italics mine because I'm a feminist and although in 1970 the issue of sexist language was still in debate, by 1984 they should have known better).

The 1940 statement is brief, to the point, and, assuming that others will experience the same trouble I had locating it (long-distance phone calls, multiple trips to the library, interlibrary loan, visits to AAUP officers), well worth including here:

> The purpose of this statement is to promote public understanding and support of academic freedom and tenure and agreement upon procedures to assure them in colleges and universities. Institutions of higher education are conducted for the common good and not to further the interest of either the individual teacher or the institution as a whole. The common good depends upon the free search for truth and its free exposition.
>
> Academic freedom is essential to these purposes and applies to both teaching and research. Academic freedom in its teaching aspect is fundamental for the protection of the rights of the teacher in teaching and of the student to freedom in learning. It carries with it duties correlative with rights ... [the rest of the paragraph is concerned with tenure and not appropriate to this discussion].
>
> **Academic Freedom**
>
> (a) The teacher is entitled to full freedom in research and in the publication of the results, subject to the adequate performance of his other academic duties; but research for pecuniary return should be based upon an understanding with the authorities of the institution. [The second half of the sentence is rarely relevant to our discussion, but I included it because it's good for a laugh.]
>
> (b) The teacher is entitled to freedom in the classroom in discussing his subject, but he should be careful not to introduce into his teaching controversial matter which has no relation to his subject. Limitations of academic freedom because of religious or other aims of the institution should be clearly stated in writing at the time of the appointment.
>
> (c) The college or university teacher is a citizen, a member of a learned profession, and an officer of an educational institution. When he speaks or writes as a citizen, he should be free from institutional censorship or discipline, but his special position in the community imposes special obligations. As a man of learning and an educational officer, he should remember that the public may judge his profession and his institution by his utterances. Hence he should at all times be

accurate, should exercise appropriate restraint, should show respect for
the opinions of others, and should make every effort to indicate that he
is not an institutional spokesman. (Joughin 35–36)

What becomes obvious as we read the basic statement, the
official interpretations, and the further interpretations and explanations by "expert" members of the profession is that academic
freedom is a policy that attempts to guarantee free speech within
the academy and between its members, not a policy designed to
guarantee free reign in the classroom.

The footnotes to the basic statement consist of both original and
editorial commentary, two of which seem pertinent to this discussion.
The second footnote defines the term *teacher*; the editor's note
comments that "[i]n practice the term 'teacher' is often replaced by
'professor' because it applies to higher education and extends to
both the research and the teaching function" (Joughin 34). Given
the language of most governance and appointment documents, the
term *professor* would mean full-time, tenure-track faculty. TAs and
part-time master's level employees need not apply.[2]

The fourth footnote concerns English teachers in particular and,
I suspect, is the basis of my hypothetical classroom monarch's con-
tention that the classroom is his sacred kingdom. The provision
confirms the right of English teachers to explore controversial
material, but it hardly makes a castle or a kingdom out of the
composition classroom and certainly avoids making any teacher an
absolute monarch. Teachers must still answer to their peers and be
willing to grant academic freedom to other members of the college
community as well as guard it for themselves. But history aside
(which is, of course, a rather radical reduction of the importance of
history), let's explore why a portfolio system doesn't violate the
tenets of Academic Freedom.

In most college and university composition courses, the individual teacher acts as the spokesperson of the academy for his or her
students and, in a sense, becomes the ruler (or as our students
would have it, the dictator) in the classroom. Student work is graded
solely by the teacher, and when a student feels that the teacher
made an unfair judgment, his or her only recourse becomes an
appeal to the department chair or the college ombud. Students
sometimes feel, and often rightly, that if they had another instructor,
their grades would have been higher.

We all know that there is some truth to professorial stereotypes.
On the one hand, the students may face Dr. Trueword, the Keeper
of the English Language, who fails them because they have too

many spelling errors but who never comments on the content of their essays. On the other hand, their roommates may have Dr. Truethought, who has been carrying on a personal battle against The System since the sixties. Truethought thinks grammar and English courses themselves are the oppressors of the voiceless and grants students As and Bs as a Statement. Truethought's students rarely file complaints (although they will protest bitterly in private that they didn't "learn anything" in the course).

In between these two bastions of pedagogy, the rest of us lurk and work with our own idiosyncrasies. Sometimes we, too, are the cause of complaints, and our chairs and ombuds struggle with matching student complaints against student rumor. But the reality of the situation remains that neither chair nor ombud has the means to determine accurately whether any of us — Trueword, Truethought, or Ordinary Folk — have adhered to a fair and open policy of grading. Most traditional departments do not have a means (or a desire) for the peer review that could promote conversation about the pedagogy a teacher employs, much less about whether or not everyone grades according to the same standards.

Departments often create elaborate rubrics, exit exams, or proficiency exams to overcome criticism of the uneven quality of instruction. "See," they report, "we may teach differently, but our students learn the same way, meet the same standards." But having a rubric or an exam does not guarantee that teachers adhere to departmental standards. Academic folklore has it that exit exams allow strict teachers to condemn the examiners for their incompetence, easy teachers to condemn the examiners for their lack of originality, and the rest of the faculty to teach to a limited and narrow version of the test.

Outwardly, rubrics and exit exams appear to bring order to a department, but without intelligent and thoughtful discussion of pedagogy and standards, the classroom remains a sovereign state. The academic freedom of the faculty is intact, but the students' freedom is violated at nearly every turn. In short, most departments promote grading anarchy; students cannot trust that the grades they receive are the negotiated results of the best thinking of the members of the department. And although they may not agree on what or how to teach in the classroom, strict and lenient teachers alike know that this distrust of the English department serves to reduce the effectiveness of instruction.

Such anarchy of grading is more likely to disappear under a system of portfolio assessment. Instead of a singular system of evaluation set up by the lone professor or some other faculty member in the ivory tower, the standards in a portfolio evaluation are the result of collaborative actions, criteria that evolve from much discussed and sometimes hotly debated issues in the discipline of composition. To institute a portfolio system indicates a willingness to participate in the business of learning on all levels. To explore the givens about good writing can be a risky and exhilarating enterprise. It calls into question what in many cases has been left unexamined since our own graduations. But this examination process is not completely alien to our experience as English teachers and critics. Most of us in the profession have long since accepted that there is no one true way to read a text; why then not admit to the possibility that there is no one true way to grade or to approach a student essay?

Reading portfolios together, determining standards, and arguing for or against various criteria for grading student writing embody the spirit of academic freedom. All members of the composition faculty decide whether or not it is reasonable to make a student repeat composition because of surface errors, and all members of the department determine whether or not content should outweigh structure. In addition, successful portfolio assessment demands that departments plan common assignments, set up common projects, think together about what they want students to learn. The individual instructor has an opportunity to vary texts, due dates, and the content of essays, but the students come to expect that they are all learning the same skills, examining the same critical issues. Students develop greater faith in the department and its goals, therefore greater faith in the instruction they receive. Faculty members feel a greater sense of participation in the goals of the department, and therefore, more control over department policies.

An additional side benefit of a well-designed portfolio system is the sense of parity it promotes among those who participate in it. Significantly, the majority of people concerned about Academic Freedom are full-time, tenure-track faculty — professors of all ranks.[3] Graduate students and instructors represent a kind of teaching Other. Lacking the status conferred by the Ph.D. and/or a tenured line, they are suspect. In some schools, "regular" professors feel an obligation to monitor the teaching of these suspicious part-timers and almost always look upon this control of the Other's classroom as a duty akin to law enforcement.[4]

Needless to say, this attitude (and its accompanying actions) rankles the soul of more than one instructor of composition. In the first place, it is unjust to subject others to rules and requirements that you would not submit to yourself. If the professor is exempted from control, so should the professionally trained instructor be, and certainly so should the graduate student, who has usually gone through a practicum devised and taught by a professor, as most graduate students are now required to do. In the second place, it is pure chauvinism to assume that being granted a Ph.D. automatically confers upon the recipient the skill and knowledge needed to teach freshman composition. Too many people with Ph.D. appended to their names have received no training in teaching composition and exhibit such a disgust at having to teach freshmen how to write that their anger affects their judgment. I think particularly of a full professor who failed half of his students for having the audacity to turn in papers with errors in punctuation and grammar. When asked about the content of the essays, he replied, "Oh, it's just that adolescent mouthing that they do. I rarely pay attention to that nonsense, and I can't respect those who do."

Just as we did with Trueword and Truethought, let's contrast this professor's attitude with the attitude held by the instructor who is far more interested in teaching self-expression or critical-thinking skills than in deconstructing Joyce. The answer is not to separate literature and composition — in most smaller institutions that remains impossible — the answer is interaction. Both of these teachers would benefit from contact with the other, not to mention other teachers with other quirks in grading. If all teachers have to negotiate over a set of student portfolios, the students in both classes might benefit. This process does not compromise their freedom to continue to do well in the university — it teaches them to negotiate the shoals of teachers who are far more arbitrary than members of the English department.

It would do us all good to remember that the focus of portfolio assessment is the student, not the instructor. A department institutes a portfolio system in order to serve students and increase teaching effectiveness — not as an attempt to destroy the careers of teachers or create empires. In a well-designed portfolio system, everyone who participates in the portfolio assessment has a chance to discuss and argue for his or her position on the issues; no one can single-handedly "rule" or "legislate" either grades or policy. While it is possible for departments to set up portfolio systems that are as unstable and arbitrary as other systems of assessment, it is less likely to happen when the entire writing faculty is involved. And even though a portfolio can be set up to answer to an outside authority rather than a department, the dialogue and interaction promoted by a portfolio system provides more opportunity for peer assessment than when the individual professor, as the sole arbiter of grades and standards, has complete control over the classroom and the student.

The concept of Academic Freedom is based not only upon the idea of the sacredness of the individual view and the necessity for diversity within the academic community but also on the belief that peer review is a necessary control in an otherwise unregulated system. The ideal system creates respect among individual members of the English department community. And while it is possible that the community might have to deal with incompetence in its membership, it is also possible that it might come to recognize the strengths of members who have previously been silent, not for reasons of intimidation, but because they have not had a forum in which to speak.

## Notes

1. Most schools that have an AAUP bargaining unit use the AAUP statement. Other colleges and universities write their own, but regardless of the source of the academic freedom statement, the content reveals the same concerns and outlines the same policies.

2. Because I see part-time and graduate-student instructors as part of the composition faculty and entitled therefore to the rights and privileges of all those who teach in the individual school community, and because others make distinctions between these members of the community and others of higher and more permanent rank, I need to provide a key to let you know whom I'm talking about at any time during this discussion: in this article I will follow the AAUP's suggestions and refer to full-time, tenure-track faculty members as *professors* and all part-time or adjunct faculty members as *instructors*; graduate students are, as always, *TAs* (teaching assistants). When I wish to refer to matters that affect all three groups, I will use the term *teachers*.

3. Although the 1970 "Interpretive Comments" redefine the concept of "rank of full-time instructor or a higher rank" (AAUP 6) to include "any person who teaches a full-time load regardless of his specific title" (AAUP 6), this definition has little to do with intellectual or economic parity. The comment supposedly clarifies qualifications for tenure.

4. Two recent articles make obvious the tensions between full-time professors, junior faculty, and part-time instructors: James A. Schultz's "Report of the Committee on Academic Freedom: Part-Timers and Academic Freedom" in the Winter 1989 *MLA Newsletter,* and Linda Brodkey's "Transvaluing Difference" in the October 1989 *College English.*

# 23

# Writing Without Testing

Cherryl Armstrong Smith
*California State University, Sacramento*

> Grading is a fact of life in all school systems. If you don't give
> grades now, in a few years someone else will. I will never get used
> to giving grades to anyone. How can a letter or number sum up
> the full work that a person has done for a term or a year? I want
> grades to help, not hinder. Once again, my inward reaction says
> they hinder. If I must grade I make the best of a difficult situation.

> —Donald Graves, *Writing: Teachers and Children at Work*

At the end of the semester, when I review portfolios of selected
papers from students in my writing and literature courses, I usually
feel that my system of assessment is fair; yet when I assign grades I
feel sick at heart. It seems almost embarassing, after the work of the
course and the spirit of inquiry and collaboration, to end the semester
on what always feels to me an awkward note, a note that may be
necessary but is beside the point for everyone, a duty like paying
taxes, or sending overdue thank-you cards. So at the end of the term
I usually look up page 93 of Donald Graves's *Writing: Teachers and
Children at Work*.

In this text that has been for me, and for writing instructors I
know at every grade level, an indispensable teaching guide, Graves
devotes only three paragraphs (the first is quoted above) to the
subject of assessment. I am usually encouraged to push through to
the end of the course not only by the reminder that Don Graves,
too, doesn't like to give grades, but that his way, too, of making the
best of it is a portfolio: "Children are graded on their *best papers*
for the marking term. The week before the end of term, I ask the
children to choose their best work. If they wish to make the best
even better at that point, they may do so" (Graves's emphasis).

I also have been helped by following Peter Elbow's suggestions in *Embracing Contraries* (167–176) to collect the best of the semester portfolio along with a record of what the student has done during the course, or sometimes, all of the work, to see what's there. This way, I count the papers the students choose for their portfolios in order to assess writing quality, but "everything else" (attendance, journals, work in writing groups, in-class writing, and so on, depending on the course) gives them credit for completing the class requirements and is counted as an adjustment to the writing grade.

In my capacity as a writing program administrator, I feel even more acutely that assessment is a matter of making "the best of a difficult situation." As a teacher, I used to enjoy introducing the required texts on the first day of class by holding up Elbow's *Writing Without Teachers* and saying, "One of my goals for this semester is to make myself obsolete." Recently, as a writing program administrator, I have made similar use of Elbow and Belanoff's articles on portfolio assessment. For, changing from an impromptu writing exit exam to portfolio assessment begins to refocus a writing program the way that initiating a student-centered curriculum refocuses a classroom. Teachers do not become obsolete, even when students are asked to read *Writing Without Teachers*; but what it means to teach — in a process-oriented course, within a curriculum that seeks to move the teacher from center stage — changes dramatically, so that "teaching" may as accurately be called "learning." Portfolios redirect writing assessment to so great a degree that I believe such assessment might also be called "writing without testing."

Perhaps it would be wise to keep secret this quality of portfolio assessment, at least long enough for portfolios to become more firmly established as a preferred alternative to impromptu placement and proficiency tests. As movements toward process instruction, collaborative learning, and toward establishing composition itself as a discipline have become more clearly articulated, movements toward skills and accountability in the public schools and, in many ways, political divisions in universities between composition and literature have also become more pronounced. The nice thing about portfolio assessment (prior to the present volume) was that it might have encouraged a *quiet* revolution. Given that students choose the best papers they have written during the normal course of events in a writing class and are evaluated on that basis, the truth about this kind of exit test is that it is not a test at all. And to focus on that facet of portfolios may make it more difficult, politically, to substitute the new assessment for the old. Having begun, however, I will proceed, admitting that my experience with portfolios has made me not so much a spokesperson for the efficacy of portfolio assessment as someone who, *because* of the success of portfolios, feels compelled to raise at least a small voice against the institution of exit testing itself.

When I negotiated a move from impromptu exit testing to portfolios in the Developmental Writing Program at California State University, Northridge, I talked to colleagues outside the writing program about the portfolio mostly as a more accurate measure of students' writing performance than could be obtained with impromptu writing tests. Providing ourselves with three or four papers including drafts and revisions instead of a single, fifty-minute writing sample obviously gave us a better look at an individual student's writing. But inside the program I introduced portfolios to the faculty by distributing Belanoff and Elbow's article "Using Portfolios to Increase Collaboration and Community in a Writing Program" (reprinted in this volume), an essay that explores the ability of such a system to direct pedagogy and staff development toward collaboration.

I believe that at most places the move from multiple-choice testing to direct assessment of writing was introduced in a similar way. As Patricia Bizzell points out in a review of recent texts on assessment, the lack of research on how best to evaluate writing undercuts arguments made by advocates of holistic assessment promoting it as a more valid measure than multiple choice testing. Certainly, essay tests appear to offer a greater possibility for accurate evaluation than any set of multiple-choice questions might provide, and it is this greater likelihood of validity that is most publicly emphasized when writing program administrators and composition specialists propose holistically scored essay exams in the place of indirect testing. But the primary impetus for essay over multiple-choice testing, and for portfolios over holistic assessments has been philosophical and political rather than research based. Composition teachers recognized the value of direct assessments, as they recognize the value of portfolios, most emphatically for the changed message they send students about the nature of the courses they teach. Direct assessment said, "This is not a course in usage and vocabulary; it is a course in writing." Portfolios say, "This is a course that focuses on the writing process and on revision." Furthermore, teachers recognize the changed status the new assessment brings them relative to the test. Whereas direct assessment allowed teacher input in a way that multiple-choice testing never did — teachers could now help choose topics and, more significantly, were directly involved in evaluating essays in holistic scorings — with portfolios, teachers readily welcome the even greater authority that comes to them. The responsibility for the course remains with the classroom teacher, for students are simply asked to include in a portfolio the best three or four essays they write during the semester. Portfolios are read by small groups of teachers who judge the quality of the writing. At CSUN, we held faculty meetings during the semester to read essays and to discuss our standards. But the real authority fell to the teachers in their small groups as they negotiated pass/fail decisions among themselves.

Having coordinated what appears to be a successful program of portfolio writing assessment, I am satisfied that portfolios do encourage a process pedagogy and that they increase the opportunity for collaboration among composition faculty and among faculty, tutors, and students. However, the result of this success is that I can no longer find a justification for exit testing. I find instead, exposed by portfolio assessment, reasons for the institution of exit testing that I either had not noticed before or had managed to disregard.

Portfolios represent an improvement over impromptu testing because portfolios take the testing out of assessment. Papers are written under normal class conditions; they are real papers that include drafts, revisions, writing-group commentary, and so on. Teachers at CSUN reported that they felt the course belonged to "real" writing once again; they did not feel obliged to "teach to the test" during the month before the impromptu exam, and those who had never felt this obligation reported that by requiring revision, portfolios allowed for a more integrated course. Many individual instructors already had been using portfolios to evaluate their students' work, and the programwide reading groups gave them valuable support.

Yet though we have managed, with portfolios, to eliminate test conditions from the final writing sample, we are using the portfolio as an exit test. Now, instead of judging by a timed writing whether a student is ready to graduate from the developmental course, or whether the student has achieved a freshman- or junior-level "proficiency," we base this judgment on a portfolio of papers written over a whole semester. In most places that use them, portfolios have been instituted as a replacement for more intrusive methods or for tests like the timed writing at CSUN, which teachers felt worked at cross-purposes to a process-oriented writing course. It is instructive to look, from the vantage point of portfolios, at the tests we have replaced.

From the perspective of portfolio assessment, timed writing

tests begin to appear inappropriate (in the worst light, counter-productive) for writing programs informed by current research and theory in composition—programs that emphasize the collaborative dimensions of writing, the complexities of invention and revision, the development of self-selected topics, the ability to work in a variety of genres, or the value of writing as a way of learning. If we were not so used to it, an impromptu, timed essay test on a prescribed topic would seem a strikingly incongruous culmination for such courses.

Impromptu writing tests are often justified by the fact that students frequently must write essay exams in college courses. But first-year composition may be one of the least appropriate of all courses for providing training for these tests. Like creative writing or studio art, other courses that focus on creating original material, there is little in first-year composition on which to be tested. Although it is true that students will write many essay exams in college, never in any course will they be tested on writing apart from being asked to examine, remember, or respond to some information that has been, itself, the subject of the course. Never will students be given a passage from some text or author they have not read or a question they have not been asked to think about before and have fifty minutes or two hours to write. And never, except in a composition class practice test, will students be examined on writing as distinct from course content.

Even in those proficiency tests for which students are given materials to study in advance and then, more fairly, are asked to write a timed response, competencies that allow writers to write well are necessarily stripped from the writing situation. Besides the unusual pressure of writing on the spot, the writer faces an unknown audience who will never respond at all to what she writes. She has no exigencies for writing that are connected to the task at hand; that is, interest or even background in the topic can be only coincidental. The writer is writing only to pass the course or fill a requirement.

And how, in evaluating this writing can we be said to measure anything more than serendipitous familiarity with the subject and degree of conventional syntax while writing quickly? An impromptu writing test may have only a tangential connection to writing per-formance in nontest contexts, and is different from timed writing situations that occur in other disciplines. In a writing course it is unlikely that, other than for an exit test, we would ever have occasion to grade first-draft writing at all.

Why then are impromptu writing exit and proficiency tests so widely established?

The first thing to be said about impromptu exit and proficiency tests is that they are identical with impromptu entrance and place-ment tests; often they are simply appropriated from placement tests when a college or school district decides an exit measure is needed. In many schools, therefore, students take a timed writing test that will determine the level of writing course in which they must enroll, and then, at the end of the freshman or junior year, they take exactly the same kind of test to determine whether they are ready to exit the course or the university. The symmetry of this process is attractive but, in terms of actually measuring writing accomplish-ment, misleading. Moreover, while a school may need to rank the writing performance of its entering population to fill appropriately the available sections of each level course it offers, there is no need to rank order student writing when a course is finished. At that point we only need to know if students have accomplished whatever it is we have agreed needs to be accomplished by the time they take the exit test. If we ask for timed writings, there is no reason to rate them any way other than pass/fail.

That impromptu exit tests are most often holistically scored on a five- or six-point scale suggests both their origins in placement testing and the extent to which scoring methods propel, indeed, are usually synonymous with, assessment. I often hear instructors talk about giving a holistic exam when they mean that a set of essays will be scored holistically. To make sense out of what we are doing in assessing writing, it is necessary to disentangle scoring from assessment, as well as placement or entrance tests from proficiency or exit tests.

The timed writing placement exam, for instance, was made possible by the development of holistic scoring procedures. Until holistic scoring was refined by Edward White and others, many writing placements did not ask students to write. Instead, indirect assessments — multiple-choice vocabulary, usage, punctuation, or reading comprehension tests — were used, and are in some places still used, to predict writing ability. And although the advantages of direct over indirect means of writing assessment were widely rec-ognized (Cooper and Odell), the real selling point for direct assess-ment was the feasibility of holistic scoring.

But the value of holistic scoring is that the members of a scoring group can achieve consistency during a particular session. A holistic test tells little about individual pieces of writing; it merely ranks them against others in the same group. This ranking of writing is always a relative matter; the top writers at one school may be the bottom writers elsewhere (Armstrong), and the use of an impromptu test is merely a matter of convenience. If nothing else is available, as is often the case at the time placements need to be made, an impromptu writing has to suffice.

At the end of a semester of instruction, however, or as a student is leaving the university, there is no reason to rely on a single, timed writing when papers and drafts are available, and no reason to rank order the writing when a pass/fail decision is all that is needed. If we look more closely at exit and placement tests some telling differences become apparent. In placement testing our goal — stated bluntly — is to fill available levels of writing courses. During 1983–84, when I taught at two campuses of the University of California, I learned that more students at UC Santa Barbara took the beginning-level writing course, Subject A, than did students at the UC San Diego campus. This information implied nothing, however, about differences between student writing abilities on each campus. There were more Subject A students at Santa Barbara because that campus offered more sections of the course. The California State University system, which has used a statewide placement reading for many years (as the University of California does now) gives campuses a numerical score for each student (the holistic score on the writing sample in combination with scores on reading comprehension and usage tests), and each of the nineteen CSU campuses makes a cutoff decision to provide a greater or lesser number of beginning, "developmental," writing courses. A student who may be termed a developmental writer at Cal State, Los Angeles, may become qualified for regular freshman composition by taking a short drive on the freeway to Cal State, Northridge, where the cutoff score is lower.

The point is that placement is a literal term. In a placement test we use writing samples, or some other measure, to place students in the various courses our campus provides. It does not matter — although we do need to be reminded — that our rankings are relative, that they are general impressions, that they are simply a convenient way to locate students for "basic" courses because we offer "basic" courses, and so on. For purposes of sorting writing samples, holistic assessment is an efficient method, because it tells us where a piece of writing ranks relative to others in the same population. Those who would propose alternative placement procedures, such as portfolios, draw our attention to the limitations of impromptu writing scored holistically for representing a student's writing ability. They draw our attention, in other words, beyond rank ordering to the evaluation of writing abilities, a subject that may be said to be beyond the scope of placement test concerns.

Proficiency, however, is another issue. Proficiency and exit tests attempt to measure accomplishment. What kind of writer is the student at the end of the course? Has she learned what we wanted her to learn? Has she improved? Should she take more writing courses before she graduates? How much does she know about writing? A great value of portfolios is that they are consistent with a process pedagogy. Inconsistent with such pedagogy is exit testing, which evaluates written products as if they alone will give us answers to these questions.

Cy Knoblauch and Lil Brannon examine such "myths about evaluation" in the last chapter of *Rhetorical Traditions and the Teaching of Writing*, arguing, among other things, for assessments that measure "attitudinal adjustments, not changes in performance" (168). Lester Faigley et al. have proposed as assessment instruments research tools, such as writers' self-reports, that attempt to measure "changes in processes of composing." Although portfolios may offer the best available means of direct writing assessment, given what we know about the complexities of the writing process and what little we seem to know about how to evaluate writing, we need to question what a collection of writing can actually tell us about how much a student has learned, or about writing competence. Are we really measuring competence when we look at writing samples? Do we want to measure improvement? Is it possible to do so? Faigley et al. caution that "practice has far outrun theory in writing assessment" (207). Ed White's comprehensive book on assessment includes a discussion of reading that serves not only to connect literary and composition theory but to demonstrate further the difficulty of reading and assessing student writing. But even if we were confident that a portfolio of writing told us what we needed to know about a student's writing accomplishment, there are important political and pedagogical reasons to question exit testing. That portfolio assessments usually ask students to include process writing, drafts, and readers' responses as well as final versions suggests ways in which portfolios make sense as a culmination to a writing course, and as a form of publication. That they facilitate collaboration indicates their value to writing programs. I want to encourage the use of portfolios but at the same time to suggest that we can have the benefits of portfolios without needing to use them as exit measures.

In most places, portfolios represent a third stage in the development of writing assessment. Within about a ten-year period, from the early seventies to early eighties, holistic assessment replaced the use of multiple-choice tests of vocabulary, syntax, punctuation, and so on, in a majority of writing programs (Edward White 19). In the late eighties, portfolios began to replace holistic assessment of writing exams for measuring proficiency. Those of us who initiated this change have had to respond to concerns about assessment voiced from the perspective of impromptu essay testing. These concerns reveal motives for exit assessment that have little to do with measuring writing ability, in the same way that, as I have been suggesting, the *benefits* of portfolios have less to do with assessment than with encouraging a process pedagogy and increasing collaboration in a writing program.

From the perspective of impromptu testing, portfolio assessment raises a number of questions and initial objections. Apart from matters of logistics, three questions repeatedly were asked about portfolios at my university:

1. What about plagiarism? How do you know that students actually wrote the essays they submit in the portfolio?

2. What about knowing how students can do on their own? These essays have been responded to by the teacher and by a peer group and sometimes by a tutor, too. Don't we need to see a student perform independently?

3. What about consistent standards among teachers? If small groups of teachers judge the portfolios, even with occasional faculty meetings, how can you be sure that the teachers all have the same standards?

All three questions raise issues of authority and control. They are not questions about whether or not we are actually measuring writing abilities.

When holistic scoring replaced indirect assessment, we knew that we could achieve scoring consistency, but we could not claim that the impromptu tests allowed us to measure proficiency; we could not claim to be examining writing competencies, those invisible qualities of mind and experience that account for writing ability. We were merely ranking writing. And surely it was closer to the purposes of writing assessment to rank writing than to rank multiple-choice test scores. But the argument holistic assessment had to win in order to replace multiple-choice testing did not focus on the evaluation of writing abilities, in any case. First, holistic assessment, like any other new program, had to prove itself cost effective. And second, it had to demonstrate reliability, that human scoring could be "objective" in the way that multiple-choice testing appeared to be, "as if," writes Ed White, "machine scored tests had been created with no human participation" (20). White reminds us that reliability in holistic scoring, and in all test scores, is usually overstated, but he does report on a study of testing in the California State University, for instance, that found a reliability of between .68 and .89, meaning that two readers disagreed by more than one point only 5 percent of the time (27). Such statistics helped to ease the move from indirect, seemingly more objective, testing to teacher-scored holistic exams. For the focus of concern, then and now, was on the need to control for variety of teacher opinion.

In a similar way, we could address the suspicions portfolios arouse by pointing out that with portfolios we not only directly read writing as we did with holistic assessment, we now have a more complete sample; but whether or not portfolios can be said to provide a good means of evaluating student writing was never a significant issue at my university. It was the more volatile issue of subjectivity that was important and that remains open. Portfolio assessment will continue to be criticized for its subjectivity not only because it cannot provide the kind of reliability data offered by studies of holistic readings but because it is, in fact, a subjective method.

> We sometimes refer to our large meetings as "calibration sessions," but that is really a misnomer. For in a true holistic scoring session, the leaders impose their standards: they choose the "anchor papers" and readers must leave their own standards and criteria at the door. The impressive speed and validity in careful holistic scoring depend on this imposed authority. But we're not trying for impressive validity. ...
> Besides, we're not tempted to set standards ourselves since we doubt they exist apart from actual papers in an actual community of readers. (Belanoff and Elbow, this volume, 28)

Teachers participating in a controlled holistic reading agree to adopt the standards articulated by the leaders, but there is no reason to consider these standards less subjective than the standards that small groups of teachers may decide upon for themselves while reading portfolios. The difference is that portfolio assessment does not attempt to moniter consistency during the readings. And it does not rely on other checks for consistency either. The papers need not be written in response to similar assignments; groups of readers may score portfolios independently from other groups, and so on. Perhaps more importantly, our discussion of the possibilities for objectivity in reading needs to be examined in terms of the ongoing conversation among literary theorists focused on contexts for reading, on the indeterminacy of meaning, and on understanding texts in ways that can only be described as subjective.

Portfolio assessment leaves the authority for decision making up to teachers and proposes no way of systematically checking up on them. Nor does it offer ways, outside the regular activities of the classroom, to check up on students. Not surprisingly, objections to portfolios will sound similar to the kinds of objections often raised to student-centered classrooms: How do you keep things from getting out of control? How do you maintain discipline? For it is right to assume that this kind of program will upset the status quo. As Nancie Atwell remarks, "The status quo regards collaboration as cheating and learning as a solitary, competitive enterprise" (37). The question most frequently asked about portfolios — the question of plagiarism — could not be asked at all from the perspective of a process-oriented course. A teacher knows that her students wrote the essays they submit because she has seen them in draft and has responded to them herself. Likewise, the question about how a student might perform independently makes little sense in a curriculum that assumes writing is always to some degree collaborative.

Belanoff and Elbow speak directly to the concerns that underlie such questions: "We make the issue one of human judgment at the one-to-one level — rather than a matter of 'test security.' That is, the student's own teacher does not forward a piece to the portfolio process unless she is confident it is the student's own work — as she sees the matter in a context where collaboration is emphasized" (this volume, 19). As for the question about scoring consistency, if groups of teachers have the final say, administrators do not. Of course, as Belanoff and Elbow point out, administrators who are after collaboration have achieved some of their purposes by instituting portfolios, just as in my classes when students realize that "what the teacher wants" is really for them to write about subjects they find worth exploring, they have, to their surprise, begun to give me what I want. A student-centered curriculum manipulates classroom outcomes to as great a degree as a teacher-centered one; similarly, by requiring teachers to come together to discuss assignments and classroom practices, as well as standards, portfolios move individual classes and writing programs toward collaboration, as tests may move classes and programs toward competition.

If portfolios work as well — even better — to give us samples of students' writing, with no test security, using the writing that students do anyway all semester, and with teachers, not administrators, having the final say, we have altered conventional assessment more than I think those we have persuaded to let us do this must realize. For the objections to portfolio assessment are objections to investing authority in classroom teachers. Portfolio reading groups operate autonomously; the administrator must initiate collaboration and then refuse to settle disputes. Unlike standardized testing, portfolio readings are personal, subjective, and in the hands of teachers themselves. Having instituted an assessment measure that does not depend on test security, that is not a test at all, the enterprise of exit testing appears before us like, well, an emperor with no clothes. Who is the test for? Why are we doing it?

Rarely do writing program administrators ask for these tests. WPAs are making "the best of a difficult situation," one that has been imposed by school districts, by college administrations, by demands for accountability from people who may not be aware of the complexity of the writing process nor the limitations of research on evaluation, and possibly, who may not particularly be motivated by an interest in writing development at all.

> Finally, testing is power, and power is a root political issue. . . . Those who ignore the politics of testing may well find themselves replaced by better and smoother politicians, and even those alert to the power pressures and power drives of administrative and political figures or of the public may wind up defeated by forces with little concern for academic matters. No one should imagine a test to be above politics or a testing program to be outside the political arena. (Edward White 238)

It does not seem to me a wild assumption to expect that writing teachers know whether their students should pass their courses, that writing teachers should assume the greatest authority for evaluation of writing. The isolation of grading and of teaching itself can be helped by portfolio reading groups. These groups are useful in the ways I have mentioned and as a forum for sharing and collaborating in the necessity for grading. And certainly portfolios are an as yet untapped source of data for teacher-research. But now that we have found a way to gather writing samples without creating artificial test situations, why turn the portfolio, which is not a test, into (of all things) a test? Why not collect the best writing a student does during the semester and spend our assessment money on publication? Students can pass into the next level course if they have done all the work for the semester. Portfolio reading groups can help teachers make the best of having to give grades. Teachers can select exemplary essays for distribution throughout the school. They can collaborate on assignments and classroom practices.

> Literature teachers seldom defend their enterprise (and are seldom asked to defend it) on the basis of their measurable success at producing "better" literary critics, or even better readers. The experience of literature, teachers would surely argue, is valued in itself

because it leads students to seek literacy and aspire to civility, though they receive neither from the literature course itself. Writing courses, we suggest, have a similar value, finding their justification in the activities they make available, the attitudes and awarenesses they foster, not the facts they convey, or their immediate performance gains. (Knoblauch and Brannon, *Rhetorical Traditions and the Teaching of Writing* 167)

The subtext of the three questions I found most frequently asked about portfolios seems to be that the purpose of exit testing is to provide an external, higher authority to check up on teachers or to check up on students. Furthermore, the questions were not appropriate to writing but to some subject that can be learned, once and for all, and then systematically tested. By using portfolios but abandoning exit tests in writing programs, we would acknowledge that teachers are authorities about the work taking place in their own classrooms, that collaboration encourages the development of writing ability and of effective teaching, and that learning to write is not a matter of passing tests but is a lifelong process.

# Portfolios: A Selected Bibliography

When we began this book, only a handful of citations about portfolio assessment could be found in the literature, and many of those citations referred to conference papers. While more articles on portfolio assessment appear with each passing month, as of the publishing of this manuscript the list is still quite small. For the reader's convenience, we have listed other discussions of portfolio assessment available through journals and ERIC documents. This list is by no means inclusive; we list only those articles that directly address portfolio assessment and have left those on general issues of assessment to other authors. We wish to express our thanks to Richard Larson for his assistance in developing this bibliography.

Anson, Chris M. "Developing a Portfolio Assessment Model." Keynote address, Conference of the Writing Program Administrators of Virginia, Lynchburg, Va., 1989.

Anson, Chris M. and Robert L. Brown, Jr. "Large-Scale Portfolio Assessment: Problems and Issues." Paper presented at the Seventh Annual Conference of the National Testing Network in Writing, Montreal, Quebec, 1989.

Anson, Chris M., Lillian Bridwell-Bowles, Robert L. Brown, Jr. "Portfolio Assessment Across the Curriculum: Early Conflicts." Panel of papers presented at the Sixth Annual Conference of the National Testing Network in Writing, Minneapolis, Minn., 1988.

Beers, Susan E. "Use of a Portfolio Writing Assignment in a Course on Developmental Psychology." Teaching of Psychology 12 (1985): 94–96.

Belanoff, Pat. "Portfolio Assessment." Paper presented at the Third Annual Conference of the National Testing Network in Writing, San Francisco, Cal., 1986.

Bishop, Wendy. "Designing a Writing Portfolio Evaluation System." *The English Record* 40.2 (1990): 21–25.

———. "Revising the Technical Writing Class: Peer Critiques, Self-Evaluation, and Portfolio Grading." *Technical Writing Teacher* 16 (1989): 13–26.

Burnham, Christopher. "Portfolio Evaluation: Room to Breathe and Grow." *Training the New Teacher of College Composition.* Ed. Charles Bridges. Urbana, Ill.: NCTE, 1986.

Camp, Roberta. "Thinking about Portfolios." *The Quarterly of the National Writing Project and The Center for the Study of Writing* 12, 3 (1990): 8–14, 27.

———. "The Writing Folder in Post-Secondary Assessment" in *Directions and Misdirections in English Evaluation.* Ed. Peter J. A. Evans. Ottowa, Canada: The Canadian Council of Teachers of English, 1985.

Camp, Roberta, and Pat Belanoff. "Portfolios as Proficiency Tests." *Notes from the National Testing Network in Writing Conference,* 1987.

Ford, James E., and Gregory Larkin. "The Portfolio System: An End to Backsliding Writing Standards." *College English* 39 (1978): 950–55.

Holt, Dennis, and Nancy Baker. "Portfolios in Barrier Testing." Paper presented at the Seventh Annual Conference of the National Testing Network in Writing, Montreal, Quebec, 1989.

Howard, Kathryn. "Making the Writing Portfolio Real." *The Quarterly of the National Writing Project and The Center for the Study of Writing* 12.3 (1990): 4–7, 27.

Hutchings, Pat, and Ted Marchese. "Watching Assessment: Questions, Stories, Prospects." *Change* 22.5 (September/October, 1990): 12–38.

Hutchings, Pat, and Richard L. Larson. "The Politics of Using Portfolios for Assessment." In Edward M. White, William Lutz, and Sandra Kamusikiri, ed., *The Politics and Practices of Assessment.* New York: Modern Language Association, forthcoming.

Killingsworth, M. Jimmie, and Scott Sanders. "Portfolios for the Major in Professional Communication." *Technical Writing Teacher* (1987): 166–69.

Krest, Margie. "Adapting the Portfolio to Meet Student Needs." *English Journal* (February 1990): 29–34.

Larson, Richard. "Using Portfolios to Assess the Impact of a Curriculum." *Assessment Update,* in press.

Murphy, Sandra, and Mary Ann Smith. "Talking about Portfolios." *The Quarterly of the National Writing Project and the Center for the Study of Writing* 12.3 (1990): 1–3, 24–27.

Parker-Smith, Bettye. *Guide to Portfolio Development* (A Manual for Students and Assessors in an Alternative Adult-oriented Degree Program). 2nd edition. Chicago, Ill.: Northeastern Illinois University, 1980.

Paulson, F. Leon, Pearl R. Paulson, and Carol A. Meyer. "What Makes a Portfolio a Portfolio?" *Educational Leadership* (February 1991): 60–63.

"Portfolio Assessment: An Annotated Bibliography." *The Quarterly of the National Writing Project and the Center for the Study of Writing* 10 (October 1988): 23–24.

Savitz, Fred R. "A Prototype for Portfolio Development." *Community Services Catalyst* 14 (1984): 13–16.

Senf, Carol. "The Portfolio or Ultimate Writing Assessment." *Technical Writing Teacher* 11 (1983): 23–25.

Smit, David W. "Evaluating a Portfolio System." *WPA: Writing Program Administration* 14 (Fall/Winter 1990): 51–62.

Soares, Eric J., and Leslie Goldgehn. "The Portfolio Approach in Business Education." *Bulletin of the Association for Business Communication* 48 (1985): 17–21.

Sugarman, Jay. "Teacher Portfolios Inform Assessment." *Harvard Education Letter* 5.3 (1989): 5–6.

Tierney, R. J., and Mark Carter and Laura Desai. *Portfolios in the Reading and Writing Classroom.* Cambridge, Mass.: Christopher Gordon, 1991.

Ware, Elaine. "Helping Students to Prepare a Technical Communications Portfolio." *Technical Writing Teacher* (1988): 56–62.

White, Edward M. "The Damage of Innovations Set Adrift." *AAHE Bulletin* (November, 1990): 3–5.

Wolf, Dennie P. "Portfolio Assessment: Sampling Student Work." *Educational Leadership* 46.7 (April 1989): 35–9.

# Works Cited

Anrig, Gregory. "The President's Report: The Constancy of Change." Education, Atlanta, Ga., June, 1989.

————. "Testing and Student Performance: Now and in the Future." Paper presented at the Fourth National Conference on Assessment in Higher Education, Atlanta, Ga., June, 1989.

Anson, Chris M. "Developing a Portfolio Assessment Model." Keynote address, Conference of the Writing Program Administrators of Virginia, Lynchburg, Va., 1989.

————. "Introduction: Response to Writing and the Paradox of Uncertainty." *Writing and Response: Theory, Practice, and Research*. Ed. Chris M. Anson. Urbana, Ill.: NCTE, 1989.

————. "Piloting Linked Courses Across the Curriculum." Office of Summer Sessions, University of Minnesota, 1987.

————. "Resistance to Writing: Case Studies of Departmental Ideology." Paper presented at the Conference on College Composition and Communication, St. Louis, Mo., 1988.

————. "Toward a Multidimensional Model of Writing in the Academic Disciplines." *Writing in Academic Disciplines*. Vol. 2 of *Advances in Writing Research*. Ed. D. A. Jolliffe. Norwood, N.J.: Ablex, 1988.

Anson, Chris M. and Lillian Bridwell-Bowles. "Piloting a Program of Linked Writing Courses Across the Curriculum." Office of Educational Development Programs, University of Minnesota, 1988.

Anson, Chris M. and Robert L. Brown, Jr. "Large-Scale Portfolio Assessment: Problems and Issues." Paper presented at the Seventh Annual Conference of the National Testing Network in Writing, Montreal, Quebec, 1989.

Anson, Chris M., Lillian Bridwell-Bowles, Robert L. Brown, Jr. "Assessment of Writing Across the Curriculum: Research for Change." Panel of papers presented at the Conference on College Composition and Communication, St. Louis, Mo., 1988.

———. "Portfolio Assessment Across the Curriculum: Early Conflicts." Panel of papers presented at the Sixth Annual Conference of the National Testing Network in Writing, Minneapolis, Minn., 1988.

Applebee, Arthur N. "Problems in Process Approaches: Toward a Reconceptualization of Process Instruction." *The Teaching of Writing: Eighty-Fifth Yearbook of the National Society for the Study of Education.* Ed. Anthony Petrosky and David Bartholomae. Chicago: U of Chicago P, 1986.

Applebee, Arthur N. and Judith Langer. *How Writing Shapes Thinking: A Study of Teaching and Learning.* Urbana, Ill.: NCTE, 1987.

Archbald, Doug A. and Fred M. Newman. "Beyond Standardized Testing: Assessing Authentic Academic Achievements in the Secondary School." National Association of Secondary School Principals, 1988.

Armstrong [Smith], Cherryl. "Redefining Basic Writing: Lessons From Harvard's Basic Writers." *Journal of Basic Writing* 7.2 (Fall 1988): 68–80.

Association of American University Professors (AAUP). *American Association of Unviersity Professors' Policy Documents and Reports.* Washington, D.C.: Saint Mary's Press, 1984.

Atwell, Nancie. *In the Middle.* Portsmouth, N.H.: Boynton/Cook, 1987.

Austin, J. L. *How to Do Things with Words.* New York, Oxford UP, 1965.

Baktin, M. M., "Discourse in the Novel." *The Dialogic Imagination.* Ed. Michael Holquist. Trans. Caryl Emerson and Michael Holquist. Austin: U of Texas P, 1981.

Beavan, Mary H. "Individualized Goal Setting, Self-Evaluation, and Peer Evaluation." *Evaluating Writing: Describing, Measuring, Judging.* Ed. Charles R. Cooper and Lee Odell. Urbana, Ill.: NCTE, 1977.

Belanoff, Pat. "Portfolio Assessment." Paper presented at the Third Annual Conference of the National Testing Network in Writing, San Francisco, Cal., 1986.

Bernier, Norman R. and Jack E. Williams. *Beyond Beliefs: Ideological Foundations of American Education.* Englewood Cliffs, N.J.: Prentice-Hall, 1973.

Bernthal, Craig A., and Jay B. Ludwig. "Teaching Composition: A Handbook for Graduate Assistants." Michigan State University, East Lansing: Department of English, 1986. (ERIC ED 293 121).

Berthoff, Ann E. *Forming/Thinking/Writing.* Portsmouth, N.H.: Boynton/Cook, 1978.

———. "Recognition, Representation, and Revision." *Journal of Basic Writing* 3 (1981): 27–37.

Beveridge, William I. B. "Observation." *The Art of Scientific Investigation.* New York: Norton, 1957.

*Biological Science: An Ecological Approach.* Dubuque, Iowa: Kendall/Hunt, 1987.

Bishop, Wendy. "Designing a Writing Portfolio Evaluation System." *The English Record* 40.2 (1990): 21–25.

———. "Revising the Technical Writing Class: Peer Critiques, Self-Evaluation, and Portfolio Grading." *Technical Writing Teacher* 16 (1989): 13–26.

———. *Something Old, Something New: College Writing Teachers and Classroom Change.* Carbondale, Ill.: Southern Illinois UP, 1990.

Bizzell, Patricia. "What Can We Know, What Must We Do, What May We Hope: Writing Assessment." *College English* 49 (September 1987): 575–84.

Blair, Catherine P. "Only One of the Voices: Dialogic Writing Across the Curriculum." *College English* 50 (1988): 383–389.

Brannon, Lil, and C. H. Knoblauch. "On Students' Rights to Their Own Texts: A Model of Teacher Response." *College Composition and Communication* 33 (1982): 157–166.

Brick, Allan. "The CUNY Writing Assessment Test and the Teaching of Writing." *Writing Program Administration* 4.1 (1980): 28–34.

Bridwell-Bowles, Lillian. "Assessing Writing Across the Curriculum: Asking the Important Questions." Paper presented at the third Miami University Conference on the Teaching of Writing, Oxford, Oh., 1988.

Britton, James, and Tony Burgess, Nancy Martin, Alex McLeod, Harold Rosen. *The Development of Writing Abilities (11–18).* London: Macmillian, 1975.

Brodkey, Linda. "Transvaluing Difference." *College English* 52.6 (October 1989): 597–601.

Brown, Robert L., Jr. "Reading Universities: Inscribed Self and Other." Paper presented at the Fifth Annual Conference of the National Testing Network in Writing, Atlantic City, N.J., 1986.

Brown, Robert L., Jr. and Carl Herndl. "An Ethnographic Study of Corporate Writing: Job Status as Reflected in Written Text." *Functional Approaches to Writing: Research Implications.* Ed. Barbara Couture. Norwood, N.J.: Ablex, 1986.

Brown, Roscoe C., Jr. "Testing Black Student Writers." *Writing Assessment: Issues and Strategies.* Ed. Karen Greenberg, Harvey Weiner, and Richard Donovan. New York: Longman, 1986.

Bruffee, Kenneth A. "Collaborative Learning and the 'Conversation of Mankind.'" *College English* 46 (November 1984): 635–52.

Burgess, Tyrrell. *A Guide to English Schools.* Harmondsworth, U.K.: Penguin, 1964.

Burnett, David G. "Giving Credit Where Credit Is Due: Evaluating Experiential Learning in the Liberal Arts." *Innovative Higher Education* 10 (1985): 43–54.

Burnham, Christopher. "Portfolio Evaluation: Room to Breathe and Grow." *Training the New Teacher of College Composition.* Ed. Charles Bridges. Urbana, Ill.: NCTE, 1986.

Camp, Roberta. "Changing the Model for Direct Assessment of Writing." *Holistic Scoring: Theoretical Foundations and Validation Research.* Ed. Michael Williamson and Brian Huot. Norwood, N.J.: Ablex (in press).

———. "Portfolios Evolving: Backgrounds and Variations." Paper presented at the Seventh Annual Conference of the National Testing Network in Writing, Montreal, Quebec, 1989.

———. "Thinking about Portfolios." *The Quarterly of the National Writing Project and The Center for the Study of Writing* 12, 3 (1990): 8–14, 27.

———. "The Writing Folder in Post-Secondary Assessment." *Directions and Misdirections in English Education.* Ed. Peter J. A. Evans. Ottawa, Canada: Canadian Council of Teachers of English, 1985.

Camp, Roberta, and Pat Belanoff. "Portfolios as Proficiency Tests." *Notes from the National Testing Network in Writing Conference,* 1987.

Charmey, Davida. "The Validity of Using Holistic Scoring to Evaluate Writing: A Critical Overview:" *Research in the Teaching of English* 18 (1984): 65–68.

Christopher Newport College. "Student Guide: The Freshman Writing Programs." Department of English, 1988.

Conlan, Gertrude. "'Objective' Measures of Writing Ability." *Writing Assessment: Issues and Strategies.* Ed. Karen L. Greenberg, Harvey S. Weiner, Richard A. Donovan. New York: Longman Press, 1986.

Connelly, Peter J., and Donald C. Irving. "Composition and the Liberal Arts: A Shared Responsibility." *College English* 37 (1976): 668–70.

Connolly, Paul, and Theresa Vilardi, eds. *New Directions in College Writing Programs.* New York: MLA, 1986.

Cooper, Charles R. "Holistic Evaluation of Writing." *Evaluating Writing: Describing, Measuring, Judging.* Ed. Charles Cooper and Lee Odell. Urbana, Ill.: NCTE, 1977.

———. *The Nature and Measurement of Competency in English.* Urbana, Ill.: NCTE, 1987.

Cooper, Charles, and Lee Odell. *Evaluating Writing.* Urbana, Ill.: NCTE, 1977.

Cross, K. Patricia, and Thomas Angelo. *Classroom Assessment Techniques: A Handbook for Faculty.* Ann Arbor, Mich.: NCRIPTAL, 1988.

Daniels, Harvey, and Steve Zemelman. *A Writing Project: Training Teachers of Composition from Kindergarten to College.* Portsmouth, N.H.: Heinemann, 1985.

Dixon, John. "English Coursework." *Times Educational Supplement* October 28, 1977.

Dixon, John, and Leslie Stratta. "Changing the Model for 'Examining' Achievements in Writing." *English in the Eighties*. Ed. Robert Eagleson. Adelaide, Australia: Australian Association for the Teaching of English, 1982.

Eiseley, Loren, "The Judgment of the Birds." *The Immense Journey*. New York: Random House, 1956.

Elbow, Peter. *Embracing Contraries*. New York: Oxford UP, 1986.

———. "Embracing Contraries in the Teaching Process." *College English* 45 (April 1983): 327—39.

———. "Trying to Teach While Thinking About the End." *On Competence: A Critical Analysis of Competence-based Reforms in Higher Education*. Ed. Gerals Grant, P. Elbow, T. Ewens, Z. Gamson, W. Kohli, W. Neumann, V. Olesen, and D. Riesman. San Francisco: Jossey—Bass, 1979.

———. *What Is English?* New York: MLA, 1991.

———. *Writing Without Teachers*. New York: Oxford UP, 1973.

Elbow, Peter, and Pat Belanoff. "Portfolios as a Substitute for Proficiency Examinations." *College Composition and Communication* 37 (1986): 336—39.

El-Khawas, Elaine. *Campus Trends, 1989*. Washington D.C.: American Council on Higher Education, 1989.

Emig, Janet. "Writing as a Mode of Learning." *College Composition and Communication* 28 (1977): 122—28.

Fader, Daniel. "Writing Samples and Virtues." *Writing Assessment: Issues and Strategies*. Ed. Karen L. Greenberg, Harvey S. Wiener, Richard A. Donovan. New York: Longman, 1986.

Faigley, Lester, and Roger Cherry, David A. Joliffe, Anna M. Skinner. *Assessing Writers' Knowledge and Processes of Composing*. Norwood, N.J.: Ablex, 1985.

Fish, Stanley. *Is There a Text in This Class?* Cambridge, Mass.: Harvard UP, 1980.

Flavell, John H. "Metacognition and Cognitive Monitoring: A New Area of Cognitive-development Inquiry." *American Psychologist* 34 (1979): 906—11.

Flower, Linda. "Taking Thought: The Role of Conscious Processing in the Making of Meaning." *Thinking, Reasoning, and Writing*. Ed. Elaine Maimon et al. New York: Longman, 1986.

Ford, James E., and Gregory Larkin. "The Portfolio System: An End to Backsliding Writing Standards." *College English* 39 (1978): 950—55.

Frederiksen, John R. and Allen Collins. "A Systems Approach to Educational Testing." *Educational Researcher* 18.9 (December 1989): 27—32.

Freedman, Sarah. *Response to Student Writing*. Urbana, Ill.: NCTE, 1987.

Freire, Paulo, and Donald Macedo. *Mass Literacy: Reading the Word and the World*. South Hadley, Mass.: Bergin & Garvey, 1987.

Freisinger, Randall. "Cross-Disciplinary Writing Workshops: Theory and Practice." *College English* 42 (1980): 154–66.

Fulwiler, Toby. "How Well Does Writing Across the Curriculum Work?" College English 46 (1984): 113–125.

———. "Showing, Not Telling, at a Writing Workshop." *College English* 43 (1981): 55–63.

Gay, Pamela. *How Attitude Interferes with the Performance of Unskilled College Freshman Writers* (Report No. 81–0202) Washington, D.C.: National Institute of Education, 1983. (ERIC ED 234417)

———. "Using Writing to Develop Visual Artists: A Pedagogical Model for Collaborative Teaching and Learning." *Issues in Writing* 1 (1988): 35–49.

Gordon, Barbara L. "Another Look: Standardized Tests for Placement in College Composition Courses." *WPA: Writing Program Administration* 10.3 (1987): 29–38.

Gould, Stephen. *Ever Since Darwin*. New York: Norton, 1973.

Grant, Gerald, and P. Elbow, T. Ewens, Z. Gamson, W. Kohli, W. Neumann, V. Olesen, and D. Riesman. *On Competence: A Critical Analysis of Competence-based Reforms in Higher Education*. San Francisco: Jossey-Bass, 1979.

Grant, Gerald, and Wendy Kohli. "Contributing to Learning by Assessing Student Performance." *On Competence: A Critical Analysis of Competence-based Reforms in Higher Education*. Ed. G. Grant, P. Elbow, T. Ewens, Z. Gamson, W. Kohli, W. Neumann, V. Olesen, and D. Riesman, San Francisco: Jossey-Bass, 1979.

Graves, Donald. *Writing: Teachers and Children at Work*. Portsmouth, N.H.: Heinemann, 1986.

Greenberg, Karen L., Harvey S. Wiener and Richard A. Donovan, eds. *Writing Assessment: Issues and Strategies*. New York: Longman Press, 1986.

Haas, Christina, and Linda Flower. "Rhetorical Reading Strategies and the Construction of Meaning." *College Composition and Communication* 39 (May 1988) 167–84.

Hairston, Maxine. "The Winds of Change: Thomas Kuhn and the Revolution in the Teaching of Writing." *College Composition and Communication* 33 (February 1982): 76–88.

Hamp-Lyons, Liz, and Rebecca Reed. "Development of the Michigan Writing Assessment, 1987–89. Report to the College of Literature, Science and the Arts." University of Michigan: English Composition Board, 1989.

Harris, John. "Assessing Outcomes in Higher Education." *Assessment in American Higher Education*. Ed. Clifford Adelman. Washington, D.C.: GPO, 1986.

Harris, Joseph. "The Idea of Community in the Study of Writing." *College Composition and Communication* 40 (February 1989): 11–22.

Hartle, Terry W. "The Growing Interest in Measuring the Educational Achievement of College Students." *Assessment in American Higher Education.* Papers presented at the National Conference on Higher Education, Columbia, S.C., October 1985. Microfiche.

Herrington, Ann J. "Writing to Learn: Writing Across the Disciplines." *College English* 43 (1981): 379–87.

Hexter, Holly, and Joan Lippincott. "Campuses and Student Assessment." ACE Research Brief Series, vol. 1, no. 8 (1990): 1–8.

Holt, Dennis, and Nancy Baker. "Portfolios in Barrier Testing." Paper presented at the Seventh Annual Conference of the National Testing Network in Writing, Montreal, Quebec, 1989.

Hopwood, Roy. "Experiment Ignored." *Times Educational Supplement* January 29, 1982.

Hornbeck, David W. "Preface." *Turning Points: The Report of the Task Force on Education of Adolescents.* Washington, D.C.: Carnegie Council on Adolescent Development, 1989.

Howard, Kathryn. "Making the Writing Portfolio Real." *The Quarterly of the National Writing Project and The Center for the Study of Writing* 12.3 (1990): 4–7, 27.

Jolliffe, David A., ed. *Advances in Writing Research.* vol. 2, *Writing in Academic Disciplines.* Norwood, N.J.: Ablex, 1988.

Jones, Nancy Lyn. "Case Study, Course Study: A Contextualized Investigation of a Writing Course." 1982 (ERIC ED 249 487).

Joughin, Louis, ed. *Academic Freedom and Tenure: A Handbook of the American Association of University Professors.* Madison: U of Wisconsin P, 1967.

Judy, Stephen N., and Susan Judy. *An Introduction to the Teaching of Writing.* New York: John Wiley and Sons, 1981.

Juska, Jane. "The Unteachables." *The Quarterly of The National Writing Project and The Center for the Study of Writing* 11.1 (1989): 1–27.

Keller, Helen. "Three Days to See." *Atlantic Monthly* 151 (January 1933): 35–42.

Keller, Kenneth. "Commitment to Focus." Office of the President, University of Minnesota, 1985.

Keller-Cohen, Deborah, and Arthur Wolfe. "Extended Writing in the College of Literature, Science, and the Arts: Report on a Faculty Survey." University of Michigan, English Composition Board, 1987.

Kleinfeld, Judith S. *Effective Teachers of Indian and Eskimo High School Students.* ISEGR Report No. 34. Fairbanks, Alaska: Institute of Social, Economic and Government Research, University of Alaska, 1972.

Knoblauch, C. H., and Lil Brannon. *Rhetorical Traditions and the Teaching of Writing.* Portsmouth, N.H.: Boynton/Cook, 1984.

————. "Teacher Commentary on Student Writing: The State of the Art." *Freshman English News* 10 (Fall 1981): 1–4.

Kolb, David A. *Experiential Learning: Experience as the Source of Learning and Development.* Englewood Cliffs, N.J.: Prentice-Hall, 1984.

Krueger, Brenda. "Improving the Credit for Lifelong Learning Process with Holistic Education Techniques." *New Directions for Experiential Learning: Building on Experiences in Adult Development.* Ed. Frederick Jacobs and Richard Allen. San Francisco: Jossey-Bass, 1982.

Larson, Richard L. "Cognitive/Analytical Activities and Composed Texts: An Approach to Evaluation of Curriculum." Paper presented at the Seventh Annual Conference of the National Testing Network in Writing, Montreal, Quebec, 1989.

————. "Making Assignments, Judging Writing, and Annotating Papers: Some Suggestions." *Evaluating Writing: Describing, Measuring, Judging.* Ed. Charles R. Cooper and Lee Odell. Urbana, Ill.: NCTE, 1977.

Latus, Thomas. "I, Sam and Science: An Exploration in Teaching." *Teaching and Learning: The Journal of Natural Inquiry* (January 1989): 3–11.

Lauer, Janice M., and William Asher. *Composition Research: Empirical Designs.* New York: Oxford UP, 1988.

Lien, Arnold J. *Measurement and Evaluation of Learning.* 3d ed. Dubuque, Iowa: Wm. C. Brown, 1976.

Lloyd-Jones, Richard. "Primary Trait Scoring." *Evaluating Writing: Describing, Measuring, Judging.* Ed. Charles Cooper and Lee Odell. Urbana, Ill.: NCTE, 1977.

Lloyd-Jones, Richard, and Andrea Lunsford, eds. *The English Coalition Conference: Democracy Through Language.* Urbana, Ill.: NCTE, 1989.

Lunsford, Andrea. "Reassessing Assessment: Challenges to the Tradition of Testing." Keynote address, Sixth Annual Conference of the National Testing Network in Writing, Minneapolis, Minn., 1988.

Lutz, William. "Legal Ramifications of Writing Assessment." Paper presented at the Sixth Annual Conference of the National Testing Network in Writing, Minneapolis, Minn., 1988.

MacCurdy, Edward, ed. *The Notebooks of Leonardo DaVinci.* New York: George Braziller, 1954.

Maimon, Elaine. "Writing in the Total Curriculum at Beaver College." *CEA Forum* 9 (1979): 7–16.

Mark, Michael, and Patricia Dewees. "Recruitment, Retention, and Alumni Development of Adult Learners through Assessment of Prior Learning." *Lifelong Learning* 8 (1984): 18–20.

Martin, Wanda. "Dancing on the Interface: Leadership and the Politics of Collaboration." *Writing Program Administration* 7.3 (1988): 29–40.

Mayher, John S. *Uncommon Sense: Theoretical Practice in Language Education.* Portsmouth, N.H.: Boynton/Cook, 1990.

Meiland, Jack W. *College Thinking*. New York: New American Library, 1981.

McClelland, D. C. "Testing for Competence Rather Than for Intelligence." *American Psychologist* 28 (1973): 1–14.

Mosenthal, Peter M. "On Defining Writing and Classroom Writing Competence." *Research on Writing: Principles and Methods*. Ed. Peter Mosenthal, Lynn Tamor, and Sean A. Walmsley. New York: Longman, 1983.

Murphy, Sandra, and Mary Ann Smith. "Talking about Portfolios." *The Quarterly of the National Writing Project and the Center for the Study of Writing* 12.3 (1990): 1–3, 24–27.

Murray, Donald. "Teaching the Other Self: The Writer's First Reader." *College Composition and Communication* 33 (1982): 140–47.

National Association of Biology Teachers. "Policy on Dissection and Vivisection." *American Biology Teacher* (March/April 1989).

Nochimson, Martha. "Writing Instruction Across the Curriculum: Two Programs." *Journal of Basic Writing* 2.4 (1980): 22–35.

Odell, Lee. "Defining and Assessing Competence in Writing." *The Nature and Measurement of Competency in English*. Ed. Charles Cooper. Urbana, Ill.: NCTE, 1981.

O'Dowd, Donald D. "Letter to the Fund for the Improvement of Postsecondary Education." University of Alaska, Fairbanks, Alaska, 1989.

Parker-Smith, Bettye. *Guide to Portfolio Development* (A Manual for Students and Assessors in an Alternative Adult-oriented Degree Program). 2nd edition. Chicago, Ill.: Northeastern Illinois University, 1980.

Perdue, Virginia. "Confidence vs. Authority: Visions of the Writer in Rhetorical Theory." Paper presented at the Conference on College Composition and Communication, Atlanta, 1987. (ERIC ED 280 058).

Perkins, D. N. "Post Primary Education Has Little Impact on Informal Reasoning." *Journal of Educational Psychology* 77.5 (1985): 562–71.

Phelps, Louise Wetherbee. "Images of Student Writing: The Deep Structure of Teacher Response." *Writing and Response: Theory, Practice, and Research*. Ed. Chris M. Anson. Urbana. Ill.: NCTE, 1989.

Philips, Susan. "Participant Structures and Communicative Competence: Warm Springs Children in Community and Classroom." *Functions of Language in the Classroom*. Ed. Courtney Cazden, Vera P. John, and Dell Hymes. New York: Teachers College Press, 1972.

Piche, Gene L. "Class and Culture in the Development of the High School English Curriculum, 1880–1900." *Research in the Teaching of English* 11 (1977): 11–27.

"Portfolio Assessment: An Annotated Bibliography." *The Quarterly of the National Writing Project and the Center for the Study of Writing* 10 (October 1988): 23–24.

Progoff, Ira. *At A Journal Workshop*. New York: Dialogue House Library, 1975.

Purves, Alan C. "Foreword." *Composition Research: Empirical Designs*. Ed. Janice M. Lauer and William Asher. New York: Oxford UP, 1988.

Raimes, Ann. "Writing and Learning Across the Curriculum: The Experience of a Faculty Seminar." *College English* 41 (1980): 797−801.

Raleigh, Michael. "Unsound, Unstimulating, Ineffectual." *Times Educational Supplement* July 4, 1980.

Rose, Phyllis. *Parallel Lives*. New York: Alfred A. Knopf, 1983.

Roth, Kathleen J. "Science Education: It's Not Enough to 'Do' or 'Relate.'" *American Educator* 13.4 (Winter 1989): 16−22, 46−48.

Ruiz, Aida, and Diana Diaz. "Writing Assessment and ESL Students." *Notes from the National Testing Network in Writing* (December 1983).

Schultz, James A. "Report of the Committee on Academic Freedom: Part-timers and Academic Freedom." *MLA Newsletter* (Winter), 1989.

Schwartz, Mimi. "Wearing the Shoe on the Other Foot: Teacher as Student Writer." *College Composition and Communication* 40 (1989): 203−210.

Scott, Patrick. *Countdown to GCSE: English*. London: Macmillan, 1986.

———. *Coursework in English: 7 Case Studies*. London: Longmans for Schools Council, 1983.

———. *Coursework in English: Principles and Assessment*. N.A.T.E. Examination Booklet no. 3. Halifax, U.K.: N.A.T.E., 1980.

Searle, J. R. "What Is a Speech Act?" *The Philosophy of Language*. London: Oxford UP, 1976.

Senf, Carol. "The Portfolio or Ultimate Writing Assessment." *Technical Writing Teacher* 11 (1983): 23−25.

Simmons, Jay. "Portfolios as Large-Scale Assessment." *Language Arts* 67 (1990): 262−68.

Sommers, Nancy. "Responding to Student Writing." *College Composition and Communication* 33 (1982): 148−156.

———. "Understanding Student Narratives: The Narrator's Rite of Passage." Paper presented at the Conference on College Composition and Communication, Seattle, 1989.

Sowers, Susan. "Six Questions Teachers Ask About Invented Spelling." *Understanding Writing*. Ed. Thomas Newkirk and Nancie Atwell. Chelmsford, Mass.: NE Regional Exchange, 1982.

State University College at Freedonia. "General College Program Assessment Report." Office of the Dean of Special Studies, Fall 1987.

Sternberg, Robert J. "Mechanisms of Cognitive Development." *Mechanisms of Cognitive Development*. Ed. Robert J. Sternberg. New York: Freeman, 1984.

Sugarman, Jay. "Teacher Portfolios Inform Assessment." *Harvard Education Letter* 5.3 (1989): 5–6.

Tchudi, Stephen, ed. *Language, Schooling, and Society*. Portsmouth, N.H.: Boynton/Cook, 1987.

Thomas, Lewis. *The Lives of a Cell: Notes of a Biology Watcher*. New York: Bantam, 1974.

———. *The Medusa and the Snail*. New York: Bantam, 1979.

Tompkins, Jane. "Fighting Words: Unlearning to Write the Critical Essay." *Georgia Review* (Fall 1988): 585–590.

United Kingdom. Department of Education and Science. Bullock Report. "A Language for Life." London: Her Majesty's Stationery Office, 1975.

United Kingdom. "Language Performance." Assessment of Performance Unit. London: Department of Education and Science, May, 1978.

United Kingdom. Her Majesty's Inspectorate. "Aspects of Secondary Education in England: A Survey by HM Inspectors of Schools." London: Her Majesty's Stationery Office, 1979.

United Kingdom. Lockwood Report. "The Examining of English Language." London: Her Majesty's Stationery Office, 1964.

United Kingdom. Kingman Report. "Report of the Committee of Inquiry into the Teaching of English Language." London: Her Majesty's Stationery Office, 1988.

University of Alaska. "University of Alaska Six-Year Plan." Fairbanks: UA Information Services, 1986.

University of Minnesota. "Report of the College of Liberal Arts Task Force on Writing Standards." Dean's Office, College of Liberal Arts, 1986.

Virginia General Assembly. Joint Senate Resolution n. 83, 1986.

———. Joint Senate Resolution no. 125, February 20, 1985.

Virginia State Council of Higher Education for Virginia (SCHEV). "Recommendations for Measuring Student Achievement at Virginia's Colleges and Universities." Richmond, Va.: SCHEV, 1986.

Vygotsky, Lev. *Thought and Language*. Cambridge, Mass.: M.I.T., 1962.

———. "Zone of Proximal Development." *Mind in Society: The Development of Higher Psychological Processes*. Cambridge, Mass.: Harvard UP, 1978.

Wauters, Joan K., Janet M. Bruce, David R. Black, and Phillip N. Hocker. "Learning Styles: A Study of Alaska Native and Non-Native Students." *Journal of American Indian Education* (Special Issue, August 1989): 53–62.

White, Edward. *Teaching and Assessing Writing*. San Francisco: Jossey-Bass, 1985.

White, Fred D. *Science and the Human Spirit: Contexts for Writing and Learning*. Belmont, Cal.: Wadsworth, 1989.

Wiener, Harvey S. "Writing Assessment: An Evaluative Paradigm." *WPA: Writing Program Administration* 10 (1986): 13—16.

Wiggins, Grant. "A True Test: Towards More Authentic and Equitable Assessment." *Phi Delta Kappan* 70.9 (May 1989): 703—713.

Young, Arthur, and Toby Fulwiler. *Writing Across the Disciplines: Research into Practice*. Portsmouth, N.H.: Boynton/Cook, 1986.

Zinsser, William. *Writing to Learn*. New York: Harper and Row, 1988.

# Contributors

**Minda Rae Amiran** began teaching English in college in 1954 and is about to return to teaching after nine years as dean (currently for Liberal and Continuing Education) at SUNY Fredonia. She was a consultant in the Department of Research and Evaluation of the Chicago Board of Education. While at Fredonia, she directed a three-year FIPSE-funded project to assess student outcomes of the general education program, the context of Fredonia's portfolio plan. Her major field is critical theory, which borders on philosophy but also on education research and hence assessment.

**Chris M. Anson** is associate professor of English and Director of Composition at the University of Minnesota, where he teaches graduate and under-graduate courses in English language, linguistics, and composition theory and research. His books include *Writing and Response: Theory, Practice and Research* (NCTE, 1989); *Writing in Context* (Holt, Rinehart and Winston, 1988); *Writing Across the Curriculum: An Annotated Bibliography* (Greenwood Press, forthcoming), and *A Field Guide to Writing* (Harper Collins, in press). He has published numerous articles on language and written communication in edited collections and scholarly journals. His research interests include WAC, response to writing, and writing to learn.

**Nancy Westrich Baker** is the coordinator of writing assessment and a member of the English faculty at Southeast Missouri State University. She is a member of the Executive Board of the Missouri Colloquium on Writing Assessment. She has spoken at conferences on writing assessment, developmental composition, and the implications of assessment for ESL students. Her research interests include prompt development and reliability in port-folio assessment. She is completing her doctoral studies in educational psychology at Southern Illinois University at Carbondale.

**Pat Belanoff**, director of writing programs at SUNY Stony Brook, is coauthor (with Peter Elbow) of *A Community of Writers* and (with Betsy Rorschach and Mia Rakijas) of *The Right Handbook*. Belanoff, who is president of the State University of New York Writing Council, has also published studies of the women of Old English literature. She has taught at Kean College, the Borough of Manhattan Community College, and at New York University, where she was assistant director of the Expository Writing Program before moving to SUNY Stony Brook.

**Wendy Bishop**, director of freshman English at Florida State University, is the author of *Something Old, Something New: College Writing Teachers and Classroom Change* (Southern Illinois UP, 1990) and *Released into Language — Options for Teaching Creative Writing* (NCTE, 1990). Her articles on the teaching of writing appear regularly in composition journals and her poetry has been published in *American Poetry Review, College English, The Chronicle of Higher Education* and many literary reviews. Before settling in Florida, she taught in California, Nigeria, Arizona, and Alaska.

**Robert L. Brown, Jr.** is a discourse theorist and ethnographer interested in the relationships between language, literacy and institutions. He is associate professor of English and composition, and director of the graduate program in English at the University of Minnesota.

**Roberta Camp** is a writing assessment specialist and development scientist in the Division of Cognitive and Assessment Research at Educational Testing Service in Princeton, New Jersey. Since the early 1980s, when she began to explore portfolio approaches to writing assessment, she has worked with teachers and school districts in a number of locations, including New York and Pittsburgh. She focuses primarily on research and development for new forms of writing assessment in which the assessment is closely linked with instruction.

**Beverly Case** is an instructor in English and co-director of freshman English at Sul Ross State University in Alpine, Texas. In teaching freshman-level and sophomore-level composition courses, she has found that the portfolio method works best, especially for basic writers and technical writing students.

**William Condon**, before assuming his current duties as Associate Director for Instruction at the English Composition Board of the University of Michigan, held positions on the faculties of the University of Oklahoma and Arkansas Tech University. In addition, he has taught in settings as diverse as Miami University (Ohio), where he earned a master's in English literature; Brown University, where he earned his Ph.D. in Victorian poetry; and a maximum security prison. His current interests include portfolio-based writing assessment, the role of the computer in composition pedagogy, and the democratization of academic writing.

**Francine Dempsey**, C.S.J., associate professor of English and American studies at the College of Saint Rose, Albany, New York, holds a doctorate from the University of Minnesota. A teacher of writing and American literature, she also directs the program in American studies. In 1981, under a grant from the National Endowment for the Humanities, she initiated and directed an evening program in American studies for part-time adult students which incorporated experiential learning. She is a published writer of fiction and frequently conducts journal workshops and retreats.

**Marcia Dickson** teaches basic writing and composition classes of all descriptions at The Ohio State University at Marion, where she is an assistant professor.

**Peter Elbow**, professor of English at the University of Massachusetts at Amherst, is author of *Writing Without Teachers, Oppositions in Chaucer, Writing with Power, Embracing Contraries*, and (with Pat Belanoff) the textbook *A Community of Writers*. The Modern Language Association and the National Council of Teachers of English have just jointly published his *What Is English? Reflections on the English Coalition Conference*. He has taught at M.I.T., Franconia College, Evergeen State College, and SUNY Stony Brook — where for five years he directed the writing program.

**Pamela Gay** is director of basic writing and assistant professor of English at the State University of New York at Binghamton, where she also serves as writing-across-the-curriculum consultant. Gay is writing a textbook that takes a portfolio approach to the development of writing abilities and helps prepare developing writers for work across the curriculum. She was awarded a grant from the National Institute of Education for her research on the role of attitude in the development of writing abilities, which was extended into a dissertation (New York University, 1983). She is a member of the Executive Committee of the Conference on Basic Writing. Currently Gay is writing about basic writers and computing and the need for a new pedagogy.

**Bonnie A. Hain** completed her doctorate at SUNY Stony Brook in August, 1988. Currently, she is an assistant professor of English at Southeastern Louisiana University where she teaches courses in genre studies, rhetoric and composition and eighteenth-century literature. She is the founder of the Aphra Behn Society and is the current president of WSECS. She and her husband, John, reside in Baton Rouge.

**Liz Hamp-Lyons** was associate director for assessment at the English Composition Board of the University of Michigan from 1986 to 1990, where she was also an adjunct assistant professor of English and testing consultant to the English Language Institute's Testing and Certification Division. She is now associate professor of English and Applied Language at the University of Colorado, Denver, where she continues her interest in the applications of portfolio assessment to all educational contexts and levels. In her other research she looks at composing strategies in the assessment context, the learning (particularly writing) needs of nonnative and other minority students in the academy, and contrastive rhetoric. Among her publications is *Assessing Second Language Writing in Academic Contexts*, in press with Ablex.

**Sharon Hileman**, associate professor at Sul Ross State University in Alpine, Texas, teaches developmental writing, technical writing, and advanced composition as well as literature survey and topic courses. Her special area of interest is women's autobiographical writing, and she has published and delivered papers on cross-cultural autobiographical fiction and letters as forms of autobiography and narrative.

**Dennis Holt** is professor of philosophy and director of the Writing Outcomes Program at Southeast Missouri State University. He earned his M.A. in philosophy at Cornell University (1970) and his Ph.D. in philosophy at the University of Oregon (1975). He joined the Philosophy Department at Southeast Missouri State University in 1976. He has published articles in the *Canadian Journal of Philosophy*, *American Philosophical Quarterly*, *Philosophical Investigations*, *The Philosophy of Thomas Reid* (Dalgarno and Matthews, eds.), and *The Journal of the Freshman Year Experience*. Dr. Holt's current interests include philosophy in gifted education, writing assessment, and writing across the curriculum. He regularly conducts workshops and makes presentations in these areas.

**Patricia Kolonosky** is an instructor of literature and composition at Kansas State University. In addition, she advises and evaluates new teachers in the composition program. In the fall of 1989, as a panel member at a composition conference at Kansas University, she presented a paper on portfolio grading at Kansas State. Other endeavors include on-going research and a paper delivered at CCCC on student maturity-levels and writing performance.

**Richard L. Larson**, whose doctorate is from Harvard, served as a teaching fellow and tutor at Harvard College, then taught analysis of case problems and written argument at the Harvard Graduate School of Business Administration, and later served as director of composition at the University of Hawaii. In 1973, he moved to Lehman College of CUNY, where until 1983 he served as Dean of Professional Studies. He is currently professor of English and staff associate of the Institute for Literacy Studies at Lehman, where he is completing work on the curriculum evaluation project discussed in this essay, and on a study of college curricula in composition. From 1980 through 1986, he was Editor of *College Composition and Communication*.

**Judith Remy Leder** received her Ph.D. in English literature from the University of California, Irvine, in 1982. After a brief tenure at the University of Cincinnati as associate director of freshman Composition, she returned to California to teach for the English Department at California State University, Fullerton. Since 1985, she has been coordinator of the CSUF Business

Writing Program, which is housed in the School of Business Administration and Economics. Leder publishes in her literary specialty (Anglo-Irish drama) as well as in professional writing.

**Denise Stavis Levine**, former director of the Junior High School Writing and Learning Project at Lehman College, is currently teaching and conducting research and professional development seminars in Community School District 2 in New York City. She recently earned her Ph.D. in language, literacy, and learning at Fordham University, where she teaches graduate education courses in reading, writing and alternative assessment. Previous articles in writing and learning across the curriculum have appeared in NCTE publications including *Language Arts* and *Classroom Practices*.

**Kathy McClelland** received her Ph.D. in English Education from New York University. She has taught composition at the college level for twelve years and currently teaches in the Program in Composition at the University of California at Santa Barbara. She serves as editor of *Writer's Bloc*, a publication of student writing. Recently, she collaborated on a research project focusing on the assumptions California high school teachers have about the expectations and practices of UC freshman English instructors and is working on articles about the findings. A fellow of the South Coast Writing Project and a LIT fellow, she was recently included in *Who's Who in American Education*.

**Karen Mills-Courts** is an associate professor of English at SUNY Fredonia, where she teaches composition, creative writing, literary theory and contemporary American poetry. She has published articles on the uses of writing in the classroom (particularly creative writing as a tool for teaching literature), the work of Emily Dickinson and William Wordsworth. She is currently working as part of the Exxon Portfolio Project, directed by Aubrey Forrest of Emporia State, to develop portfolios as assessment tools. Her first book, *Poetry As Epitaph*, a study of the relationships between theory and poetry, was published by Louisiana State University Press in the fall of 1990.

**Roberta Rosenberg** is an associate professor of English and the writing program administrator at Christopher Newport College. She holds a Ph.D. in English from the University of North Carolina, Chapel Hill. Her publications include *An Historical and Textual Introduction to Wolfert's Roost by Washington Irving* (G. K. Hall, Boston) as well as several articles on writing and literature. She is currently working on a book that analyzes the relationship between women's history and literature entitled *Social History and Women's Literature, 1945 to the Present* for G. K. Hall/Twayne in Boston.

**Patrick Scott** has worked in schools and colleges in Britain and is now the advisor for English and drama for Cleveland (UK) Local Education Authority. Between 1984 and 1986, he was chair of the National Association for the Teaching of English. He edited the report of a NATE working party funded by the Schools Council to examine how portfolio assessment alters curriculum provision—*Coursework in English: 7 Case Studies* (Longman, 1983). His most recent publication, entitled *Reconstructing A Level English* (Open University Press 1989), considers whether the English curriculum for sixteen to nineteen year olds in Britain is an appropriate one for the last decade of the twentieth century.

**Kathryn Seltzer** began teaching at Kansas State University in 1981 after coauthoring several journal articles and completing a master's degree in curriculum and instruction. Seltzer joined the English Department in 1982 where she continues today as an instructor of composition and in Kansas State's Writing Laboratory. Seltzer is also a member of the Composition Committee and is one of four advisors who assist new instructors and graduate students in the Composition Program.

**Anne M. Sheehan** is assistant professor of English at the College of Saint Rose where she teaches literature, writing, and the teaching of writing and also serves as supervisor of the Writing Center and chairperson of the Writing Across the Curriculum Committee. She has assisted in developing a system of writing placement for the college and is project director for assessing outcomes for the English Program: "Growth in Writing of English Majors." Anne has also given numerous presentations and workshops in the areas of technical writing, writing in the disciplines, and writing assessment.

**David Smit** is an assistant professor and director of composition at Kansas State University. His articles on stylistics, collaborative writing, and portfolio evaluation have appeared in *The Henry James Review*, *Style*, *The Journal of Advanced Composition*, and *WPA: Writing Program Administration*. His book *The Language of a Master: Theories of Style and the Late Writing of Henry James* was published in 1988 by Southern Illinois University Press.

**Cherryl Armstrong Smith**, assistant professor of English at California State University, Sacramento, and Associate Director of the South Coast Writing Project, formerly taught in basic writing programs at Harvard University and at California State University, Northridge. She publishes poetry as well as work in composition and teaches courses in both fields.

**Jeffrey Sommers**, professor of English at Miami University, has been using portfolio grading in his writing courses since 1979. He has published essays on responding to student writing in *College Composition and Communication*, *Freshman English News*, *Teaching English in the Two-Year College*, the *Journal of Teaching Writing*, and *Writing and Response: Theory, Practice, and Research* (NCTE, 1989). The author of *Model Voices* (McGraw-Hill, 1989), Sommers is currently secretary-treasurer of the Council of Writing Program Administrators and past executive director of the Miami University Center for the Study of Writing.

**Joan K. Wauters** is an associate professor of English and director of writing at the University of Alaska Southeast in Juneau. She received a Doctor of Arts in English from the University of Michigan and has been active in presenting and publishing research on learning styles of minority students and implications for writing instruction. Her students have won numerous state wide and national essay-writing contests and are represented in the third edition of *Student Writers at Work and in the Company of Other Writers: The Bedford Prizes*. Wauters also teaches and writes fiction; in 1989 she was awarded first place in *Redbook* magazine's short story contest for 1989–90.

**Kerry Weinbaum** has taught seventh and eighth grade in the Bronx, New York, for thirteen years, the past eleven at the Elizabeth Barrett Browning Intermediate School 115. For the past four years she has served as a teacher-consultant for the New York City Writing Project where, in addition to teaching, she consults with colleagues on ways to use writing in their subject areas. Weinbaum is also an adjunct lecturer in English under the auspices of the New York City Writing Project at Lehman College, Bronx, New York. She has an M.S. from the University of Pennsylvania and a B.A. from Lehman College.